# THE ORVIS® GUIDE TO FLY FISHING FOR COASTAL GAMEFISH

THE

# ORVIS®

GUIDE TO

# FLY FISHING FOR COASTAL GAMEFISH

AARON J. ADAMS

An imprint of Globe Pequot Press

Guilford, Connecticut

Lyons Press is an imprint of Globe Pequot Press.

Project editor: David Legere
Layout artist: Mary Ballachino

Photos by Aaron J. Adams unless otherwise noted.

Library of Congress Cataloging-in-Publication Data is available on file.

ISBN 978-0-7627-7912-3

Printed in United States of America

10 9 8 7 6 5 4 3 2 1

# CONTENTS

# ACKNOWLEDGMENTS

As with previous efforts, this book benefited from the input of numerous people. Sandi Adams, Bob Miller, and Maria Cochran were helpful editors. Many fishing friends too numerous to mention contributed words of wisdom. The information on snook diet in Charlotte Harbor is courtesy of David Blewett of the Florida Fish and Wildlife Research Institute. The chapter on sight and sound benefited greatly from the input and advice of Dr. Andrij Horodysky, whose research focuses on fish sensory abilities: if any mistakes remain, they are mine.

# PREFACE

This book is written first for the saltwater angler who wants to learn more about where he or she fishes and to apply this new knowledge to improve his or her fishing. The more we know about the fish we pursue and the habitats they use, the more often we will be in the right place at the right time with the right fly tied to the tippet. But this book is also written so that saltwater anglers can become better stewards of the coastal habitats and gamefish that give us so much pleasure. The more we learn about these fish and their habitats, the better stewards we can become. If we want to continue to have quality fisheries, we have to work to protect them.

Coastal environments provide a unique opportunity for fly fishing. They are at once intimate and infinite, secluded and expansive, seductive and unconquerable. Perhaps it is this mix of extremes that grabs anglers after they wet a fly line in salt water. Or perhaps it's the size and power of a fish that feeds in water so shallow that its back is exposed, then eats a fly and flees at warp speed through water only inches deep. And surely the beauty of the coasts—where land meets sea and where salt water meets fresh—is a factor; there is a special excitement to catching a fish while surrounded by the unbridled colors and sounds of coastal environs. While scanning a flat for bonefish, I've often wondered how many hues of blue and green nature can pack into a single frame. On the better fishing days this wonderment is broken by a tailing bonefish. On the slower days the wonderment continues uninterrupted.

Despite all these attractions, the aspect of saltwater fly fishing that most appeals to me is the diversity. In a single outing I might encounter shallow grass flats, steep drop-offs swept by strong current, rocky outcrops, and sandy beaches. I might find the same species of fish around each turn or tangle with a handful of species in a single day. The diversity of prey available to these gamefish is just as impressive—many species of shrimps, crabs, worms, clams, small fishes, urchins, brittle stars, and a seemingly endless number of baitfish species—many of which can be imitated with a fly. There is a certain sense of satisfaction that comes from catching a fish with a fly you created to imitate a prey species you found while exploring gamefish habitats.

On some days a single fly might be all that is necessary. On other days a single species of gamefish might change preference of prey as the day progresses: Tailing red drum that eagerly ate a fly imitating a mud crab in the early morning may prefer small shrimp patterns as the sun floods the flat and the mud crabs head for cover. I once fished a pair of flats within sight of one another; the bonefish on one flat pounced on a Gotcha without hesitation, but bonefish on the seemingly identical flat just a mile away shunned the Gotcha in favor of a small crab fly. Helping the fly angler to understand why these changes in fish behavior occur and to use this information to find and catch fish is what this book is about.

I am doubly lucky. First, I've been a fisherman since the age of five. One of my first memories involves a fishing rod in my hand, rod bent double as a fish headed for the depths. That first big fish was a bullhead catfish—a five-pound fish is a whopper for a five-year-old. Hooking that fish didn't take any special knowledge, just a worm on a hook with a bobber. But just as vivid is the memory of my first experience with tides—a favorite bluegill hole on the tannin-stained edge of a tidal river was mysteriously full and then dry from one visit to the next. Realizing that fish change location and behavior due to water movement was my introduction to the importance of scientific literacy to fishing.

I fell naturally into a career in marine science. I'm not sure exactly when this career path started (probably back at that bluegill hole), but almost without planning I've progressed through jobs and degrees in marine science to where I am today—a marine biologist who fishes and an angler who studies marine science. For me it is the perfect combination.

My goal in writing this book is to bring some of the science of coastal systems into the larger picture of saltwater fly fishing and to present this information in angler's terms. There are plenty of books that describe in great detail what flies work for different gamefish and which fishing tactics are useful for catching these fish. Some of these books even tell you where to go, what time of day to fish, what fly to use, and how to fish the fly—all in order to catch your favorite gamefish. This approach provides useful information for a particular place or time but doesn't provide enough of the "why" that is necessary to truly become a better angler.

That said, this book is by no means exhaustive. With each read through my drafts of the text, I noted new items I could add. Local nuances were the most common new items for inclusion—the differences between northern and southern Indian River Lagoon, for example. But I quickly realized that the local nuances are endless and that I could probably spend the rest of my life revising and updating each chapter and still never include everything.

I must reiterate my opening statement in many of my fishing club presentations—although I am a fly angler and the examples in this book are of fly fishing, any saltwater angler will benefit from reading this book. The information on habitats, prey, and gamefish behavior is just as applicable to all coastal anglers. If you are a lure fisherman, for example, you can easily replace my examples of a particular fly with an appropriate lure. And although the examples in this book are of warm-temperate, subtropical, and tropical waters, with only a minor mental revision they apply equally as well to more northern waters.

Rather than provide a book that is old news after a single read, I hope this book can be used as a reference, with new insights gained from the book as your experience level increases and as you venture on to new locations. New anglers will learn a lot from this book. But after years of fishing experience under their belts, they can reread the book and learn even more. Experienced anglers will be better able to connect the dots of their fishing experiences and to improve their fishing.

# INTRODUCTION

Whether you've waded or boated the waters of warm-water coasts for the first or the fifth or the fiftieth time, you've discovered how perfect they are for fly fishing. Not only have you found these picturesque, diverse, and dynamic coastal habitats relatively shallow and accessible from shore by wading or from small boats, you've also realized that they are home to many species of gamefish willing to take a fly. We anglers can feel fortunate to be fishing at a time when modern equipment makes success possible for anyone with the desire and motivation to venture into coastal habitats.

But do you know that life cycles of many gamefish depend on coastal waters such as beaches, estuaries, and wetlands? And that this dependence is what makes these gamefish accessible to fly anglers? For some species, it is the younger fish that inhabit these inshore areas and are caught by fly anglers, whereas the largest fish reside mainly in deeper waters. Red drum, for instance, generally follow this pattern—the majority of red drum in estuaries are immature or young adults, and the adults are primarily offshore. Conversely, for other species both young and adult fish inhabit shallow coastal waters for all or part of the year, and fly anglers will encounter a variety of sizes of those fish. Bonefish are an example of such a species.

Now that our sport has tools that make saltwater fly fishing as accessible to the fly angler as is freshwater fly fishing, it is essential that we learn about the environments we are fishing, just as the freshwater trout anglers did many years ago. *The Orvis Guide to Fly Fishing for Coastal Gamefish* draws from scientific research and literature and from my scientific and angling experience to provide relevant information in angler's terms, so in a sense it is a saltwater version of the science-based books for freshwater fly anglers that have existed for decades.

This book contains what I think has been lacking in the world of saltwater fly fishing: information on the *types* of habitats where gamefish can be found, the *types* of prey gamefish prefer, the *ways* gamefish behave in and use their environment, and the *ways* gamefish pursue different prey. In a sense, the coastal environment from a fish-eye view. When they use this information, my hope is that saltwater anglers will be able to figure out what tactics and flies might work best in a given situation. This is a book for the thinking angler.

The newness of scientific information in the world of saltwater fly fishing is certainly not the fault of the pioneers of fly fishing the salt. The pursuit of saltwater gamefish with a fly rod is relatively new and is just now maturing to the point where this type of book and those that have preceded it is appropriate. The entomology books so common now in freshwater fly fishing were also a step behind the earliest freshwater fly anglers, but those books are now standard on freshwater anglers' bookshelves.

Much as freshwater entomology and ecology books did for trout anglers years ago, this book aims to teach saltwater fly anglers about the ecosystems they fish so they are better able to figure out a fishing system on their own. It is also my hope that in the process of learning how coastal environments work, my fellow anglers become more than just occasional visitors and become better stewards of these unique coastal treasures.

What attracts many of us to fly fishing—the enjoyment of casting and bringing a fish to hand, a connection with gamefish environments, and a growing appreciation for the gamefishes' world—will be enhanced by the different approach you will find in these pages. I'll present information on gamefish habitats, the different prey available in those habitats, and the ways gamefish use these environments under different conditions. After you are connected to this ecology of gamefish, you can build on what you learn here and formulate your own strategies for many gamefish, in many habitats, and under many scenarios. Trout anglers take stock of stream conditions and use that information to select a fly. Saltwater anglers should be doing the same.

The anglers just beginning in saltwater fly fishing may at times be overwhelmed by sections of this book—information overload. But as beginners spend more time on the water and gain more experience, the information contained in this book will make more sense and will become part of the learning experience. In time my hope is that their experience combined with this book will make them better anglers.

Because this book is about how gamefish use their habitats, the more you know about gamefish, the more you will learn from this book. I think that even a seasoned angler will learn something new. Seasoned anglers might get a better understanding of why a fish behaves a certain way than they had before reading this book or might suddenly be able to connect the dots or fill those elusive gaps in their fishing knowledge.

*The Orvis Guide to Fly Fishing for Coastal Gamefish* examines coastal habitats through the eyes of gamefish or at least as close as scientific research can get us. In this book I'll present characteristics of coastal habitats used by gamefish and their prey—such as how the type, size, shape, and density of seagrass blades influence the types of prey a gamefish will find and how a gamefish's predatory behavior might change in response.

This book includes a lot of marine science, and when many people hear the word *science*, their eyes immediately glaze over and their minds wander. Fear not; this is not that kind of book. There are no complicated formulas or confusing graphics. The science I refer to is the research that has been done on the ecology of coastal marine communities, especially gamefish. This includes what gamefish eat and when, how gamefish diets vary among regions, habitats, and seasons, how the age of a gamefish might influence its diet, and how different habitats provide different opportunities and challenges for both gamefish and anglers. I have done all the sorting through the volumes of information that are of interest to scientists but not to anglers, present here only what I consider to be the useful points, and present them in straightforward terms. I am, after all, also an angler.

I combine the scientific research information with my experiences as an angler, and I provide examples throughout the book to mesh science with angling. I have also incorporated the knowledge I have gained from fishing with and talking to some great anglers—knowledge that has been ingrained in my fishing. This is, in every sense, a book about fishing.

## HABITATS AND GEOGRAPHY

To hasten your connection to the world of gamefish and their prey, I've divided the coastal environment into five primary habitat types—seagrass, mangroves, oyster reefs, marshes, and beaches—with a sprinkling of secondary habitats (rubble, open bottoms of mud or sand). Each habitat has unique characteristics that make it attractive to gamefish, and each habitat will have a different mixture of prey.

Although the basics of each habitat type are similar across latitudes, there are enough important differences that I've divided the warm-water coasts into three geographic zones defined by average and low temperatures, plant and animal distributions, geological history, and many other well-established scientific criteria. The zones are:

Tropical—includes the Caribbean, the Florida Keys, and the Bahamas

Subtropical—southern Florida, southern Texas, and the Gulf of Mexico coast of Mexico

Warm-temperate—the Gulf of Mexico from central Florida through Texas and the southeastern Atlantic coast from central Florida to Cape Hatteras

## THE GAMEFISH

One of the strengths of the approach of *The Orvis Guide to Fly Fishing for Coastal Gamefish* is that because the information is presented from a gamefish's perspective, the habitat-based information is applicable for pursuits of any gamefish that use these habitats. Combining your knowledge about what a habitat has to offer and what types of prey a gamefish prefers will allow you to formulate a strategy for the gamefish of your choice. So, although the examples and fishing strategies offered in this book focus on the most common gamefish in coastal habitats, the strategies are much more broadly applicable. The list of gamefish covered in this book includes tarpon, bonefish, permit, snook, barracuda, snappers, jacks, ladyfish, red drum, spotted seatrout, weakfish, bluefish, striped bass, cobia, cero mackerel, and Spanish mackerel.

## GETTING THE MOST OUT OF THIS BOOK

Consider this book to be another tool in your tackle box. On the one hand, it is an outline of the ecology of gamefish and their prey and of the habitats in which they live. It's a primer on the complex life cycles of coastal species and how subtle changes influence everything from diet to location to behavior. Anglers will come to understand that without success in *all* of the life stages, *none* of the life stages will exist. Your appreciation for the importance of coastal habitats will grow beyond what brought you to saltwater fly fishing in the first place and make it a much richer experience. And your knowledge of the life stage of the species you're pursuing will increase your enjoyment of our sport. To understand basic life cycles is to understand how, when, and why gamefish use different habitats and what they are likely eating in each habitat.

On the other hand, consider *The Orvis Guide to Fly Fishing for Coastal Gamefish* your "direct connect." It provides the elusive but essential connection between scientific data and your success. You'll learn to combine facts such as type of habitat, time of year, and fish behavior with your own experience to create the most effective flies and fishing strategy. And as you work with the book, what you learn about fish life cycles will translate into a richer angling experience.

Chapter 1 outlines the life history of gamefish and their prey and focuses on the basic concepts and information you will find referenced throughout the book. It serves as an introduction to ways gamefish and their prey use coastal habitats and why at certain times of year gamefish seem to prefer certain habitats or feed on particular prey.

Chapters 2 and 3 provide background information on factors that are the same for all habitats and gamefish and are essential for saltwater anglers to understand—tides and how fish use sight and sound.

Following are separate chapters for each of the five primary habitats and a chapter addressing the secondary habitats. Each chapter begins by outlining the ecology of the habitat, which forms the foundation for the rest of the chapter. I then dive into specifics on where, when, and why gamefish use the habitat and which prey they are most likely to find. I pause at numerous points in each chapter to summarize the information that has been covered and to provide examples of fishing strategies—sections called Applying What You've Learned. The imaginative reader will be able to formulate fishing strategies that go beyond the examples I provide.

A word of caution—don't give in to the temptation to skip straight to the chapter that covers your favorite habitat. I suggest you read the chapters in order. Because the general ecological themes are similar in all habitats, rather than repeat these themes in each chapter I introduce and describe an ecological concept as the opportunity presents itself in the early chapters and refer to these concepts in later chapters without further explanation. By skipping ahead you may miss important points to consider when fishing in your favorite coastal habitat. In addition, you may find that some strategies and examples I offer for one habitat may be equally applicable in another habitat.

Because this is a book about the habitats from a gamefish's perspective, specific gamefish are addressed within the context of the habitats. For example, bonefish are most often found in seagrass, mangrove, and sand bottom locales, so they are covered in the sections focusing on these habitats. In contrast, red drum use seagrass, oyster bar, mud flat, mangrove, and beach habitats, so aspects of red drum ecology that are important to fly anglers are addressed in most chapters.

Because common names for fishes change from region to region and can be confusing, I use the standard common name for each gamefish species as it appears in fish science texts. Thus, I use red drum instead of redfish, channel bass, or spot-tail bass. When first mentioned, the common name is followed by its scientific name. Standard scientific notation is used for species names, with the genus capitalized, the species in lowercased, and both italicized. For example, the scientific name for permit is *Trachinotus falcatus*. The scientific name is provided to allow certain identification and to make it easier for you to do additional research. You'll find, for example, that an Internet search for *Cynoscion nebulosus* will result in more useful information on diet, habitat, and growth than a search for spotted seatrout. In addition, for those of you who want to do your own follow-up on the science, a search through scientific literature will necessitate use of the scientific nomenclature.

The final chapter focuses on stewardship specific to the habitat. As active participants in the coastal environment we must act as good stewards to protect the valuable gamefish resource. To paraphrase friend Chico Fernandez, gone are the days when we could go fishing, have a good time, and forget about it until our next fishing trip. If we want to make sure we have future fishing trips, we have to become involved.

The References and Further Reading section lists the sources used in writing this book as well as other references you may find useful, such as books for species identification. Although not an exhaustive list, it provides the interested reader with a jump start on additional resources. After all, no single book can cover everything; there is always more.

Finally, Appendices A and B list the common gamefish and prey, respectively, covered in this book. These tables provide a quick point of reference for connecting the habitats, gamefish, and prey.

# 1

# Life Cycles of Marine Gamefish and Their Prey

Coastal habitats are essential to the survival of many gamefish and to the species they depend on for food. But what many people don't realize is just how intricately intertwined our favorite gamefish are with coastal habitats and the implications this has for formulating fishing strategies. The food, shelter, temperature, salinity, and overall water quality of coastal habitats are some of the characteristics that make these areas so important to so many gamefish, which in turn makes so many gamefish accessible to fly anglers.

Prior to presentations that I give to fishing clubs, I am sometimes asked, "Why do I need to know about gamefish life cycles to catch more fish?" The simplest answer is that the more you know about the gamefish you are fishing for, the more likely you are to be in the right place at the right time with the right fly tied to your tippet. Lefty Kreh once told me that he couldn't figure out why so many fishermen think that all gamefish ever want to do is eat and that fishermen are disappointed when the fish aren't biting or are acting strangely. Gamefish behavior depends on a lot of things in addition to getting a meal, and understanding what influences that behavior is a big part of the puzzle that fly anglers need to solve to catch more fish.

How and when gamefish use different habitats depend, in many ways, on their life cycle patterns. To understand how, when, and why species—both gamefish and their prey—use coastal habitats is to take a giant step toward approaching fishing from the fish's perspective of coastal habitats. You will also understand why habitats you might never fish—like tiny marsh creeks—are essential

*Knowing about gamefish life cycles helps you to find the right place at the right time to catch more nice fish like this one.*

to the survival of your favorite gamefish and why some locations are productive fishing spots only during certain times of year.

Challenges confronting fish in coastal habitats are complex and vary depending on a fish's size and age. Among the challenges: competing with other fish for food and shelter; finding appropriate food while avoiding becoming a meal for a larger fish; and finding an area with the right type of habitat, salinity, and temperature. And these challenges change as the fish grows. The type of food required by a juvenile fish is usually different than that required by an adult, and the way a fish uses a habitat changes. For example, a juvenile gamefish in a seagrass bed can search for food and can hide from a predator among the grass blades. An adult gamefish in a seagrass bed will search for larger prey than a juvenile of the same species and won't be able to feed on the small items among the grass blades as efficiently as a juvenile. And whereas the juvenile gamefish might use camouflage coloration to blend in with the seagrass to avoid being eaten, there is no place to hide for such a large fish in a seagrass bed, so adults may be more wary in these shallow habitats than their juvenile counterparts and more likely to flee than hide when predators appear.

Most saltwater fish species pass through three distinct life stages in their lives: larval, juvenile, and adult. The species that follow this progression, which include all of the gamefish species discussed in this book and most of their prey, reproduce through a behavior known as broadcast spawning: Adult females and males (either as pairs or in groups) release their eggs and sperm into the water column where fertilization takes place—they "broadcast" the eggs and sperm into open water rather than lay eggs in a nest as do largemouth bass or trout. (The "water column" is the water between the bottom and surface.) Although this seems to be a risky approach to reproduction, females of many species can produce hundreds of thousands to millions of eggs for a single spawning period, so even though there is no parental care, sheer numbers virtually ensure that some larvae make it to the juvenile life stage.

## THE LARVAL STAGE

The fertilized eggs hatch within hours to days depending on the species and water temperature. The time for an egg to hatch is different for each species, and within the range of temperatures that a species can tolerate the warmer the water, the shorter the time needed to hatch. After they hatch, the larvae live as plankton—small, free-floating individuals in the open waters of the ocean or estuary.

Although larvae are able to swim, their swimming abilities are not great, so they are unable to fight strong currents and can be transported where these currents take them. Recent research has shown that larvae of many species are able to migrate vertically in the water column to take advantage of different currents at the surface and below and in this way maintain some control over where they travel. Larvae of some species remain in coastal waters, whereas others may be transported out into the open ocean. Where and when the larval stage occurs depend on both a species' requirements, such as where and when the adults spawn, what type of environment the larvae need to survive, and the best season for growth and survival of larvae and juveniles, among other factors, and luck.

For example, snook in Florida, which are associated with estuaries for their entire lives, spawn in passes and channels at the mouths of estuaries near the end of an outgoing tide, most often during a full or new moon during the summer (May through September). Adult snook spawn at the mouths of estuaries because the eggs and sperm require salt water to be viable, and farther into the estuary the salinity might be too low. After the eggs hatch, the larvae ride incoming tides that carry them far into the estuary. The tides around the new and full moon—known as spring tides—are the strongest tides, so these tidal currents will carry the larvae farthest into the estuary. Summer is best because the warm water temperatures result in faster growth rates of larvae than would occur in winter and because adult snook are most active in warm months. And because juvenile snook require the difficult-to-reach backwater creeks and wetlands to survive, the wet season (summer) is best because this is when the creeks experience the highest freshwater flows of the year, which floods these areas and gives the small snook access to the backwaters.

The larvae live as zooplankton (animal plankton), eating small phytoplankton (plant plankton) and other zooplankton for periods of days to months depending on the species. The average time in the planktonic phase for bonefish larvae, for example, is fifty-three days. Depending on currents and how long they spend as plankton, surviving larvae may end up close to their place of origin or far away—even drifting from one island to another in the Caribbean, for example. In fact, juvenile bonefish have been captured along beaches on Long Island, New York, during summer, obviously the result of spawning that occurred in the tropics. These juveniles likely died at the end of the summer when water temperatures cooled.

Most larvae are not only small (less than 1 inch) but also look absolutely nothing like their parents. Many larvae are transparent or nearly so, which is great camouflage in clear ocean water. Some larvae have all kinds of spines and other protrusions for protection,

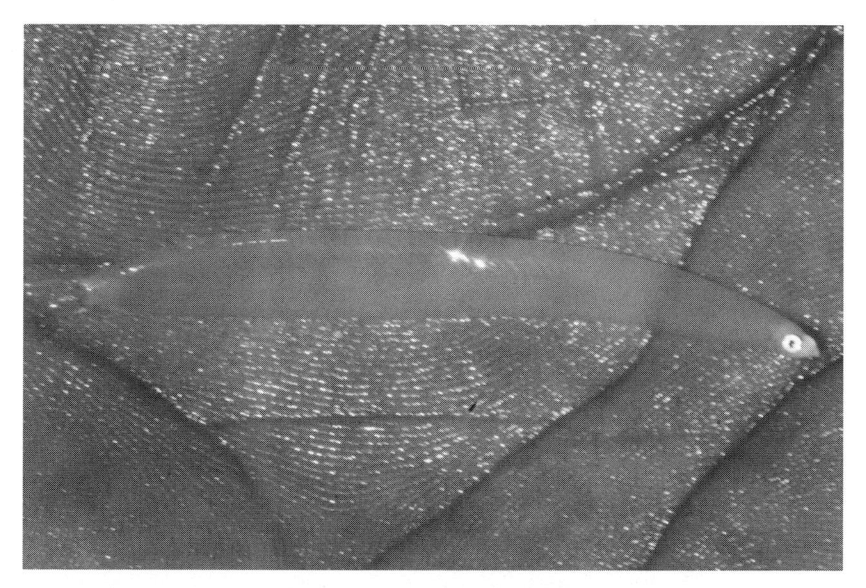

*If it's lucky, this larval bonefish will one day become an adult and contribute to the fishery.*

and many aren't even shaped like adult fish. Most, however, are voracious predators, taking on their predatory behavior early in life. Despite their camouflage and long spines, typically more than 99 percent of larvae are eaten or die. That seems like a lot, but remember that 1 percent of millions of original eggs and larvae is a substantial number. This is a strategy that has worked well for many species for a long, long time.

## THE JUVENILE STAGE

At the end of the larval life stage, surviving larvae undergo a rapid and drastic transformation, changing from mostly clear, often spiny larvae to a form that we would all recognize as miniature fish, thus starting the juvenile life stage. At the same time that the larvae are getting ready to transform into juveniles, they are searching for the right type of bottom habitat.

For some species, like tarpon, these new juveniles are miniature versions of the adults and can be easily identified. For other species, like amber jack, the juveniles have a different coloration than the adults and change color, becoming more like adults, as they grow. The juveniles of many species of jacks are difficult to distinguish from one another.

Because many larvae are riding the same or similar currents toward their nursery habitats and many were spawned at the same time, many will reach the larvae-to-juvenile transformation stage at the same time. And because larvae often arrive at juvenile habitats on spring tides, the juveniles often appear in distinct pulses over short time periods.

This is also true for gamefish prey, which can be reflected by gamefish showing a preference for a particular prey and even a particular size of prey. You can often detect distinct size groups of juveniles that reflect these pulses; understanding these dynamics will aid in the selection of flies for different times and locations.

The seasonality of pinfish (*Lagodon rhomboides*), an important prey species for fish in subtropical and warm-temperate regions, is a good example of this. Pinfish spawn in coastal waters from late autumn through winter. Small juveniles of 1 to 2 inches become abundant in estuaries in winter and early spring. Small, yellow-and-white, high-bodied flies are good pinfish imitations for this early season fishing. As summer progresses, these same pinfish will have grown to greater than 3 inches in length and will have been joined in the estuaries by larger adult fish (6 inches or longer) from previous years that have migrated back to the estuaries for the summer. So, by late summer your 1-inch flies from spring will likely be too small and should be replaced by pinfish imitations 3 inches long or larger.

Knowledge of the occurrence of pulses of prey might also help to explain those instances when you see fish actively feeding, but your normally successful fly patterns don't get even a first look. It might be that the fish are feeding on a brief but intense occurrence of a particular prey species. With some effort, you might be able to figure out the time of day, season, type of habitat, tide, temperature, and other conditions when such an event occurs and be ready for it the next time it happens. The famous crab and worm "hatches" of tarpon lore are good examples.

## JUVENILE NURSERY HABITATS

For many saltwater fish, and especially the gamefish species covered in this book, coastal areas provide many of the habitats that are essential for the survival of juveniles. Habitats important to juveniles are known as nurseries. These habitats are essential because without them few juveniles would survive to become adults, and we would have no coastal gamefish.

Shallow coastal habitats, including seagrass beds, mangroves, marshes, oyster reefs, and shorelines are heavily used by juvenile fish because these habitats provide the best food and shelter needed for the juvenile life stage. In the most general sense, there are two types of nursery habitats—those with plants and those without. I'll first give an overview of the characteristics of plant-based habitats that make them good nurseries for gamefish. Although plants, such as seagrasses, mangroves, and marsh plants, are not necessary for an area to support juvenile fish, plants do provide several advantages over other habitats.

Shallow coastal areas furnish two commodities important for supporting plant growth—appropriate nutrient levels and sunlight. In turn, plants provide three important habitat functions to juvenile gamefish as well as to gamefish prey. First, plants are able to harness sunlight and nutrients into a form many prey species can use. Prey species feed on plant material or on the smaller organisms associated with the plants and are in turn fed upon by juvenile gamefish. Second, by holding sediments together, plants keep the bottom, shoreline, and associated habitats intact, which protects the integrity of the habitats. Stable habitats are good habitats for juvenile gamefish. Furthermore, the rooted plants trap organic matter, which is food for crabs, shrimp, small fish, and other prey of juvenile and adult gamefish. Third, plants create habitat structure that provides shelter from predators for the juvenile fish. Many of the same features that attract juvenile gamefish to these habitats also support species that are prey for juvenile, adolescent, and even adult gamefish.

The combination of food and shelter creates great habitat for many species, which results in a diverse community. Juvenile gamefish are able to take advantage of this dual bounty of shelter from predators and abundant food to grow quickly. And because larger fish are less likely to get eaten by predators than are smaller fish, the faster the juvenile gamefish can grow, the better.

Juvenile tarpon and snook are most abundant in the shallows found at the headwaters of tidal creeks and in backwater mangrove lagoons, often in low-salinity water. As the juvenile snook and tarpon grow, they gradually move down the creeks toward the open estuary, which is one reason why mangrove creeks are good places to find baby tarpon and snook through much of the year.

Juvenile barracuda are abundant among and near mangroves when very small (1–2 inches). When they are this small they look and behave like small twigs suspended, often vertically, near the water surface. As they grow to catchable size, some barracuda will remain near the mangroves, and others will find good feeding areas along shallow beaches and near coral reefs.

Juvenile red drum can be found in seagrass, marsh cordgrass, and tidal creek habitats depending upon the location and the types of habitats available. As they grow they widen their use of habitats and can be found in just about any habitat with appropriate food.

Juveniles of many species of snapper and grouper use shallow seagrass habitats before moving to deeper habitats as adults.

Not only juvenile gamefish but also a host of other organisms use these areas as nurseries. For example, juvenile blue crabs are dependent on estuarine seagrass and shallow wetland areas, and juveniles of numerous coral reef fish, like grunts, use seagrass and algae in lagoons. The list of organisms that use coastal habitats as nurseries is large indeed, and in many cases it is these organisms that we attempt to imitate with our flies. Many of these prey species will be addressed in later chapters that focus on the habitats where the prey are most often found.

Coastal habitats without plants also support juvenile gamefish, though generally not as many as areas with plants. Often, these are areas that have appropriate levels of nutrients but may be too deep or too murky for sunlight to penetrate, have too much variation in salinity to support seagrass, or have too much current for plants to become established. A variety of organisms that don't need sunlight is able to take advantage of these areas and can provide habitat for juvenile fish. Oyster reefs, mussel reefs, and reefs made of worm tubes are examples of this type of live coastal habitat. In the tropics, rocky shorelines and tidepools provide habitat for juveniles of numerous species of gamefish. Like plants, these structures provide shelter from predators and support communities of organisms that are food for juvenile fish.

You are likely to find juvenile members of the jack family (family Carangidae) along beachrock shorelines in the Caribbean.

Juvenile horse-eye jacks (*Caranx latus*), barjacks (*Caranx ruber*), blue runner (*Caranx crysos*), and jack crevalle (*Caranx hippos*) are the most common. Some of these juvenile jacks along beachrock shorelines will be large enough to catch with a small Clouser Minnow. Casting a size 2 chartreuse-and-white Clouser with beadchain eyes with a six-weight rod is one of my favorite ways to fish for jacks along beachrock shorelines. Sometimes much larger jacks show up, which adds some excitement to the day.

Coastal habitats like sand or mud flats, with neither plants nor other habitat like oyster reefs, support fewer juvenile gamefish. Although some organisms, such as worms, clams, crabs, and some small fishes like gobies and blennies, may inhabit these areas, there is little shelter for small fish. In general, survival of juvenile fish is higher in areas with shelter than in areas of open bottom, like sand or mud. Gamefish species that use shallow open bottom areas as juvenile habitat include flounder and, in some locations, red drum.

The presence of these nutrient-rich, diverse communities in coastal areas might prompt you to ask, "Don't large predatory fish know about all of this?" Of course they do, and that's one reason why large individuals of many gamefish are often accessible by fishing from shore or by wading. These shallow, rich habitats and the communities they support attract large fish within range of shore-bound fly anglers. And this brings us to the adult stage.

## THE ADULT STAGE

After surviving the gauntlet of the open ocean and then escaping predators in their nursery habitats, remaining juveniles grow to adulthood. The transformation from juvenile to adult is not as rapid or drastic as from larvae to juveniles. For some species, this juvenile-to-adult transition occurs within the same general area as the nursery, so juveniles and adults can be found together. Spotted seatrout (*Cynoscion nebulosus*), for example, use estuarine seagrass habitats as juveniles, young adults, and adults. However, juveniles are usually found in dense seagrass, whereas adults will venture into patchy seagrass. For other species, individuals gradually move from nursery areas to adult habitats. Juvenile and young adult tarpon often use mangrove lagoons, whereas larger adults generally use more open areas and often undergo lengthy seasonal migrations.

Usually, a fish's diet and behavior will change as it grows, allowing the fish to take advantage of a wider array of habitats and prey. Knowing this fact can help you in choosing flies to target what is available in a given situation. Spotted seatrout are a great example. Juveniles and young adults tend to associate in schools, whereas larger, older fish (often called gators) adopt a more solitary existence or a looser affiliation with other larger spotted seatrout. Also, as spotted seatrout grow, they move from a small juvenile's diet of small mysid shrimps to increasingly larger shrimp species as young adults and eventually to a more varied diet consisting of shrimp, fish, and crabs as older adults.

Red drum show a similar change in diet with age, subsisting on small crustaceans (shrimp and small crabs) as juveniles before moving to a more varied adult diet of shrimp, larger crabs, and fish. A similarity among the life stages is that red drum often school as both juveniles and adults. Casting a size 1/0 deceiver at a juvenile red drum may get the interest of the young drum but is just as likely to send the fish swimming in the other direction. That same fly cast to a larger adult fish has a decent chance at being eaten because fish such as mullet become an important part of the diet of larger adult red drum.

## SEASONALITY OF GAMEFISH PREY

You've probably noticed seasonal changes in the abundance of your favorite gamefish in coastal waters and maybe even changes in their diet. Although the reasons for this seasonality are many, food availability and temperature are major factors. Juveniles of many of the organisms that use coastal habitats as nurseries are most abundant in spring and summer. This is true even in the Caribbean, where abundance of juvenile fish is highest in summer months. Gamefish and other predators may shift their diet and feeding locations to take advantage of this seasonal abundance of prey.

Speckled seatrout, for example, undergo seasonal shifts in diet. In Indian River Lagoon, Florida, adult speckled seatrout feed mostly on shrimp in summer and early winter but switch to a diet dominated by small fishes in late winter and early spring. Of course, there are always exceptions to general rules, but choosing a fly based on these general seasonal trends is a good start. In the Virginia portion of Chesapeake Bay, speckled trout venture into shallow grass beds in the spring (May and into June) in search of juvenile and shedding adult blue crabs.

In contrast, the closely related red drum (both speckled trout and red drum are in the drum family, Sciaenidae) has a diet similar to that of speckled trout (fish, shrimp, and crabs) but may have different diet preferences depending on location. Along Florida's Gulf of Mexico coast, studies of red drum populations revealed that red drum in coastal habitats prefer small fish such as menhaden and anchovies in winter and spring and crabs and shrimp in summer and autumn. Along the coast of Mississippi, many red drum prefer shrimp in winter, crabs in spring and summer, and small fish in the autumn.

This type of information comes from studies of populations of red drum in certain locations and reflects the overall amounts of different prey items in the stomachs of fish captured for the study. In other words, for the studied population of gamefish, certain prey items appeared in stomachs more often and in greater numbers than did other prey items. This information should help you decide what types of prey items to imitate with your flies but shouldn't be interpreted as being a complete list of prey. Although gamefish have diet preferences, they are also opportunistic and might take advantage of what they perceive as an easy meal and take a fly that is not high on the list of common prey items. There are also local variations. For example, in contrast to the study that showed that red drum on Florida's Gulf of Mexico coast prefer bait-fish in winter, I found that the diet of red drum feeding in estuarine seagrass beds in winter was dominated by crabs and shrimp.

### Applying What You've Learned

#### Seasonality of Prey Species Life Cycles

While living on St. Croix, U.S. Virgin Islands, I discovered another example of seasonality of prey in the Caribbean. A small baitfish, known locally as "fry" (a type of silverside), forms into dense spawning aggregations along the shores of protected coves in early April. These large schools of fry attract a host of predatory fish, including tarpon, bar jacks, and barracuda. But most exciting is that bonefish feed aggressively on these schools of fry (they strafe the schools of fry much like a jack) and are suckers for a white Crazy Charlie. At other times of year, these same bonefish feed mostly on shrimp and crabs, so a Norman's Crab or a simple tan Gotcha is the most productive fly. In areas of the island where large schools of baitfish are not present, the bonefish feed almost exclusively on bottom organisms such as clams, crustaceans, and worms, and baitfish imitations are typically not productive.

### Applying What You've Learned

#### Taking Advantage of Juvenile Prey

My experience on a summer research expedition to the Caribbean provides a vivid example of gamefish use of seasonal prey. I had just finished a session of intensive field work. Using SCUBA, colleagues and I had been counting juvenile fish on coral reefs. After being underwater for more than six hours a day for three weeks, I had seen all the juvenile fish I cared to for a while. I was taking a couple of days of R&R before heading home, and on this particular day I was wading across a large sand flat in search of bonefish. Out in the middle of the flat I came across a broken-down piece of old, dead mangrove that must have been washed onto the middle of the knee-deep flat in a storm. The closest live mangroves were more than a half-mile away along the shoreline.

I slowly walked over to the old mangrove to see if it might hold some small snappers because mangroves provide important habitat for juvenile snapper. Small snapper would be perfect for my six-weight rod and small Clouser Minnow. As I reached the old mangrove I saw two torpedoes speed off—bonefish! This really piqued my curiosity because I had never before seen bonefish so closely associated with structure in this fashion, especially on a shallow sand flat where I expected to see them cruising and feeding, not lurking among the branches of a dead, submerged mangrove.

After I was close enough to the mangrove, I saw why the bonefish were so attracted. There were hundreds of 1-inch-long juvenile grunts (family Pomadasyidae—similar in appearance to snappers, family Lutjanidae) huddled among the mangrove branches and roots. From their size I figured the juvenile grunts had made the transformation from larval to juvenile stage about a month before. I concluded that those two bonefish had found the jackpot and were content to feed to their hearts' content until tide, or an angler, forced them away. An event like this would happen only in summer, when juvenile grunts are in their greatest numbers. Had I anticipated this, I might have fooled the bonefish with a small yellow-and-white Clouser Minnow. Lesson learned.

## SPAWNING GAMEFISH

Another reason to learn about the life cycles of fish is the influence of spawning on their location and behavior. For example, knowing where and when adult snook spawn narrows where to look for adult snook in summer months. Between the major spawning events (that is, between the full and new moons), snook will feed along ocean beaches and in grass beds that are near the passes, often in very shallow water. As they get ready to spawn, large groups of fish can be found "staging"—gathering in groups—near passes and channels.

I've found the best snook fishing along the beaches to be in the early- through late-morning hours, when snook can be found as close to shore as the water depth will allow. One of my favorite spots for summertime fishing for snook along an outer beach is about 1 to 2 miles from a pass where snook spawn. I like to stand high enough on the beach that I can see approaching snook and cast to fish as they cruise by on their way to the pass. I've found that fish will often travel in small groups of three or four, with the occasional large, solitary females. How do I know the big fish are females? Snook are known as protandrous hermaphrodites, which means that most snook first mature as males and then undergo a sex change to become females after they reach a larger size. So most of the monster snook of legend are females.

In contrast, bonefish spawn in deeper water outside reefs and thus aren't accessible to shoreline anglers and rely on off-shore currents to carry their larvae to the appropriate juvenile

*Snook and other gamefish will feed in only inches of water along sandy beaches.*

habitat. In the Caribbean, spawning occurs near the full and new moons, from late autumn through spring. During the few moons each season that seem to be the main spawning events, this might mean fishing may be less than stellar for a few days. But when the bonefish return to the flats from spawning, they'll be hungry. This time of year is also when anglers tend to encounter the largest bonefish, which may be due to large adults that are normally in deeper water spending some time inshore as they wait for the next spawning event.

Although the impact of catch-and-release of spawning fish is unclear, the conservative approach is to not target fish that are actively spawning. Spawning consumes a lot of the fishes' energy and may also make the fish more susceptible to large predators such as dolphin and sharks. Prior to spawning, many fish are ravenous as they build up an energy stockpile and can be just as hungry after spawning as they replenish their lost reserves. I think these pre- and postspawn fish are generally in good health and can handle catch-and-release fishing.

## TEMPERATURE

Fish are cold-blooded, and each species' physiology operates most efficiently within a limited temperature range for which the species is best adapted. Some species migrate long distances to take advantage of the largest area they can to stay within their preferred temperature range. Some tarpon, for example, migrate thousands of miles as they follow prey and participate in spawning, all in water that is mid-70s or higher. Other species remain in a region throughout the year but alter their behavior and habitat use patterns to remain within acceptable temperatures. Red drum are present in North Carolina throughout the year but can be hard to find during the cold fronts of winter when they hide out in deeper waters.

Regardless of the strategy that gamefish use to stay in an appropriate water temperature, the result is seasonal changes in gamefish availability. These temperature-related changes in gamefish abundance and behavior are most notable in warm-temperate and subtropical areas but also occur in the tropics. In general, the number of gamefish species is greatest during the warmer months. Species that spend the cold winter months offshore where water doesn't get as cold as along the coast or that migrated south when autumn arrived return to subtropical and warm-temperate coastal habitats as the shallow water warms in spring. In addition, many of the species that remained throughout the winter become more active with the warming waters of spring. So, summer brings the widest variety of gamefish to shallow coastal habitats.

In contrast, other species seem best adapted to the cooler temperatures of winter—spotted seatrout in the subtropics and some warm-temperate areas, for example—and the dog days of summer can send these species into deeper water. In the subtropics, red drum may become scarce in shallow habitats during summer and either feed in the shallows at dawn or dusk or move to cooler ocean waters outside their normal estuarine haunts. This is because during summer the water in shallow coastal habitats can become too warm, so fish seek out the relative coolness of deeper water. Spring and autumn, or even winter, can be the best times of year for these species, even though they are present and can be caught throughout the year.

Autumn is a special time in warm-temperate and subtropical regions because so many species are aggregating for autumn migrations. Not only the seasonal gamefish but also the species they depend upon for food are ready to move out. And these gatherings of large groups of prey bring out the resident gamefish for some prewinter feeding. These coinciding migrations can result in some amazing action as gamefish gorge on tightly packed schools of panicked baitfish. Most exciting for fly anglers is that these large concentrations of prey often occur along shallow beaches or even in shallow protected bays and so are within easy reach.

## LOCAL NUANCES

It's important to remember that every location will have its own nuances, so there is no single recipe for a successful strategy. You will have to investigate your home waters to figure things out. More-experienced anglers who are reading this probably already have experiences from their home waters similar to my Caribbean bonefish experiences. The obvious patterns are easy to figure out, but many more-subtle activities will require more study. But regardless of your local knowledge, your understanding of the general patterns described here will help you to be in the right spot at the right time casting the right fly. Of course, if in doubt, a local shop may be able to give you tips, and you can match those tips with information you'll gain from this book for a successful outing.

Now, with the information on fish life cycles as a foundation, we'll next examine the basics of tides and fish senses before launching into the full descriptions of coastal habitats and how they are used by gamefish.

# 2
# Tide Basics

Despite the importance of tides to coastal anglers, the ins and outs of tides and the way tides influence gamefish behavior are misunderstood by many. In this chapter I present basic information on tides to increase angler awareness of their importance to coastal gamefish and to enhance discussions of gamefish, habitats, and tides in later chapters.

## TIDE BASICS

Tides are the result of gravity and inertia. The gravitational pull of the moon creates a bulge of water on the side of the Earth facing the moon. The inertia of the water on the side of the Earth opposite the moon caused by moving water in response to the moon's pull creates a second bulge of water that is kept from leaving the Earth all together by the gravitational pull of the Earth. These two bulges of water, one on the side of the Earth closest to the moon, the other on the opposite side of the Earth, correspond to high tides. Halfway between the bulges of water are areas of extra-low water, on opposite sides of the Earth from one another, that correspond to low tides. As the moon revolves around the Earth, and the Earth spins, the bulges of water remain aligned with the moon, so the areas of high and low water rotate around the Earth. The changes in water height that correspond with the passing of the high and low water are called tides.

Because it takes slightly longer than a twenty-four-hour day for the moon to complete a full revolution around the Earth, a tidal "day" takes twenty-four hours and fifty minutes. This is why the timing of high and low tides changes daily—each tide approximately fifty minutes later than the day before—and follows a lunar cycle that takes slightly more than a month to complete.

The sun has about half the influence on tides as does the moon. But the sun's influence is sufficient to enhance or dampen the moon's effect on tides. When the sun and moon are aligned (either both are on the same side of the Earth or on exact opposite sides of the Earth), they exert their combined gravitational pull so that the bulges of water are larger than when the sun and moon are not aligned. And when the bulges of water are larger, the amount of water between the bulges is less, which translates to higher-than-normal high tides and lower-than-normal low tides. These extreme tides are called spring tides and are associated with new and full moons. And as if that wasn't enough, the pull of the moon and sun varies depending on how close they are to the Earth, so the severity of the spring tides can vary. Amazingly, gamefish and their prey are tuned in to these phenomena.

When the moon and sun are at right angles to one another, they partially negate each other's gravitational influence, resulting in a more-even distribution of water over the Earth's surface and a less-than-normal tidal range. These less-than-normal tides occur at the times of quarter moons and are called neap tides.

So within the monthly tidal cycle, every two weeks a flat will experience spring tides and on the alternating weeks will experience neap tides.

Because the Earth is round, you might expect all locations on Earth to get two high and two low tides per day, but this is not the case. Differences occur due to the topography of the oceans and continents and the inclination of the moon's rotation relative to the Earth. Some locations get two high and two low tides of approximately equal height per day (called semidiurnal tides), others get only a single high and low tide a day (diurnal tides), and some locations get two high and two low tides of unequal height per day (mixed tides). In addition, some areas have extreme tidal ranges (a 50-foot spring tide range in the Bay of Fundy, for

*From left to right: During the new moon, the sun and moon align on the same side of the Earth, creating disproportionate bulges of water, resulting in more-extreme spring tides; at the moon's first quarter, when the sun and moon are at right angles to the Earth, a weaker neap tide occurs; when the moon is full, the sun and moon are on exact opposite sides of the Earth, again creating spring tides; during the moon's last quarter, the sun and moon are again at right angles, causing weaker neap tides.*

example), whereas others have only a minor tidal range (a spring tide range of 1½ to 2 feet in most of the Caribbean).

As the height of the ocean changes with the tides, currents are created. Rising water travels around and over obstacles via currents, filling coastal bays and flats. As the tidal bulge passes, water level drops, and the ebbing tide drains the shallows. Because the amount of time between high and low tides for any given area is always the same, regardless of the tidal range, the strength of tidal currents varies between spring and neap tides. During spring tides, when tidal range is greatest, the greater volume of moving water creates stronger currents, whereas the weak neap tides cause the weakest tidal currents.

## Spring Tides

When spring high tides flood the shallows at the new and full moons, many gamefish take advantage of the higher water to forage in areas that they normally can't access or that are too shallow under neap tide conditions for them to feel comfortable. Shallow sand and grass flats, shorelines, shallow mangroves, and especially salt-marsh habitats hold many prey that are accessible for only a few days every couple of weeks during spring tides. High spring tides are also the best times to fish for gamefish like red drum along the ridges of oyster bars and flats that don't have mangroves or shallow shorelines. And it is usually during spring rising tides that you find bonefish, red drum, snook, and other gamefish feeding and resting in the skinniest water. Spring tides are my favorite for searching for red drum along shallow muddy shorelines lined by black mangroves or stalking bonefish in large backwater flats of stunted mangroves.

Many gamefish that ambush prey also take advantage of the stronger currents during spring tides. Snook, for example, will often hide behind submerged mangrove prop roots in creeks, darting out to grab small fish that are swept by in the current. Snook use this strategy especially during an ebbing tide. And striped bass are famous for holding in tidal currents, picking off

*At extreme low spring tides, some mangrove flats will be completely dry. Often, when the incoming tide covers these flats, bonefish are close behind.*

prey—from sand eels to menhaden—that are at the mercy of the strong currents of spring tides.

During spring tides the fishing can be fantastic but is often compacted into short time blocks. Red drum provide a great example for the flats, but with a few tweaks the same tips that follow can be applied to bonefish and other gamefish that prowl the flats. As the tide rises, red drum wait along the edges of salt marshes for the water to enter the marsh grass. As soon as the water is deep enough, red drum will move onto the low marsh flat, first through creeks and troughs, then out into the flooded marsh grass. They are searching mostly for crabs (fiddler crabs and portunid, or swimming, crabs) and to a lesser extent for the juvenile shrimp and small fish that also rise into the marsh with the tide. Similarly, as the tide rises into black mangrove stands, red drum first prowl the edge in search of food, then continue to push inward looking for fiddler crabs that are a bit too greedy and don't make it back into their burrows. In general, though, red drum don't stray too far from the safety of deeper water.

*Fiddler crabs emerge from their holes to feed at low tide and hide in their holes during high tide. Red drum will target these areas on rising tides, hoping to catch fiddler crabs that stay out of their holes too long.*

Why is this type of fishing often compacted into short time periods? Because the amount of time between high and low tide is always the same, regardless of whether it is a spring or neap tide, so the drop in water level is very fast during spring tides. Gamefish have to be concerned about becoming stranded too far from deep-water refuge as the tide ebbs.

In areas with large tidal ranges, the latter portion of the flooding tide and first portion of the ebb can be difficult fishing. As the tide continues to rise, the amount of habitat available to gamefish for feeding expands, and the amount of area to cover in search of fish can become overwhelming. High water during spring tides can make normally shallow grass and mud flats too deep for tailers and for sight-fishing, for example, and can even allow gamefish to access flooded areas, like mangrove forests, where they are inaccessible to anglers. This doesn't mean that it's time to go home. Those same gamefish that rode the rising tide into those inaccessible places will ride the ebbing water back out. So as the tide ebbs, the fish slowly move out of the flooded areas, often using the same avenues they used to access the shallows on the flooding tide.

As the tide drops out of the mangrove forests and marshes and pours out of the estuarine creeks, don't be tempted to leave too early. I am repeatedly amazed at how late in the ebbing tide some of the largest gamefish wait to emerge; I have seen the water so shallow, for example, that the backs of bonefish are exposed as they leave mangrove flats and move into deeper water. This has also been true in my experience with red drum, snook, and striped bass.

### Neap Tides

During neap tides, tidal range is at its minimum for the monthly tidal cycle. The skinny water where you found schools of tailing fish at high tide just the week before might not even be deep enough to hold fish during a high neap tide. Many salt marshes, black mangrove stands, and oyster bars, for example, will not have enough water on them to cover a gamefish. The gamefish are obviously still feeding and keyed to the tides but often will feed in different areas.

During the slow currents of neap tides, rather than set up feeding stations or push into the shallows to tail for prey, gamefish will often cruise in search of prey or try to ambush prey in habitats like potholes in seagrass beds. These tides are also good for looking for laid-up fish in the shallows. Troughs next to oyster bars and along red mangrove shorelines are good places to find gamefish during these tides. And the fish may be actively feeding in deeper areas, such as over grass beds, along channel edges, and in depressions and troughs between flats, providing fishing opportunities throughout the tidal cycle.

## BAROMETRIC PRESSURE AND WIND

Because tides are caused by movements of such massive areas of high and low water, you might think tides are impervious to influence from any other force, but this is not the case. Both barometric pressure and wind can greatly influence tides on a local scale and can significantly change tidal heights from the predictions of a tide chart. And although the wind- or barometric pressure-induced differences in tide may sometimes seem minor to us, they can influence gamefish behavior significantly.

Much is written in the fishing literature about the effect of barometric pressure on marine gamefish. Interestingly, colleagues who study fish physiology tell me that fish don't really have sensory structures that would allow them to feel changes in barometric pressure that would warn them of changing weather. And some claim that the changes in barometric pressure associated with a change in weather would be drowned out by even minor changes in depth by the fish. But if you've spent enough time on the water, you know that fish behavior changes with approaching changes in weather, so they are able to figure it out somehow. I think that we just haven't yet figured out how fish assess changes in weather. For example, a number of years ago, in two separate instances, colleagues conducting work on shark movements recorded juvenile sharks leaving an estuary as a tropical storm and a hurricane approached, only to return a day or two later after each storm had passed.

Regardless of whether fishes are able to detect changes in barometric pressure, barometric pressure changes can influence water level. During periods of low pressure, there is less pressure from the atmosphere pressing down on the water, so overall water level (and thus both high and low tide heights) can be higher. In addition, low barometric pressure is most often associated with either a warm or cold front, so a region may experience a weather change in association with a change in barometric pressure. In contrast, when barometric pressure is high, overall water level (and thus high and low tide heights) is suppressed, so tides may not be as high as predicted. High pressure is usually associated with fair weather.

While living on St. Croix, U.S. Virgin Islands, I remember multiday periods, sometimes weeks, of especially low or high water levels that didn't seem associated with a particular weather event or wind pattern. The reason for was explained when I was attending a science conference. One of the presentations was by an oceanographer who showed that he and his colleagues had measured average sea level changes associated with low or high pressure areas that moved across the tropics from Africa to the Caribbean. Sometimes these areas moved slowly or even stalled and explained my observations of abnormal water levels on the flats.

Wind can also have a dramatic effect on tides. For example, strong onshore winds can make high tides higher than predicted and in extreme conditions can even prevent low tides from occurring—in effect creating a ghost tide. Offshore winds will have the opposite effect—both high and low tides will be lower than predicted. When wind and high or low barometric pressure combine, the effects can be significant.

In many cases, a strong wind won't prevent tides from occurring but will delay the onset of the ebb or flood. For example, a strong onshore wind may lengthen the duration of high slack tide, but eventually the force of the ebbing tide is too much, and the water level drops quickly in the short amount of time remaining in the ebb. Also possible, and a potential source of danger, is the delay of a rising tide by offshore winds. Sandbars that are great spots for fishing can suddenly become overwashed with a delayed flooding tide, and the trek back to safety onshore can become treacherous, so be careful. This is more likely to be true in areas with a large tidal range—like New England or Georgia, where tidal range can be up to 8 or 9 feet—than in areas with a small tidal range, like the Gulf of Mexico.

The degree that wind influences tide levels depends on water depth and the shape of the basin. For example, a shallow enclosed bay will be more affected by wind than will an area with no surrounding land or shallows to restrict water flow. For enclosed basins depending on how long and strong the winds blow and the size and depth of the area affected, it may take a day or two for tides to return to normal after the wind subsides. This is why the tides of the Gulf of Mexico are more notably influenced by weather than are their Atlantic coast counterparts. The shallow continental shelf, shallow coastal bays and marshes, enclosed geography, and small tidal range allow wind and atmospheric pressure to have a greater influence than they do along the Atlantic coast with deeper water, greater tidal range, and a coastline that is relatively straight.

### Applying What You've Learned

#### Winds and Tides

In areas with a narrow tidal range and extensive shallows, wind and barometric pressure can have a greater effect than a normal tide and can influence the behavior of gamefish much the same as spring and neap tides. The potential effects of wind and changes in barometric pressure on bonefish, for example, are numerous. First, a strong offshore wind (and to a lesser extent strong high pressure) might completely offset the high water expected from a spring tide, which will prevent bonefish from accessing the shallows as they normally would. The extreme low spring tide will then be even lower than expected, perhaps forcing bonefish off the flats altogether. If the same wind blows during a neap tide, the minor high tide that was predicted might not happen, so it will seem like low tide throughout the tidal cycle. In these scenarios, strong offshore winds may mean that the edges of flats, deeper holes and troughs between flats, deeper grass beds and sand basins, and the deeper water on the back sides of fringing coral reefs may provide bonefish the best feeding opportunities.

In contrast, a strong onshore wind (and to a lesser extent strong low pressure) may give bonefish an extended stay at the shallow water buffet. A strong onshore wind can push a spring high tide even farther into the shallows and mangrove flats, can delay the onset of the ebbing tide, and can keep the water level from becoming as low as predicted at low tide. In a sense, the predicted tide heights shift up a notch. The extra water gives bonefish a wider selection of locations and, potentially, a longer time to forage. In general, when the wind and tide are working in concert to push more water onto the flat, the result is more bonefish on the expansive shallows.

## Bonefish

Bonefish are experts at using the tides to their advantage, which allows them to maximize the benefits in the tradeoff between feeding and avoiding predators. I guess you'd expect this from bonefish because they've been perfecting their behavior for millions of years. Bonefish try to get away with as little travel as possible in their search for a meal, and if a flat provides food and protection from predators, it makes no sense to swim long distances in search of food. This is one reason why bonefish don't stray far when retreating from a flat during low tide. This was verified by acoustic tagging research conducted by Robert Humston when he was a graduate student at the University of Miami. And research by Mike Larkin, also at the University of Miami, showed that most bonefish tagged with dart tags (aka spaghetti tags) were recaptured within 5 miles of where they were tagged.

At low tide or the earliest stages of flood tide, you can often find a bonefish or two feeding slowly along a shallow edge of a flat. But these fish can be tough to catch because they are often skittish in the skinny water. These "early" fish are typically not feeding aggressively because the tide hasn't begun to move. In contrast, after the tide begins to flood, more fish will move onto the flat and begin to feed in earnest.

Bonefish will often follow traditional routes onto and off the flats. Many of these access routes are nothing more than small troughs that cross a flat. (These access routes are different than the deeper, more obvious channels adjacent to flats that often hold bonefish at low tide.) Favorite bonefish avenues are the troughs only a few inches deeper than the surrounding flat that lead from deeper edges to the flat's interior. Often these access channels are hard to discern when the flat is covered in water, so visit a flat on a late dropping tide and make a note of where the fingers of water are draining. These troughs are also the first to fill on the rising tide and usually where bonefish make their first appearance. As you gain experience on particular flats, figure out which of these troughs are the traditional (most used) access routes. Of course, it's not always that simple—the routes might vary depending on the tide height and the strength of the current, such as the differences you might find between spring and neap tides or on windy versus calm days.

### Spring Tide

When spring high tides flood the shallows, bonefish are quick to take advantage of the higher water to forage in areas they normally can't access. Being able to reach very shallow habitats coupled with the limited time they can remain there can result in bonefish grouping along the edges of flats in anticipation of the incoming tide. Early in the rising tide and late in the outgoing tide, find the bonefish travel avenues, and you should have brief-yet-intense periods of casting to cruising fish.

As the tide rises, move onto the shallow sand and grass flats, shorelines, shallow mangrove flats, and the shallow ridges of sand flats accessible to bonefish only during these spring high tides. Such habitats often hold a lot of prey, and bonefish know this. Much of the bonefish feeding during spring tides, for example, is concentrated from the midrising through early falling tide. Bonefish often feed so actively near high tide that they may actually take a break or leisurely nibble as they move off the flat to wait for another foraging opportunity during the next incoming tide.

During low tide, bonefish often rest in flat-side channels waiting for the next flooding tide. From their perspective, why expend energy unnecessarily? In the hour or so on either side of the low tide, stalk the edges of flats searching for bonefish laid up or cruising slowly in slightly deeper water. I've even landed some bonefish blind-casting into these channels that are just a bit too deep to sight-fish.

## Neap Tide

During neap tides the skinny water where you found tailing bonefish or redfish at high tide just the week before might not be deep enough to hold fish. The shallow mangrove flats that attracted so many bonefish into their shadows may still hold water but are probably empty of bonefish. Even areas that seem to have enough water may lack redfish or bonefish because during neap tides they're too far to allow travel from deep water. This means you need to change where you search.

Bonefish will still move from the edges of flats onto a flat as the tide rises but won't venture as far onto the flat. Perhaps because bonefish aren't traveling far to get to shallows accessible only during spring tides, they're more likely to feed throughout the tidal cycle during neap tides. Edges of flats are good places to search for cruising bonefish during weak neap tides. Bonefish may be actively feeding in deeper areas such as over grass beds, along channel edges, and in depressions and troughs between flats, providing fishing opportunities throughout the tidal cycle.

Because the water level isn't rising as high on the flats, and the tidal currents aren't as strong as during spring tides, the travel avenues used by bonefish may be different during neap tides than during spring tides. Shallow troughs that provided access to backwaters during spring tides may not be used during neap tides because those backwaters aren't feeding areas during low water. Instead, feeding may occur on different parts of the flats—adjust your search pattern accordingly.

## Final Thoughts

High tides during full moons can work against an angler. During full-moon spring tides, bonefish sometimes venture into the shallows at night to feed. Conventional wisdom is that when bonefish (and other gamefish) feed at night they eat less aggressively during the day. One way to combat this potential problem is to fish at dawn and dusk, when nighttime bonefish may be ending or beginning their feeding. If bonefish seem to be dining less aggressively than usual, try working the fly more slowly to accommodate slower-moving fish.

During warm times of year when water temperatures in the shallows rise above the bonefish comfort level, tidal currents carry cooler water from adjacent deeper areas onto the flats with the rising tide. As the tide rises, the cooler water flows first along the edge, and, if the incoming tide is strong enough, it will also flood the flat. Under these conditions bonefish will initially remain along the edge of the flat, moving onto the flat only with the cool water of the rising tide. In other words, it may take a little longer for bonefish to move onto the flat during warm weather.

In contrast, during cold seasons the sunny days may warm the water in the shallows, or water flooding onto a flat may absorb the warmth of the sun-baked bottom. This brings bonefish into the shallows as the water temperature rises. Although you might think of the temperature changes of the tropics as minor, to bonefish and other tropical species a few degrees can make a big difference.

# 3
# Sight and Sound

Many anglers make assumptions about what fish see and hear, and many of these assumptions are wrong. I've been told, for example, in no uncertain terms that fish can't see color. This is not true. Although very few studies have been done on fish to address whether they truly discern different colors, the eyes of most marine fishes have one to four optical pigments (which are needed to detect the wavelengths of light for different colors) in contrast to humans, who have three optical pigments. In any case, different species of fish have different photo pigments, which means that they likely see different portions of the light spectrum (i.e., different colors). In addition, some fish can see portions of the light spectrum that we cannot, such as ultraviolet wavelengths of light. Therefore, knowing what colors can be seen by your favorite gamefish is important for designing and selecting flies.

The issue of color vision by fish is complicated, however, by the behavior of light in water, which influences, among other things, which colors can be seen at different depths and at different distances. The information contained in this chapter will help you to make sense of light in water and fish vision and help you better understand how fish react to their surroundings—including your fly.

Because fish don't have external ears, many people think they can't hear. This is also not true. Water is 850 times denser than air, so sound travels very well in water. Sensing that sound is very important for fishes, both to find prey and to avoid predators as well as for social behavioral purposes such as finding and communicating for reproduction. Dropping items in a boat, splashing while wading, making a splashy presentation of a fly are all actions that send sound waves propagating rapidly through the water, alerting fish to your presence. But designing flies that put out vibrations as they are stripped through the water—vibrations are low-frequency sound waves—can be deadly in bringing in fish. Understanding how fish detect sound and how sound travels through water can also be useful in creating and selecting flies as well as in strategizing how flies are fished under different conditions.

This chapter provides brief overviews of sight and sound for anglers: how light and sound waves behave in water and how fish detect them. The chapter is intended as a primer—enough of the basics to satisfy many anglers and enough of a foundation to give more-curious anglers the means to pursue more-detailed explanations.

## BASICS OF LIGHT IN WATER

Visible light (the portion of the light spectrum that we are able to see) is composed of many wavelengths (colors). The general makeup of these colors is red, orange, yellow, green, blue, indigo, and violet plus all of the small transitions in between. Beyond either end of the visible spectrum are wavelengths of light that we are unable to see—infrared on the outer end of the red end of the light spectrum, for example, and ultraviolet past the violet end of the spectrum. Each of these colors has different wavelengths, which means they interact differently with the material through which they are passing. The color with the longest wavelength is red, and wavelengths become shorter toward the violet end of the spectrum.

Why does wavelength matter? Because, in general, the longer the wavelength, the faster the light is absorbed in water. I say "in general" because there is more than just water molecules in water; there is a lot of other stuff that also influences the behavior of light in water.

In clear, open ocean water, and to a lesser extent on tropical flats, the color red is no longer visible below 20 feet or so. Orange and yellow are lost soon after. By the time a depth of 30 feet is reached, blue and violet are pretty much the only colors left. In deep water, everything takes on shades of gray and black.

The behavior of light differs, however, in coastal and estuarine waters. Many coastal waters contain a lot of plankton, which absorbs short-wavelength light (such as blue), and longer wavelengths are absorbed by the water. This leaves green as the dominant color remaining in coastal waters because it penetrates to the greatest depth. In coastal waters with a lot of suspended particles—estuaries, for example—green is also absorbed and scattered, which leaves red, orange, and yellow as dominant remaining light wavelengths, at least as far as they can penetrate into the water.

Patterns of color attenuation also occur horizontally, and loss of light is often more extreme in the horizontal plane. So, although you may be able to clearly see the colors of a red fly 1 foot below the surface in clear ocean water, a fish that is only a few feet away may not see the color red. This is because light in the vertical, downward plane (your perspective) can be much brighter than light in the horizontal plane (the fish's perspective). For example, at high noon the light in the downward, vertical plane can be 10–100 times brighter than in the horizontal plane. And then when you add in the angle of sunlight hitting the water, color visibility becomes even more complex. So, a big consideration when choosing colors for flies is how far away the fish will be when you make your fly presentation.

Interestingly, even bright fluorescent colors are not always visible. For example, fluorescent colors are stimulated by the ultraviolet end of the light spectrum, so you might expect that they can be seen farther away in all conditions, but this is not necessarily true. In turbid and stained waters, ultraviolet light barely penetrates, so fluorescent colors might not be very visible. In contrast, in clear tropical waters, where ultraviolet light penetrates considerable distances, fluorescent colors should be more visible over a greater distance than some other wavelengths. This may be why a tuft of fluorescent orange on a bonefish fly seems to be attractive to bonefish.

The detection of color in the horizontal plane by gamefish is further complicated by what happens to light after it is in the water. Light is also lost over distance (attenuated) by scattering and absorption by objects. For example, when light travels through the water, some light is reflected by particles that are suspended in the water. This reduces the amount of light that continues to pass through the water and thus reduces the intensity of the light at greater depth. Other light is absorbed by objects, such as rocks, and the light is converted into heat. Light is also absorbed by plankton, which use it for photosynthesis. And still more light is absorbed by the water and converted to heat. At one extreme, in murky, plankton-filled coastal waters, light doesn't penetrate very far. At the other extreme, in tropical oceans light penetrates for hundreds of feet.

The scattering of light by particles is an important concept to understand, even when fishing apparently crystal clear waters of a bonefish flat. Often, water that seems to begin clear from the surface is not so when viewed from below. This is because the light that enters the water reflects off suspended particles, scattering light in all directions. This results in decreased ability to see colors when looking horizontally.

As light hits the water surface, some is reflected back into the air, and some enters the water. The amount of light that enters the water tends to be greater on days with waves than on days that are flat calm. This may seem counterintuitive—after all, days with waves or chop can produce a lot of glare that is tough for an angler to see through. But the glare the angler experiences has more to do with the angle of the water on the waves in relation to the angler's angle of looking into the water than it does with how much light is entering the water.

When light enters the water, it is refracted (in a sense, it is bent). This is because air and water are of different densities, so light travels faster in air than in water. When the angle of the water surface changes in relation to incoming light, such as on a wavy water surface, the relative angles that the light is refracted change, which creates the undulating motion of light and shadow underwater.

The amount of light play underwater can have an influence on how well objects are seen by fish. In general, I think that on days with wave action it is harder for fish to see small objects—they can become lost in the mix of light and shadow that results from the refraction of light through the multiple angles of the water surface. So, on days with wave action, try using larger flies. In contrast, on calm days when there is less underwater light play because the light is being refracted at mostly the same angle, small flies may be more appropriate.

## A GAMEFISH'S POINT OF VIEW

One way by which prey tries to hide from gamefish is through cryptic coloration (colors and patterns of colors that help them blend into their surroundings). For many baitfish, this takes the form of countershading (darker on the dorsal [top] surface and lighter on the ventral [bottom] surface) or even bars and stripes to break up their profile. However, the effectiveness of the prey and the ability of a gamefish to see the prey change with the amount of light, direction of light, and the relative orientations of the gamefish and prey to one another. Important factors are water type, depth and the angle of view, elevation, and direction of the sun.

How a gamefish visually detects its prey depends a lot on the relative positions of the gamefish and the prey. For example, although the scattering, absorption, and other factors affecting light in the water may limit color visibility when objects are viewed horizontally, these same factors mean that the silhouettes of prey are easier to see when viewed by a gamefish from below. This is because light falling down from the sun is 100–1,000 times brighter than light emanating from below, so a gamefish viewing a prey from below against the sun can see that prey's silhouette regardless of the prey's coloration. In fact, research has shown that the conventional wisdom that white ventral (belly) coloration in aquatic animals makes them less visible from below is false. This is because the amount of light from above is so much brighter than light from below that it overwhelms the white coloration (or even a mirror reflecting downward) or even a reflection from the underside of the prey, thus producing a silhouette.

When searching for baitfish, a gamefish may change its location in the water column to achieve different perspectives. For example, moving shallower or deeper will provide a different perspective, allowing gamefish to sight prey as silhouettes from below or perhaps detect their coloration from a horizontal perspective. Gamefish might also circle to change their location relative to the angle of the sun to, for example, see the baitfish as silhouettes against the bright light of the sun. The low angle of the sun early and late in the day can be especially advantageous for gamefish. This is because virtually no light emanates from below, and this contrast with the light from above makes the prey more visible as silhouettes.

The changing visibility of prey in relation to the orientation of gamefish and prey is an important consideration as you determine how, where, and when you present a fly. You may notice, for example, that sometimes gamefish will take only flies that are fished in a certain direction or when the gamefish are oriented in a certain direction relative to the angle of the sun. This may also be why sometimes gamefish appear to attack schooled baitfish from a specific direction—they likely attack from the direction that gives them the best view of the prey.

This was especially apparent to me during a day of fishing on Cape Cod in early autumn. I was sight-fishing for striped bass along a shallow sloping beach and had good success with sight-fishing for cruising stripers. Late in the afternoon I came upon a school of small menhaden (peanut bunker in New England parlance) that was pushed up against the beach by a few dozen stripers. The stripers would meander away from the beach and circle back toward the menhaden from the 10 o'clock direction (12 o'clock was perpendicular to shore). Casting to the stripers that were moving away from the menhaden or moving parallel to shore brought no reaction, but when a striper turned toward shore and the school of menhaden, it reacted well to a fly thrown into its path. The sun was low in the sky and over land, so it was shining toward the water; when the stripers approached from offshore the menhaden (and my fly) likely stood out as stark silhouettes and were easy for the stripers to spot.

The scattering of light presents even more of a challenge in murky or muddy water. There are so many particles in the water that light is reflected in all directions, making visibility very difficult. To get a better grasp of this, think about driving through a fog bank at night. You can see more with your low-beam headlights on because less light is being reflected back at you than when you have the high beams on. Dark objects tend to show up best in murky water conditions because they provide the maximum contrast against the otherwise murky, backlit background against which a light-colored fly won't stand out. This is a major reason why black flies are productive in murky water. It's also true that larger objects can be spotted from farther away, so in these conditions you may want to consider using larger flies.

## FISH VISION

The eye of most gamefish is similar to the human eye—it has a cornea, lens, and retina with rods and cones. Gamefish are able to regulate light entering the eye through a pupillary aperture, which acts similar to the iris in the human eye via contraction and dilation. Some fish also have behavioral characteristics that place them in situations with light levels to which they are best adapted, such as moving up and down in the water column or feeding exclusively during the day or night. Other gamefish have types of flaps that can be used to moderate the amount of light entering the eye. This is often the case for fish that feed on the bottom—they have a flap that blocks some of the bright light from above so that they have better vision as they focus on the bottom (this is similar to anglers reducing glare by using a wide-brimmed hat and side flaps on sunglasses to reduce glare when sight-fishing on the flats).

Within the retina are specialized cells called rods and cones. These cells contain pigments that absorb the light and send signals to the optic nerve that connects to the brain. Rod cells are best suited to low-light conditions and provide sensitivity to light, especially to images in low light. During high light-intensity conditions (daylight), many rods are protected by a specialized pigment that shades the rod cells. This is when cone cells are most important during daylight conditions and are most responsible for color vision and visual acuity. As light levels change, the ratio of active rod and cone cells changes to maximize vision. This is not an instantaneous process, which is why it takes a while for eyes to "adjust" to drastic changes in light levels.

In general, a fish species's vision is the result of the habitats to which the fish is best suited and the fish's behavior. A species of fish that feeds nocturnally or is limited to regions with murky coastal water, for example, will have eyes that are highly sensitive. This species does not need much light to see its prey and surroundings, but this trait comes at the cost of visual acuity. In contrast, a species that is adapted to clear water with high light intensity, like tropical flats, will be less sensitive to light but have better resolution (in good light conditions, the species will have good visual acuity). In addition, fish that specialize in feeding in high light conditions tend to have eyes capable of processing fast-moving images, such as a Spanish mackerel chasing a scaled sardine. In contrast, red drum are adapted to generally murky estuarine and coastal waters with lower light levels and thus likely have lower speed vision.

Also related to fish habitat and behavior is the field of vision, that is, where a fish is looking. Because cone cells are responsible for visual acuity and color, they are typically most dense on the part of the retina that is exposed to the portion of the field of vision that is most important to the fish. For example, fish that look upward for their prey tend to have high concentrations of cone cells on the lower region of their retina. Similarly, tuna, which forage in open waters, have cone cell concentrations that focus on forward and upward portions of the field of vision. Interestingly, research by Andrij Horodysky shows that striped bass also have cone cell concentrations that focus forward and upward.

With those basics out of the way, we get to the question of color. Even though scientific research shows that fish can detect different wavelengths of light, there is really no way of knowing if fish see colors in the same way that we do. This is something to keep in mind when designing and selecting flies. We also know that many fish can detect wavelengths in the ultraviolet end of the spectrum but don't know the details on how fish use this information, much less what these ultraviolet wavelengths look like to the fish.

Once again, fish are likely to be most sensitive to colors that give them the most information in the environments they typically inhabit. For example, red drum see green and blue rather well and to a lesser extent orange and yellow. Red is not detected as well by red drum. Perhaps because they generally dwell in shallow waters, spotted seatrout see purple and blue rather well, green to a lesser extent, and red not well at all. To my knowledge, no research has been done on color vision of bonefish, tarpon, or permit.

## BASICS OF SOUND IN WATER

Sound is more important in water than most anglers realize. Much of the misunderstanding likely results from a property of sound waves—they typically don't travel from one medium to another, from water to air, for example. The densities of water and air are too different for most sound to travel from one to the other, so anglers fishing on a boat or wading are oblivious to most of the noise that exists below the water surface. Similarly, fish are generally unaware of sound traveling through the air above them.

A sound wave is a pressure wave that includes two linked components—pressure and particle motion—that are difficult to separate, so for the remainder of the discussion I will use the term *pressure* to refer to both. In any case, these waves displace particles as they travel through air, water, or another medium. Sound in water travels approximately 4½ times faster (and also travels farther) than in air. Low-frequency sounds tend to travel farther than high-frequency sounds. This means that the noise made by dropping a reel onto the deck of the boat is detected almost immediately by fish within a significant radius of the boat—the boat hull acts as an amplifier, and because it is in the water, the sound of banging against its hull is transmitted through the water.

Pressure waves are also generated by objects moving through the water—whether a swimming fish, a scurrying prey, a moving boat, or a wading angler. These waves travel through the water in the same fashion as sound waves. This is why stealthy anglers are more successful when wading than when moving quickly across the flat, pushing a wave of water as they move. This also explains why a fish reacts to a fly that plops loudly into the water.

When sound travels through water, its intensity diminishes with distance. This is because as a sound wave travels through water, it is weakened by scattering and absorption. Scattering is the reflection of the sound wave in directions other than its original direction of movement. This can be caused by structures such as rocks and by the bottom or water surface, both of which are of different densities than water. This is especially true in shallow water, where the bottom and water surface are close to one another and greatly limit the distance that a sound wave can travel relative to the open ocean. In deeper waters the bottom and water surface aren't as influential, and sound can travel farther. Absorption is the conversion of the sound energy to other forms of energy and doesn't differ between shallow and deeper water.

## FISH HEARING

The propagation of sound and other pressure waves in water means that detection of these waves is an essential characteristic possessed by gamefish, their prey, and their predators. Fish have two means for detecting these sound and pressure waves (and the associated particle displacement)—an inner ear and a lateral line.

A fish's inner ear is composed of a series of fluid-filled canals and chambers. The inner walls of the chambers are lined by cells with hairlike extensions that protrude into the chamber. In these chambers are small bones called otoliths. As the otoliths move around in the chamber, the cilia detect the movements and send a signal to the brain. This is how, just as with our inner ear, fish can control their equilibrium—the otoliths lying on the bottom, side, or top of the chamber tell the fish it is swimming upright, on its side, or upside down, respectively.

More important to this discussion is how this setup is used to detect sound. As a sound wave travels from the water to the otoliths, it is moving between substances that have different densities. This causes the sound wave to change shape and causes the otoliths to vibrate differently than the rest of the fish. The vibration of the otoliths stimulates the cilia, which send a message to the brain. The brain then has to determine whether the sound is of consequence and whether it is from a prey or predator. The sound waves traveling through the fluid within the inner ear can also be detected.

To use the pressure components of sound, some fish use their air-filled swim bladder to increase their hearing ability. The air within the swim bladder is compressed by the sound waves and thus is more sensitive than the inner ear. In many fish the swim bladder is connected to the inner ear, which allows the air bladder to act as an amplifier of sound (the swim bladder acts like a transducer, reradiating the pressure components of sound as particle motion to the otoliths). Even in many fish without a direct connection between the swim bladder and inner ear, an extension of the swim bladder is close enough to the inner ear to at least partially amplify sound. The inner ear system of fish is good at detecting sounds at both close range (30 feet or so) and at a distant (1 mile or more).

A great complement to the inner ear system of fish is their lateral line system. The lateral line is a series of pores, through which specialized cells extend. The lateral line extends along the length of the fish, from just behind the head to the base of the tail. Sticking through the pores are specialized cells, called neuromasts, that contain sensory cells embedded in a jelly-filled casing called a capula, which extends into the pore. As pressure waves pass over the fish, the capula is moved, which in turn moves the sensory hairs within it, which sends a signal to the brain. The lateral line detects the particle motion aspect of sound from near sources, 30 feet or less.

The movement of pressure waves through the water and the ability of fish to detect them are why flies such as Seaducers, muddlers, sliders, and poppers can work so well. All of these patterns produce pressure waves as they move through or across the water. So, even in low light or murky water, fish are able to detect these flies. But don't reserve these flies just for low-light or murky water conditions—fish likely first detect prey (or your flies) from a distance using sound (or pressure waves from motion) and then rely on sight only in close quarters.

## Applying What You've Learned

### The Science of Flies

When strategizing the creation, selection, and presentation of flies, I start with the basics and add components if the situation requires. Step 1 is to determine the conditions in which I'll be fishing. Do I need to be prepared for murky or clear water, backcountry water that is tannin-stained, or the crystal-clear water of a tropical flat? It's always a good idea to have flies for sunny as well as cloudy days. What about the species I'll be targeting—is it adapted best to feed in bright or dark conditions, clear or murky water? The answers to each of these questions are critical to designing, selecting, and presenting flies in coastal waters.

Let's start with murky coastal waters because I think this situation allows the most basic approach. Because underwater visibility is greatly limited, gamefish primarily use their lateral line and inner ear to locate prey, and vision becomes important only at close range. For this reason, a fly's motion and sound are the most important characteristics to consider. A whistler with a full, webby hackle collar pulsates with every strip, sending out pressure waves that can be detected by gamefish. Similarly, Mangrove Muddlers and other similar patterns that push water as they are stripped can be located by gamefish in murky waters. Of course, poppers can be very productive in poor visibility conditions—the "pop" sends out strong pressure waves, followed by weaker pressure waves from water drops splashing down. Plus, you can alter the strength of the popper's pressure waves by changing how strongly you strip the fly.

Do artificial noisemakers actually work to attract gamefish? Despite the prevalence of rattles and other noisemakers on the market, we don't know the answer to that question. Rattles, for example, likely create sound at a frequency that is too high for most gamefish to hear. However, items such as "clackers" likely produce sound at a lower frequency, which gamefish are more likely to hear. In either case, it's important to not overdo it. Remember that prey tend to minimize their output of pressure waves—whether sound or motion—to escape detection by predators, so too much noise emanating from a fly can actually keep gamefish away.

In murky water conditions, it's important to work the fly slowly. Doing this gives a fish the chance to find the fly. Your strips of the fly can be varied—from strong and fast to gentle and slow—but you should give ample time between strips to allow the fly to stay in the water for a sufficient amount of time. Keeping the fly in the water longer allows time for the waves generated by the fly to travel through the water and be detected by the fish's lateral line or inner ear and for the fish to determine the source of the movement, to move toward the fly, and, after it is close enough, to visually identify the fly and eat it.

After the fish determines the source of the movement and locates the general location of the fly, it has to see it. Remember that in murky water with a lot of suspended matter, light is reflected off all those particles, so things are backlit in almost every direction. Generally in these situations, light-colored flies are tough to see—they have little contrast to their surroundings and thus are much tougher for fish to see than are darker flies. In fact, a lot of prey fishes, such as mummichogs, in murky water are very lightly colored so that they are more difficult to see. So, in murky water situations, darker flies are usually best because they contrast the most to their surroundings and stand out well against a backlit background (i.e., provide a good silhouette).

Because sound/motion and contrast are most important in these situations, color and detail are secondary considerations at best. Because the fish is using sound/motion to find the fly, much light has been attenuated quickly, and much of the remaining light is reflected to make most objects backlit, I think it's most important to focus on fly profile and action—does the fly have a shape, size, and movement of a prey the gamefish expects to see?

Murky water is on one end of a continuum that covers the range of relative importance of sound and sight to gamefish pursuing prey (and flies). Other conditions present similar challenges for gamefish to locate prey, such as nocturnally feeding fish. Dusk and dawn are a bit along the continuum, where the relative importance of sight increases. This should be reflected in your flies and how you present them. Under each of these conditions (dark of night, dawn, and dusk), gamefish rely heavily on motion/sound to locate prey, and the relative importance of sight changes with the changing conditions.

At night there is so little light that sound/motion and contrast are the only factors I consider for flies. A fly that moves water can be located by a gamefish, and because I expect a nocturnally feeding fish to be adapted to seeing in low-light conditions, I use a black fly that contrasts well with the star- or moon-lit sky to a fish feeding from below. This strategy works well for anglers fishing for striped bass at night.

At dawn and dusk the gamefish is exposed to constantly changing light conditions—at dusk there is less light with each passing minute, whereas at dawn light is increasing over time. When fishing for tailing red drum in late evening and into dusk, I usually start with a fly that contains a flash of colors that red drum can see. Gold or copper and green flash on tan or brown flies are my favorites. As dusk approaches, I often switch to a fly that is darker and moves water, such as a muddler, Seaducer, or even a surface fly such as a gurgler.

Dawn patrol provides a bit of a different challenge. Light is initially very low, so flies that move water and provide good contrast are essential. As light levels increase, however, color can become important very quickly, so even the flies that rely on motion and contrast for low-light dawn conditions should have appropriate colors. The importance of light at dawn changes quickly enough, I believe, that if you rely on changing flies to keep up with these light changes, you will be forever behind the curve. This is why, when fishing at dawn for tarpon, I usually tie on a purple Toad—the toad provides the motion necessary for tarpon to find the fly in low-light conditions, purple provides sufficient contrast in low light (though not as good as black), and as light levels increase, tarpon are able to see purple (which appears to be a portion of the light spectrum that they can detect well).

At higher light levels and clearer water, the relative importance of color in flies is greater. But even under the best of conditions, remember that light is lost just as quickly in the horizontal as it is in the vertical. Your fly still must have the motion, size, shape, and contrast to get the gamefish close enough to the fly to see color. Then at closer quarters the colors you use for the fly help to close the deal.

This is where knowing what portions of the light spectrum gamefish can see comes in handy. Red drum, for example, can see most wavelengths of visible light but are best able to see green, followed by yellow and orange. Similarly, spotted seatrout best see wavelengths of 460 nanometers, and striped bass are well adapted to see yellow-orange, green, and blue. To the best of my knowledge, there has been no research on what portions of the light spectrum can be seen by bonefish, tarpon, and permit.

For fish such as bonefish, tarpon, permit, and a lot of other gamefish with no research on their vision, a little bit of field research with flies of different colors is useful. It's something worth exploring if you have sufficient time while fishing for these species. Also helpful is taking into consideration the water in which you typically encounter these fish. Some thought on the habitats and behaviors of the gamefish you are targeting is also useful.

## Applying What You've Learned

### Changing Light

Throughout a day of fishing, conditions can change, even during the middle part of the day when light levels are high. It's important to pay attention to your surroundings so you can adapt to these changing conditions. Water clarity and light levels, for example, often change during the course of the day, which influences which colors are best seen by gamefish and the relative importance of sight and sound for fly selection. A day of fishing for tarpon along an ocean sandbar provides a good example of how changing flies as conditions change can result in more fish.

When we arrived at the sandbar at about 9:30 in the morning, the skies were clear. The water was very slightly murky—not from sediment but rather from some type of plankton bloom. The plankton was very thick in some patches but relatively light in most areas. The plankton gave the water a slightly tan coloration. Given the slightly "off" water color, we tied on flies with yellow in them. To our eyes, the yellow showed well when the fly was in the water, and under these conditions we thought that yellow should also be visible to the fish. The tarpon reacted well to the yellow flies, and we got some to eat, giving us confidence in our decision.

A bit after midday, water currents switched direction with the change in tide. The plankton slowly disappeared, and the water became clear with a slight greenish tinge. The tarpon began to ignore the yellow fly. When we switched to a fly with a green swash, the fish once again turned on and ate the fly well.

If you've spent enough time on the water, you likely have seen this type of phenomenon before—the color of fly the fish prefer changes. Sometimes this happens during a day, as it did with tarpon; at other times it may be one day to the next. And you've also probably watched fish react entirely differently to the presentation of the same fly pattern from one day to the next. One day the fish seem attracted by the splash of the fly landing on the water. On another day the fish head for the hills when the fly hits the water. All of these changes are reflections of how the fish are interacting with their dynamic environment. Understanding how fish detect sight and sound and how sight and sound are influenced by environmental conditions will help you design better flies and fish the right flies at the right time.

# 4
# Seagrass

Seagrass beds are my favorite coastal and estuarine habitats to fish. Seagrass beds are where many juvenile gamefish and prey get their start, are full of species that gamefish use as prey, and are used as feeding areas by many adult gamefish. Seagrass beds come in different forms: They can be thick, dense stands of continuous grass; thick grass pockmarked by deep, sandy potholes; a patchwork of seagrass and open bottom; or sparse seagrass blades scattered over an otherwise open sand or mud bottom. And what's more, numerous species of seagrass can make up a grass bed, each with unique characteristics that make a difference to gamefish and their prey. The combination of how a grass bed is arranged, the different types of seagrass, and a grass bed's location pose different opportunities and challenges for both gamefish and anglers. Information in this chapter will improve your understanding of how gamefish perceive seagrass habitats, what prey species are most common, and how best to approach fly fishing in these diverse habitats.

At first glance, seagrass beds may seem like lush underwater lawns with a limited number of organisms living among the blades of grass. But on closer inspection, an observant angler will see a habitat teeming with life. Because seagrass beds are shallow and very productive areas that provide food for many species, they are attractive areas for numerous small organisms, many of which are cryptic (well camouflaged to match their surroundings) and very adept at using the seagrass blades for shelter. Many of these organisms are prey for gamefish.

Although seagrass habitat provides shelter for small organisms, such as shrimps, crabs, and small fish, there is inadequate shelter for large fish. This is one reason why large fish often forage in shallow seagrass beds but retreat to deeper water when they feel threatened. (In areas with thick growth of seagrass, however, redfish and spotted seatrout will burrow into grass in an attempt to hide from predators.) Figuring out the strategies that gamefish use to capture prey while avoiding predators in these shallow habitats is the focus of this chapter and will help you find and catch more gamefish in seagrass beds.

After I summarize the ecological requirements of the species of seagrass that make up grass bed habitats, I will delve into examples of the many species of prey that use grass beds for food and shelter and then examine how the abundance, seasonality, and behavior of these prey species influence feeding behavior of gamefish.

## SEAGRASS BASICS

"Why," you might ask, "should I read about the ecological requirements of the different species of seagrass?" One answer is that the more you know about the gamefish's home, the more you know about the gamefish and the more fish you are likely to catch. Another answer might be that the more you know about what these habitats need to exist, the better equipped you'll be to make sure these habitats remain healthy so you can continue to catch fish in the future. And learning about what makes these habitats tick will give you clues that will help you choose the best times and locations to fish.

Seagrass beds are widely distributed in shallow, protected, coastal waters throughout the tropics and subtropics and to a lesser extent in warm-temperate environments. In the Gulf of Mexico, seagrass beds are common as far north as the Florida Panhandle. Seagrass beds along the northern Gulf of Mexico coast (western Florida Panhandle through eastern Texas) are scattered and sparse compared with the Gulf coast of Florida and the tropics. Seagrass beds become more prevalent again beginning in southwest Texas and south into Mexico and Central America. Along the Atlantic coast, seagrass beds are present as far north as Indian River Lagoon, Florida, and then largely absent until North Carolina's Outer Banks and associated sounds.

Seagrass beds of the tropics, subtropics, and warm-temperate regions may contain as many as nine species of seagrass, but you are most likely to encounter only four species: turtle grass (*Thalassia testudinum*), shoal grass (*Halodule wrightii*), widgeon grass (*Ruppia maritima*), and manatee grass (*Syringodium filiforme*). In the tropics you will mostly encounter turtle grass and manatee grass as well as shoal grass in the shallows, whereas you may regularly encounter all four species in the subtropics. Seagrass beds in warm-temperate North Carolina contain mostly eel grass (*Zostera marina*), with some shoal grass in the southern Outer Banks of North Carolina and some widgeon grass in backwater areas.

All seagrass species require sunlight for photosynthesis and thus are limited to shallow coastal waters. The depths to which you will find seagrass depend on water clarity—the clearer the water, the deeper you will find seagrass. You can find seagrass at depths of 30 feet or more in clear tropical waters (though you won't likely be fishing this deep), whereas it is uncommon to find seagrass in greater than 10-foot depths in Florida estuaries and the northern Gulf of Mexico.

Seagrass serves an important ecological function by acting as a baffle, reducing the velocity of currents that flow over grass beds so that sediment particles suspended in the water by these currents settle to the bottom. This acts as a filter, keeping sediments from reaching reefs and keeping the water clear. Too much sediment, however, can smother seagrass, so in addition to blocking sunlight from penetrating the water, high amounts of waterborne sediment can overwhelm seagrass that is already established. This is why areas that have high amounts of sediment suspended in the water will support seagrass in only the shallowest locations.

In some locations there is not much sediment in the water to influence the amount of sunlight, but the water can be stained the color of coffee from high loads of tannins from mangroves and other wetland and shoreline plants, a natural phenomenon. The color in the water decreases the depth that sunlight can penetrate and thus will decrease the depth that seagrass can grow. Still other areas have soft bottom sediments that are easily stirred up by waves and currents, and the water is frequently too murky for sunlight to penetrate, so frequently that seagrass can't survive.

Seagrass also requires low-energy conditions. As those of us who have been caught by a wave in the surf know, water can exert extreme force. In high-energy environments, such as beaches with strong wave action or areas with strong currents, grass blades can be broken and entire plants ripped out of the bottom, so these types of areas aren't suitable for grass beds. Plus, waves and currents move sediment, and the shifting bottom makes it difficult for seagrass to become established and to grow. This is why seagrass is most abundant on the lee (protected, downwind) sides of barrier islands (like the Chandeleur Islands and the back sides of the barrier islands on the Outer Banks), in estuaries and lagoons (like Indian River Lagoon), on protected flats (like the backreef flats on many Caribbean islands), lagoons (such as at Turneffe Atoll, Belize), and along coastal areas (like Apalachee Bay, Florida) that receive little in the way of wave energy.

Seagrasses are able to tolerate a wide range of salinities (salinity is a measure of the salt content of water and is measured in parts per thousand [ppt], with typical ocean salinity around 35 parts per thousand), but too much variation in salinity may prohibit seagrass from becoming established or may eradicate existing seagrass beds. Each species of seagrass has a preferred range of salinities but can tolerate brief periods (usually up to a couple of weeks) of salinity outside its normal range. Long periods of high salinity followed by long periods of low salinity, in contrast, are usually too stressful for a species of seagrass to become established. In the tropics and subtropics, where there are distinct wet and dry seasons, the area where a river runs into an estuary may be full ocean salinity during the dry season and almost full freshwater during a strong wet season. In such an area, the conditions are too salty for freshwater grasses during dry season and too fresh for seagrasses during wet season, and the result is an open bottom of sand or mud.

The shape and number of seagrass blades can be influenced by salinity. Turtle grass blades tend to be wider, longer, and brighter green in color and to occur in dense stands in areas where salinity is high and doesn't vary much, like in the lower portion of an estuary or lagoons protected by reefs in the tropics. In the upper portions of an estuary, where salinity is often lower and more variable because of river flow, turtle grass blades tend to be thinner, shorter, and dark green, and there are generally fewer blades of grass per area of bottom.

When you put their basic requirements (light, low energy, salinity) together, you get a good idea of where you are most likely to find healthy seagrass beds, which can help you formulate a fishing strategy. The first locations to eliminate in a search for seagrass are the mouths of rivers that carry heavy sediment loads. Beaches that are exposed to strong waves and areas that are exposed to strong currents are also off the list. You can eliminate the deep spots, although the actual depth depends on where you are fishing. The clearer the water, the deeper and more widespread you will find seagrass. Locations that seem to have muddy water a lot of the time are also not likely to harbor seagrass beds because not enough light gets to the grass blades, or the grass blades get smothered as the sediment settles out of the water column. In regions with notable wet and dry seasons, seagrass is often absent from the lower portions of rivers and where rivers meet estuaries or ocean because of changes in salinity—even if the river flows are not full of sediment. And within an estuary, the thick, dense grass beds tend to be closer to the estuary mouth and farther from the rivers because these areas experience the least variation in salinity. For example, in Pamlico and Albemarle Sounds in North Carolina, the most extensive grass beds are on the inland sides of the barrier islands, with only smaller pockets of seagrass farther into the sounds and in the rivers. Similarly, seagrasses are largely absent from areas near rivers along the Central American coast.

Now that you have a short list of the types of locations where you are likely to find healthy seagrass beds, you need to know which species of seagrass will grow where and how these different types of grass beds are perceived by gamefish.

## SPECIES OF SEAGRASS AND THEIR ENVIRONMENTAL REQUIREMENTS

Each species of seagrass has advantages over the others under different environmental conditions, and each species grows best and is most common where it has the advantage. You will often find beds with mixed species of seagrass, but you will also find grass beds that are composed entirely of one species or grass beds where different species of seagrass grow in different parts of the overall grass bed.

The type of seagrass present in a location reflects the long-term conditions at that location—tides, current, salinity, depth, and wave energy. In other words, the types of seagrasses that are present on the flat are a store of information about the typical conditions. Gamefish know the typical conditions for a grass bed and when those conditions are off and behave accordingly. Knowing the environmental requirements of each seagrass species will help you to decipher patterns from one location to another and to devise an effective strategy for fishing those locations.

### Turtle Grass

Turtle grass is the most common seagrass in shallow coastal and estuarine areas of the tropics and subtropics and is the species of seagrass you most often see in the beautiful panoramic pictures of clear, tropical grass flats. Of the four most common seagrass species in the tropics and subtropics, turtle grass blades are the widest. That width helps to act as baffles against the current and cause deposition of sediment, which can create a soft bottom.

Although turtle grass can tolerate salinities as low as 3.5 ppt and as high as 60 ppt, it grows best in salinities between 24 ppt and 35 ppt. Turtle grass tolerance for salinities below 15 ppt is limited by time of exposure. Periods longer than a couple of weeks will cause turtle grass to become stressed and die. This means that turtle grass won't grow in locations that receive significant amounts of fresh water for an extended period of time.

In the tropics, turtle grass will grow throughout the year, but in the subtropics and the areas of warm-temperate northern Gulf of Mexico where it grows, turtle grass can become dormant during winter. In these more seasonal areas you may notice a thinning of the grass beds during winter as the blades of turtle grass that die or break off are not so readily replaced as during summer or may remain short for extended periods. In summer these same grass beds will have more densely packed and longer blades. During peak growing season of summer in some areas, turtle grass blades can grow fast enough to replace old blades about once a month, quite a high rate of turnover. And the blades can grow very long—I once measured blades of turtle grass at 36 inches long.

Turtle grass is usually found in relatively shallow water due to light requirements for photosynthesis. In clear, tropical water, you might find beds of turtle grass as deep as 30 feet, whereas in less-clear waters of estuaries turtle grass is usually found in waters less than 10 feet in depth. Of course, as fly anglers we are most interested in grass beds 6 feet or less in depth, so that is where I will focus the discussion.

Turtle grass can tolerate occasional exposure to air during low tides, but it won't grow in spots that are dry too frequently or for too long a duration. During periods of extra-low spring tides, you might find turtle grass in shallow areas with blades burned brown from exposure to the sun and air. These blades will soon be replaced by new growth after tides become less extreme. But if the rhizomes (their version of a root system) are exposed to air too frequently or for too long, the plants will die.

In the Caribbean, turtle grass is the dominant species on the flats, so it is common to find shallow grass flats with burned turtle grass blades during periods with extra-low tides. In contrast, in the subtropics and northern Gulf of Mexico, although you may also find turtle grass in very shallow areas, you will often find shoal grass beds dominating the shallows.

## Shoal Grass

Like turtle grass, shoal grass has a pretty wide range of salinity tolerance—from 12 ppt to much greater than 35 ppt—and although shoal grass is also unable to tolerate extended exposure to fresh water, its tolerance is greater than that of turtle grass. Shoal grass can be found growing among the blades of turtle grass and is often overlooked because shoal grass blades are so much thinner than turtle grass blades. Shoal grass is often overlooked even in areas where it sometimes dominates because during winter in subtropical and warm-temperate regions plants can become dormant and blades can break off entirely, leaving a bare sand bottom. When water warms in spring, the buried root system sends new growth

*Shoal grass (left) and turtle grass (right) are important habitats for many gamefish prey.*

into the water column. These newly emerging, springtime grass beds will quickly attract small organisms (shrimp, crabs, small fish, etc.) that are readily eaten by gamefish. And during winter, when the bottom is not entirely covered by shoal grass, many of the crabs, shrimp, and small fishes remain. This makes it a bit easier for gamefish to find prey, so these locations are worth checking out.

The main advantage that shoal grass has over turtle grass is that it is better able to tolerate recurrent exposure to air and wave energy. Because of this advantage over other seagrass species, shoal grass is often most abundant in the shallowest areas (thus the name). This doesn't mean that other grass species won't also grow in areas that are exposed at the lowest of low tides, but it does mean that, in general, shoal grass will be your best indicator of where the shallowest areas are on a grass flat, even during periods of higher water. It's important to realize that, depending on the tidal range, the difference in depth between shallow shoal grass spots and deeper turtle grass spots may be only a couple of inches—changes in depth that are difficult for an angler to detect but are known by gamefish.

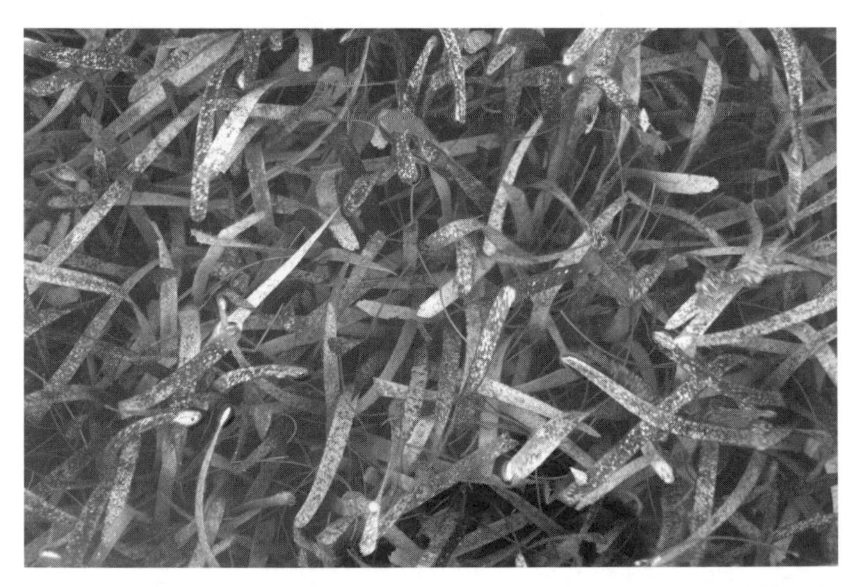

*This dense thicket of turtle grass, with some shoal grass mixed in, holds a lot of gamefish prey.*

## Drift Algae

During winter in the subtropics, because grass blades (especially those of turtle grass and shoal grass) are not being quickly replaced as they die or break off, you might think that grass beds don't provide good shelter. Fortunately, many do. In most locations, the loss of seagrass blades isn't so great that the grass beds disappear. Plus, at the same time seagrass growth slows or stops in late autumn and winter, drift algae becomes more abundant, reaching its peak in late winter into early spring.

Drift algae is like the tumbleweed of the sea because, although sometimes attached to grass blades, the algae is carried by tidal- and wind-driven currents and deposited in areas where the current slows. As the drift algae grows through the winter and is moved around by currents, it often collects in depressions and along windward shorelines. Sometimes there is so much drift algae that it carpets the bottom and can be more than 2 feet deep. I've found that areas with such thick accumulations of drift algae don't hold as many prey and don't make for the best fishing. You'll find much better fishing in areas with a mixture of seagrass and drift algae.

*Drift algae provides habitat for a lot of gamefish prey, including these juvenile pinfish.*

## Eel Grass

Eel grass is found from the Outer Banks of North Carolina north to Canada and is limited in its southern range by warmer temperatures. Similar in shape to turtle grass, eel grass blades have a width between that of turtle grass and shoal grass. This means that eel grass provides good habitat for small organisms and juvenile gamefish. Eel grass has a wide range of salinity tolerance (7 ppt to 35 ppt) but prefers the upper end of the range and thus grows well in the estuarine waters of the Outer Banks, Chesapeake Bay, and northeast bays and lagoons. Strong currents, waves, and areas exposed to frequent strong winds that muddy the water limit the growth of eel grass. In the warm-temperate region, the most extensive eel grass beds can be found on the leeward sides of the barrier islands of the Outer Banks and in shallow, clear areas protected by marsh islands. Only isolated beds grow close to the rivers.

## Widgeon Grass

Widgeon grass has many blades branching from each stalk and thus provides good hiding places for small organisms. Widgeon grass grows in shallow water, in depths similar to turtle grass and shoal grass, but is often outcompeted by these species. Widgeon grass's greatest advantage is its wide salinity tolerance, from 2 ppt to 70 ppt, and its ability to tolerate high and low salinities for extended periods. You will likely find the greatest concentration of widgeon grass in areas that experience large changes in salinity that last for weeks at a time. Shallow mangrove or marsh creeks that drain large wetland areas experience low salinities during the wet season and high salinities during the dry season. In such areas, widgeon grass may occur seasonally, with highest growth in the wet season. Similar shallow, coastal areas, such as in Louisiana backcountry where water is clear enough, are also good places to find widgeon grass.

Widgeon grass is a good indicator of backcountry areas that receive significant fresh water during part of the year. Usually, the grass will persist even during dry periods. And the presence of widgeon grass also means that the area, though shallow, is covered by water in all but the most extreme situations. So, if you are scouting an area and come across widgeon grass, make a note of it. This area will probably hold gamefish, such as snook or redfish, during certain times of year.

Widgeon grass is also rather tolerant of warm water temperatures that occur in backwater lagoons that don't get much water exchange, even in the tropics. In these locations, although there is little connection to open water, the presence of widgeon grass often means there are also gamefish. I know of a few lagoons in the tropics that are cut off from the ocean for years at a time when a hurricane builds up sand across the entrance. All of the organisms are trapped in these lagoons until a heavy rain event or another storm reopens the connection to the ocean. These organisms include bonefish, permit, snook, and tarpon. These lagoons all have abundant widgeon grass.

## Manatee Grass

Of all the seagrasses mentioned here, you will probably have the least direct contact with the round-bladed manatee grass. Manatee grass is usually the deepest growing of the four species, is found in low-energy conditions, and has little tolerance for exposure to air. Manatee grass has the least tolerance for fresh water, with a narrow preferred salinity range of 24 ppt to 35 ppt. Manatee grass often grows among turtle grass blades in deep grass beds and grows in patches or sparsely arranged blades in deeper water as well. Manatee grass can be a great indicator of deeper sand holes that don't get a lot of current, have clear water, and offer good places for gamefish to hold while waiting for higher water to get onto a nearby flat. Look for areas with a greenish hue to the bottom. This is also an area where gamefish may pass through but are not likely to hold and wait for baitfish to be swept through on currents. I know of a couple of spots with deep patches of manatee grass that are good places to stake out and wait for tarpon.

## Local Nuances

The most notable exception to these general rules is the Laguna Madre of south Texas. Because the southern Laguna Madre is mostly enclosed, isolated from the Gulf of Mexico, and receives almost no fresh water, salinities can be extremely high (greater than 50 ppt in many places). Nonetheless, seagrass grows in the shallow waters of the Laguna Madre, and you can find plenty of red drum, spotted seatrout, and other gamefish. Before the lower Laguna Madre was connected via dredging, the dominant grass was shoal grass, but now that the salinities are lower, turtle grass and manatee grass dominate.

### Applying What You've Learned

#### Reading Seagrass

Having learned the general environmental conditions required for seagrass beds, you now know where to look for seagrass when exploring new areas. You also know that different species of seagrass grow best in different conditions, so you know how to interpret different types of grass beds. As you put it all together you will find that even if you encounter a grass flat that is just too deep at high tide for good fishing, you can get an idea of how the flat might look and where fish will most likely be at a better fishing time near low tide. Here is a likely scenario.

Picture yourself fishing in a subtropical estuary. At high tide you encounter a grass flat with a mixture of grasses. Some areas on the flat are mostly turtle grass, whereas others are mostly shoal grass. You think the flat will be good for sight-fishing for tailing red drum near low tide, but it is an expansive flat—if you are in the wrong spot you might never see the tailing red drum you are certain will be there. Your increased understanding of environmental factors influencing seagrass distribution will help you figure out where the shallow spots and deeper troughs will most likely be located. You can position yourself in the spot where you are most likely to see fish expose their positions as they travel through and feed in the shallowest water and the most likely avenues they will use to retreat during low water.

A typical response to using the type of seagrass to determine depth is "I can look at the bottom and see which area is deeper, so why should I care which type of seagrass is where?" Most anglers are able to tell changes in depth only on a rough scale—say, the difference between 1 and 2 feet. But the difference in depth that might determine whether you find tailing fish is often measured in inches, and the depth differences that the gamefish are reacting to are in inches or even fractions of inches. A red drum might move along a trough of turtle grass, for example, that is only a few inches deeper than a ridge of shoal grass and can feed without showing a tail. If you have enough sunlight to sight-fish, you can position yourself along the higher ground and search for fish feeding in that trough. If you are unable to see fish because of low-light conditions or murky water, but you still want to cast to sighted fish, find the shallower ridges and wait for tailing fish to move onto these areas to feed as the tide rises.

The presence of shoal grass might also indicate exposure to waves, such as the outer side of a shallow sandbar. If environmental conditions are consistent enough to cause a distribution of turtle grass on the inside (protected side) of the bar and shoal grass on the outer side of the bar, these conditions are also likely to influence fish distribution. Under rough sea conditions, your first choice to search for tailing fish is on the inside of the shallow bar. During calm periods, you might find that fish take advantage of the calm and feed on the outer edge of the bar in the shoal grass.

When you are fishing on the inside of the bar in turtle grass, your best strategy will be to use an unweighted, weedless fly. On the outer side, where the shoal grass will likely be comparatively sparser and doesn't pose as much of a fly-snagging challenge, a lightly weighted fly that gets to the bottom quickly might be a better choice.

Here is an example from the tropics of the importance of reading seagrass. In much of the eastern Caribbean, the difference in water depth between a typical high and low tide is less than 10 inches. Despite the slight change in water depth, permit enter shallow backreef flats to feed on the latter half of incoming tides and are usually absent after the first hour or so of dropping tides. The difference in water depth is almost imperceptible to an angler but sure makes a huge difference to the permit. After you know the requirements of turtle grass you can figure out locations of feeding and travel lanes that permit are most likely to use on a flat. Sparse, short grass blades (maybe some of the blades are burned brown from a recent extra-low tide) indicate a shallow spot. A trough of more and longer blades probably indicates a slightly deeper area. As the tide rises you might find permit using the deeper trough as a traveling lane to get access to the shallow feeding area, so choosing ambush spots should be relatively straightforward.

## Applying What You've Learned

### Spotted Seatrout

Spotted seatrout frequently hang out in deep spots at low tide and ride the rising tide into shallow grass beds to feed. During winter, rising tides heated by the midday sun seem to bring the most spotted seatrout into shallow grass beds, whereas the rising tides of dusk are best in the heat of summer. In either case, if you find deep water next to shallow grass beds, whether drop-offs at the edge of the grass bed or deeper potholes within the grass bed, there is a good chance you will find spotted seatrout on a rising tide. One of my favorite places to fish for seatrout is a large bed of turtle grass separated from deep water by a series of sandbars and troughs, with sparse shoal grass growing on the bars and lusher stands in

*Spotted seatrout are commonly found lurking among seagrass blades, waiting to ambush unsuspecting prey.*

the troughs. At low tide, I like to pole along the bar and cast into the thicker patches of shoal grass in deeper spots in the troughs. On the good days, a handful of spotted seatrout rest in many of the small holes, waiting to ride the flooding tide into the shallow turtle grass flat. The holes that hold fish are usually close to a trough that cuts through a sandbar, which provides a travel avenue from the deeper holes to the turtle grass flat.

Another good location for spotted seatrout is deep beds of turtle grass that grow on a bottom that slopes into shallow water. These grass beds allow spotted seatrout to find the most comfortable water temperatures by moving between deep and shallow water without ever having to leave the food-rich seagrass bed. In the heat of summer, you'll find spotted seatrout using the deeper areas during the day to remain cool and moving into the shallows in the evening. The movements of spotted seatrout during winter are exemplified in the Big Bend area of Florida, where fish will remain on the deep grass to avoid the cold water of the shallows and move into the shallows on warm, sunny days to warm up in the midday sun.

## SEAGRASS AS HABITAT

Now that I've outlined the basic environmental requirements of seagrass and the particular needs of each species, I'll delve into how the characteristics of seagrass habitats combine to make these areas such great places to find gamefish.

One of the most important functions of seagrasses is their ability to harness sunlight and nutrients in the water and sediment, thereby producing food and providing shelter for other organisms. Many organisms (like snails and numerous species of fish) graze directly on the seagrass blades and are in turn eaten by larger predators. Other organisms don't graze on the seagrass but instead live on the grass blades: the diverse array of algae and invertebrates that attach to the surface of the grass blades are called epibionts (the algae are called epiphytes, the invertebrates are called epifauna, and both groups combined are called epibionts).

Seagrass also holds sediments in place, just as plants on land help to prevent soil erosion. A stable bottom habitat will attract and support a wide array of species that is prey for gamefish. The ability of seagrass to act as current baffles is also very important. Even in areas where you find current strong enough to bend over grass blades, the water near the bottom of the grass blades will be nearly still. The slowing of currents as water passes over a grass bed causes many particles that are suspended by moving water (sediment, broken blades of grass) to fall toward the bottom. Microorganisms often coat the floating material, and as the sediment and decaying plant material fall to the bottom they provide food for numerous organisms that feed on the microorganisms. This collection of sediments, plant, and animal matter is called detritus.

The productivity of seagrass beds supports the rich food web that brings larger recreational fish into these shallow waters. In simplified form, the food chain can be summarized this way: Sunlight and nutrients support seagrass, which creates sediment and detritus, which feed epibiont invertebrates and algae (the latter also use sunlight), which feed larger invertebrates and small fishes (which feed on small invertebrates and graze on algae and seagrass blades), which are prey for larger fishes (including gamefish).

The shelter provided by seagrass beds sustains high abundances of small organisms that are potential prey for gamefish. The high numbers of prey attract gamefish to these shallow habitats. But knowing why gamefish are so often found in seagrass beds searching for a meal is only the first part of the equation.

The second part of the equation comes from understanding how prey use seagrass as shelter. The behavior of prey influences when gamefish are most likely to find a particular prey, in what types of seagrass beds the prey will be found, and the different strategies that gamefish use to pursue different prey. When you understand the habitat, the feeding behavior of a gamefish will often tell you which prey it is pursuing.

Seagrass beds support an incredibly wide diversity of species of fish, crabs, shrimp, isopods (think potato bugs), amphipods (miniature shrimplike creatures), worms (a broad category including many groups), algae, echinoderms (urchins and sea stars, among others), and a host of other groups of organisms that are potential prey for gamefish. Although many of these organisms aren't appropriate for imitating with a fly (amphipods would require a size 30 hook), they are all important prey for juvenile or adult gamefish. And although only a few of the fish species found in seagrass beds are targeted by recreational anglers, many of these small fish are potential prey for gamefish. It's a complex food web that suffers if any part is missing.

Not all seagrass beds will have exactly the same prey species. The abundance and types of species found in a seagrass bed may change depending on location. So, although the general list of prey species available to gamefish may be similar, the actual prey eaten by gamefish often varies among locations. This, in part, explains why some flies are pounced upon by fish on one seagrass flat but are completely ignored by fish in other locations. However, if you have a general list of prey species that a gamefish will feed on, you can move quickly through a short list of flies to find an appropriate imitation for just about any situation.

One reason why the species of prey is different among grass beds is that each seagrass species provides different advantages and disadvantages to gamefish and their prey. Turtle grass has the widest blades and seems to provide the most shelter to small organisms. For example, a grass shrimp will actually move around a grass blade, keeping the blade between itself and the gamefish, in order to hide. Although this is an effective strategy with turtle grass, the strategy is probably not as successful with thin-bladed shoal grass. The grass shrimp is wider than the blade of shoal grass and thus is more likely to be spotted by a gamefish. If you examine stomach contents of speckled trout, you might find that trout that have been feeding on grass shrimp have some grass blades in their stomachs as well. A mouthful of shrimp and seagrass is better than no shrimp at all.

Another reason why different types of prey are found in different grass beds concerns how the grass beds are arranged. If you compare the number and types of small fish, crabs, shrimp, and other potential prey species found living on an open sand bottom with those of a nearby seagrass bed, the difference is immediately apparent. Far more species in far greater numbers will be found in seagrass. This is because seagrass provides food and shelter from predators. Small fish, for example, will feed on epibionts living on the grass blades and will flee into thick stands of grass to escape a pursuing predator. The small fish is able to find sufficient food and escape predation, which seems straightforward. But there's a catch.

In a world without predators, small fish might be found in equal numbers in areas of open bottom and in a bed of dense seagrass. This is because the small fish is a predator, too—it is eating even smaller organisms that are also using the seagrass as shelter. From the perspective of the small fish as predator, the less shelter its prey has to hide in, the more efficiently the small fish can find and eat prey. So, although there are things in the seagrass bed for the small fish to eat, there are also things to eat on open bottom, and they are much easier to get to.

Now throw a gamefish into the mix. The small fish not only has to be concerned with finding something to eat but also must find shelter to keep from being eaten. So, with a predator around, you are unlikely to find many small fish in the open bottom habitat because most will be in the seagrass. The small fish can't feed as efficiently as if they were on the open sand bottom, but they have less chance of getting eaten by a gamefish. This trade-off—between eating and being eaten—is an important factor that helps determine which seagrass beds hold more prey and more gamefish.

The comparison between open bottom and a bed of dense seagrass is a comparison of extremes—all or nothing. Yet, between open bottom and dense seagrass is a range of seagrass habitats: thick, dense stands of continuous grass; thick grass with scattered patches of open bottom; a patchwork of seagrass and open bottom; or sparse seagrass blades scattered over open bottom. The same trade-offs—between eating and being eaten—also apply in different types of seagrass beds.

The density (the number of seagrass blades growing in a section of bottom) and landscape (how the mixture of seagrass and open bottom is arranged) of seagrass play heavily into the dynamics of eating and being eaten. This helps to explain why some seagrass beds consistently hold more gamefish than others.

Beds of dense seagrass hold a lot of prey, but they can be difficult areas for gamefish to capture prey. For example, dense seagrass may be too thick for a gamefish to swim through, so it will be forced to swim above the seagrass blades. It is also easier for small fish to swim above the grass blades, but they can usually see the gamefish approaching and quickly dive into the cover of the dense seagrass until the gamefish has passed. In these situations, a good strategy is to use an unweighted streamer fly and either strip it slowly so that it hovers above grass blades or use quick, short strips. The slow, hovering fly is a good imitation of a small fish that has not seen an approaching predator and thus might trigger an ambush attack by a gamefish. The quickly stripped, darting fly imitates a small fish that has seen a gamefish and has elected to flee over the grass rather than dive into the grass blades.

In the subtropics, spotted seatrout will often rove through dense seagrass beds looking for unwary prey and are suckers for streamers fished just above the grass blades. In the tropics, barjacks cruise above the dense grass blades at high speed, hoping to surprise an unsuspecting small fish. Jacks are suckers for chartreuse-and-white Clousers with beadchain eyes that are not so heavy that they sink into the grass but whose jigging action imitates a small fish searching for the cover of seagrass.

In dense seagrass, you are likely to find gamefish searching for organisms they can root for in the bottom rather than chasing fish among the grass blades. Red drum, permit, and bonefish can be found rooting for shrimp, crabs, and worms in the bottom of dense seagrass beds. The challenge for the fly angler in these situations is twofold—first is seeing the fish in the midst of the dense seagrass, and second is getting a fly into the fish's strike zone. Meeting the first challenge comes with practice: A flicker of the tip of a tail above the water may be all that gives a fish away; or you may pick out the well-camouflaged body of a bonefish sliding through the grass blades. Spotting these brief signatures of a feeding gamefish becomes second nature that is developed only over time. After you've spotted a fish feeding in dense seagrass, you must meet the challenge of making an accurate cast—close enough so the fish sees the fly among the grass blades yet gentle enough to not spook the fish. Of course, weedless flies are a must in these situations.

Areas of sparse seagrass usually don't have as many prey species as you will find in dense seagrass. However, these areas are easier to fish because it is easier to spot a fish, there is less seagrass to snag a fly, and the sparse seagrass means a gamefish is more likely to see your fly.

Beds of sparse seagrass can be good places for gamefish—such as jacks, ladyfish, and even cobia—that are moving in search of baitfish or other tasty prey, but you have to be there at the right time to intercept these fish. Sparse seagrass beds can be good places to find red drum or bonefish tailing on a rising tide as they root for worms, shrimp, and crabs that burrow into the bottom. And snook will visit sparse seagrass beds that are exposed to current and pockmarked by potholes.

Jacks—crevalle jacks, barjacks, horse-eye jacks, and others—can provide great fun on flats of sparse seagrass. Jacks cruise through these areas, often at high speed, hoping to surprise baitfish. You can often spot cruising jacks by the bow wake they push as they move through shallow water. When casting to a fish in this situation, remember that the fish is at least a couple of feet ahead of the wake (the distance the fish is ahead of the wake depends on the speed the fish is moving and how close to the surface it is—the faster it is moving and the deeper it is, the farther ahead of the wake it will be), so lead the fish by at least 5 feet. At other times you might actually see the fish. Don't be fooled: These fish are probably moving faster than it appears. Force yourself to lead the fish with your cast more than you think is necessary, especially if the jacks are in deeper water.

Another way to track jacks across a flat is to follow the chaos they create. Without actually seeing the fish, I have been able to track jacks as they cruise across a flat by following the track of small eruptions of baitfish. I connect the dots of baitfish activity to guesstimate the path of the jacks and cast into the area I think they will be in next. The strategy has worked well enough to catch fish I would otherwise never have sighted. Small streamers (Clouser Minnows, deceivers) work well for these fish. You will get some refusals, but more often than not a well-placed cast will result in a strike because the jacks are cruising the shallows in search of a meal.

In areas that lack seagrass, to some extent other habitats fill a similar ecological role for gamefish and their prey. Coastal Louisiana, for example, has plenty of marsh mud bottom yet little seagrass in most areas but still has plenty of red drum. Although there are areas with seagrass, the ecosystem in this area is centered around marshes, mud bottom, and oyster bars, and the types of prey are different than in seagrass beds. Red drum are able to use the marsh and mud bottom areas with great success even though seagrass is not common. Some of the characteristics of marshes and mud bottoms that make these areas attractive to gamefish will be addressed in later chapters.

## FISHING IN PATCHY SEAGRASS

So, beds of dense seagrass hold a lot of prey but can be tough to fish, whereas bottoms with sparse seagrass don't hold as many prey or gamefish but are easier places to see and cast to fish. What's a fly angler to do? Find the best of both worlds—areas of mixed open bottom and dense seagrass. A mixture of seagrass and open bottom supplies good habitat for shelter (seagrass) with good areas for easy feeding (open bottom).

Overall, there are probably more species and more total numbers of prey items in the areas of thick grass, but the feeding efficiency of gamefish is higher in more open areas. This is one reason why you might find snook lying in wait in an open patch in the seagrass to ambush small fish and why speckled trout will often hide among the grass blades near the edge of a seagrass bed and dart out into the open to grab a fly as it passes by. These open areas are also easier for fly anglers to fish because the fly is more visible to the gamefish and there are fewer snags.

Areas of open bottom in seagrass beds are often called potholes because they are often slightly deeper than the surrounding seagrass-covered bottom. Most gamefish species that are found in seagrass beds will use potholes or edges of seagrass beds as places to ambush prey. Some species use the ambush strategy

*Patchy seagrass (a mixture of dense seagrass and open bottom) provides great fishing because anglers can focus on the open areas when sight-fishing for gamefish.*

extensively. Barracuda, snook, tarpon, seatrout, and snapper will often rest near the edge or bottom of a pothole waiting for small fish, shrimp, or other prey to venture out of the protection of the seagrass and into the pothole. Other species will rest in potholes between feeding forays into the seagrass or while waiting out low tide but will certainly take advantage of an easy meal. Red drum and bonefish will often use potholes as rest stops but always seem to have an eye open for a potential meal. Snappers will often reside in larger potholes during the day and venture into the grass bed at night to feed. But just like red drum and bonefish, snappers are opportunistic feeders if prey ventures into the pothole. Finally, jacks will cruise from pothole to pothole if the water is deep enough in the surrounding grass bed.

Another advantage to fishing in open bottom areas in seagrass beds is that these habitats are more amenable to using flies that imitate some of these prey species. For example, most worms move slowly (or not at all) along the bottom of the grass beds and thus are difficult to imitate with a fly in areas of thick seagrass. Casting a fly that imitates a worm into a dense stand of seagrass and letting it sit are rarely productive. But casting the same fly so that it sinks to the bottom in an open area in the path of a bonefish, permit, or red drum is a worthwhile endeavor. Similarly, weighted flies are needed to imitate small, bottom-dwelling species like blennies and gobies. These flies quickly sink among the grass blades where it is difficult for gamefish to find them but can be hopped across the open bottom of potholes and make easy prey for gamefish.

Drift algae tends to be more common in areas of mixed open bottom and seagrass. And as you might expect, many of the small animals that reside in seagrass also take refuge in drift algae. Grass shrimp, pink or brown shrimp, pipefish, mud crabs, juvenile blue crabs, gobies, blennies, and brittle stars are present throughout the year and use both drift algae and seagrass. Juvenile fishes also use drift algae during winter, when drift algae is most abundant, because the complex shapes of drift algae provides good shelter. All of these species will be eaten by one gamefish or another.

I have seen red drum rooting in clumps of drift algae with such intensity that they do not hear my approaching skiff. In a couple of instances I have been able to drift over the feeding fish, its head buried in drift algae, before it spooks from the shadow of the boat. I've examined the stomach contents of red drum feeding in areas with drift algae and have found, in order from most to least abundant: mud crabs (often the common mud crab, *Panopeus herbstii*), snapping shrimp (genus *Alpheus*), and small gobies and blennies. The mud crab can be imitated with many of the common crab fly patterns in olive green, size 4. The snapping shrimp is also olive green and about 1 to 2 inches long. Gobies and blennies are easily imitated by small brown streamers such as weighted muddler minnows.

So far in this chapter you've learned where you are most likely to find seagrass and why, how the types of seagrass provide clues on currents, tides, and waves to tell you where and when to fish an area, and how the density and landscape of seagrass will affect prey and feeding strategies of gamefish. Now it's time to take another breather and translate this knowledge into a practical situation. I'll use one of my favorite activities—fishing for tailing red drum in subtropical Florida—as an example.

## Applying What You've Learned

### Tailing Red Drum

The tide was so low that I had to get out of my small skiff and push it over the sandbar that had only a sprinkling of shoal grass, indicating the bar was probably exposed frequently at low tide. As the boat slid off the sandbar into slightly deeper water, the shoal grass became denser, with scattered clumps of turtle grass mixed in.

I jumped back onto the skiff and slowly poled across the mirrorlike water surface. As the water got just a little deeper, the grass changed to mostly turtle grass, and the tips of the blades poked into the air in scattered bunches. The tide had just turned and was starting to flood. I hoped to find red drum feeding in the grass bed in the slightly deeper water between the sandbar and the mangrove shoreline some 200 yards away.

With the morning sun at my back, I could make out the network of seagrass and open bottom. Some areas were covered by large sections of dense turtle grass, and I could picture the flurry of activity among those grass blades as grass shrimp, snapping shrimp, gobies, brittle stars, mud crabs, and many other species moved about in search of food. Although a suite of animals also lives in the sections of open bottom, many live within the sediment, so it appears less active above ground than does the seagrass.

With a quick sideways push of the pole I turned the boat and headed into my favorite section of the grass bed—a mixture of turtle grass interspersed with open bottom. I knew that the thick seagrass provided shelter and food for some of the red drum's favorite prey items, and the open bottom gave me a better chance to see these fish as they meandered across the flat.

The patches of open bottom and sparse seagrass provided areas where the feeding drum could more easily capture prey that ventured from the shelter of the seagrass to feed and, most importantly, gave me perfect opportunities to cast my flies to feeding or cruising fish. In these open or sparsely vegetated patches, red drum were more likely to see the fly, and the fly was less likely to get snagged on the grass. I targeted these open areas so I could use crab and shrimp flies that sank quickly to the bottom and could be moved ever so slightly (if at all) with a short, quick strip, just like the real prey. These same quick sinking patterns would get lost among dense grass blades before a red drum could see the fly and would easily snag in the grass.

As soon as I had turned the boat, I saw the reflection of the morning sun on the square copper tail of a red drum as it broke the water surface about 50 yards away. I gave a good shove to the push pole to send the boat moving toward the tailing fish, and immediately I saw another tail waving, this one much closer. I quickly stowed the pole, grabbed my fly rod, threw a quick backcast, and shot the fly toward the tailing fish. The olive-colored crab fly plopped down in front of the fish just as it stopped tailing and was readying to move forward. This was a lucky break for me because the fish saw the fly as it dropped the 10 inches to the bottom. The line jumped as the fish surged forward and took the fly, and with a strip strike the fight was on.

Other grass beds where I've found and fished for tailing red drum are full of thick, dense turtle grass and offer a different challenge. In these situations I use an unweighted, weedless shrimp fly that I cast just about on top of a tailing red drum's head. If I'm lucky, the tailing fish hears the plop as the fly hits the water and investigates the source of the noise. If I'm unlucky, the splashdown of the fly scares the scales off the fish, and it speeds off. If the fish doesn't hear the fly hit the water and doesn't spook, I let the fly slowly drop toward the bottom in front of the fish, giving the fly slight twitches and hoping the red drum sees the fly among the grass blades. When the drum does see the fly, there is no mistake as the fish rushes the fly, pushing a bow wake in the process. This is real excitement that will test your patience—despite the urge, don't strike too soon and pull the fly from the fish's mouth.

In areas with dense seagrass, I like to cast the fly on top of the fish's head because if the fly is more than a few inches from the fish, the fly will be hidden by seagrass blades and never seen. I liken casting to these fish in thick grass to casting to a moving teacup, the teacup being the red drum's circle of vision as it moves and feeds in the thick grass. I think this is one reason why red drum can appear "picky"—despite your perfect cast, the fish just never saw the fly among the many grass blades. With these conditions, you can see why so many prey species prefer the shelter provided by dense seagrass habitats.

Black drum also inhabit grass flats in some locations, Florida's Mosquito Lagoon hosts perhaps the largest and best-known schools of shallow-water black drum. Schools of black drum also appear in shallow water in large numbers in the autumn through early winter, and although they don't provide the feeding frenzy action of other species, they are fun shallow-water gamefish (it's all about the presentation and take for the lumbering black drum; no blistering runs here). The strategies for red drum are also good for fishing to black drum, with a slight difference—slower (or no movement at all) is better when giving action to the fly.

## GAMEFISH PREY

So far in this chapter I've covered the attributes of seagrass beds. Now, information on the common prey species living in grass beds and strategies for imitating these prey with flies will complete the puzzle for fly fishing in seagrass habitats.

Although the number and types of species may vary among locations, most seagrass beds have members of particular families of organisms living among the grass blades. We can use this information to narrow the list of probable prey items we might find and to choose the best selection of fly patterns with the greatest potential for catching fish.

In Chico Fernandez's book *Fly-Fishing for Bonefish,* in a chapter on bonefish prey I provide a summary of the findings of numerous scientific studies (some published and some unpublished) that examined the availability of bonefish prey, food preference, and overall diets of bonefish found in shallow water habitats, including seagrass, in Puerto Rico, Florida, and the Bahamas. In each of these locations, the types and abundances of prey species varied, as did bonefish prey preferences and diets. For example, most Florida bonefish had crustaceans in their stomachs, whereas clams were most frequent in stomachs of bonefish from Puerto Rico. And big bonefish in Florida seem to like eating toadfish.

I found similar differences in prey preferences for permit in the U.S. Virgin Islands. On St. Croix, where permit come into backreef flats of shallow seagrass mixed with coral rubble to feed, analysis of stomach contents revealed a preference for small clams and small sea urchins. At locations in the nearby British Virgin Islands, where permit are most often found in shallow seagrass beds intermixed with sand flats, crabs and shrimp are high on the permit menu. These differences in diets of bonefish and permit among locations are most likely due to differences in the abundances of prey items rather than particular prey preferences.

I'd be hard pressed to come up with a workable fly pattern that imitates a clam, so in the areas where bonefish and permit eat a lot of clams it is best to focus on the next-most-common items in their diets or to throw them something too good to be true—a shrimp or crab. Some species of shrimp and crabs are widespread, whereas numerous other species have smaller ranges. This is one reason why the species of crustacean that bonefish or other gamefish eat can vary from place to place. And, of course, there can even be variation in coloration of the prey—green in one location and mottled tan and green in another—to match the surroundings. Although this variation in species and color might make your head spin with all the fly pattern possibilities (you'd need a caddy to carry all of your fly boxes), fear not: There is a common theme throughout that will allow you to use a few fly patterns to cover many possibilities.

## Crustaceans

An important characteristic of crabs and shrimp is that although the species and color pattern may vary from region to region or location to location, the general colorations and behaviors within each group can be strikingly similar. Swimming crabs (family Portunidae) and walking crabs (there are numerous families of walking crabs) are both present in seagrass beds. Crabs from both families will be colored so they are well camouflaged in their surroundings—whether green in areas of thick turtle grass or mixed tan and green in areas where coral rubble, shells, or rocks are mixed with the seagrass. Most importantly, most of these crabs will scurry for cover rather than try to outrun a pursuing fish.

### *Crabs*

#### *Swimming Crabs*

Species of swimming crabs are present in all three regions, are similar in shape (think blue crabs to give you an idea of body shape), and are probably the most active crabs in grass beds. They can be voracious predators and scavengers and thus are always on the move. Their color varies from the olive green of blue crabs to tan with eyespots for small tropical species. Swimming crabs can be found along the bottom of grass beds, clinging onto grass blades, swimming near the surface, or digging small holes in patches of open bottom as they excavate a clam dinner. When chased, swimming crabs may make a quick dash to escape—either by scurrying along the bottom or swimming quickly through the water—before rapidly burying themselves in the bottom or hiding under shells, rubble, or rocks. When fleeing a gamefish, swimming crabs usually swim sideways. When cornered and unable to bury themselves, swimming crabs will attempt to ward off a gamefish by waving and slashing with their claws, regardless of the relative sizes of crab and gamefish.

The shape, coloration, and behavior of swimming crabs should already have you thinking about fly patterns and ways to fish the flies. The first consideration is color. Mottled green and tan are among my favorite color combinations for crab flies because this combination includes the colors present in a grass bed. All green and all tan are also in my arsenal in the event that the gamefish are keyed in on a particular color, and so I am prepared for whatever species of crab might be on a flat. A second consideration is orientation and shape of the fly. You'll need a fly that, when stripped, will appear to swim sideways, so the fly should be longer along the axis of the hook shank. Finally, the fly must be weighted so it sinks to the bottom where natural crabs seek shelter when chased by gamefish (a swimming crab may try initially to swim away from a gamefish but will dart for the bottom when the gamefish closes in).

After you've chosen your fly pattern and color, the action you give the fly will have to convince a gamefish that it is an easy meal. A nice thing about fishing flies that imitate swimming crabs is that you can give the flies substantial motion to get the gamefish's attention because a natural crab will first attempt to get out of the neighborhood without being seen. After it realizes that it's been spotted, a crab will attempt to hide. You can mimic the same behavior with your fly. First strip the fly so that it swims through the water until seen by the gamefish. Then let the fly sink to the bottom as if to hide. Often, the gamefish will take the fly as it drops to the bottom.

I have found blue crabs measuring up to 4 inches across in the stomachs of 18-inch speckled trout. Although a 4-inch crab is a bit too large to imitate with a fly, this gives you a good indication of how much speckled trout and other gamefish like to prey on blue crabs. Cobia will also venture onto grass flats in search of blue crabs and can be taken on crab flies. Permit are well known for their crab-laden diet—live blue crabs are a favorite bait for permit anglers using spinning gear. Like speckled trout, cobia and permit eat blue crabs whole.

Bonefish also like blue crabs but sometimes do not eat the crabs whole, especially if the crabs are large. Instead, bonefish will pick at the crab to dismember it and then eat the mortally wounded crab. This can be frustrating for anglers casting a blue crab imitation to bonefish. For this reason, the crab flies I use for bonefish are typically small—sizes 4 and 6. When bonefish feed on a crab fly in this manner, you have to patiently wait for the bonefish to turn with the fly in its mouth before setting the hook. Juvenile blue crabs of the size preferred by gamefish are most abundant in summer in warm-temperate latitudes but can be present throughout the year in the subtropics and tropics.

### *Walking Crabs*

Numerous species of walking crabs can be found in seagrass beds, the species varying by region. In the tropics, reef crabs (members of the spider crab family Majidae)—usually colored green in areas with seagrass and algae and tan in areas with a lot of coral rubble—are the most common. In subtropical and warm-temperate areas, mud crabs (family Xanthidae) can be found throughout the year in seagrass beds in soft bottom. Mud crab color in seagrass beds will vary from place to place but will normally be a dark shade of green with or without brown and black spotting.

Walking crabs always maintain a close association with the bottom. In the tropics, reef crabs are often found feeding among rubble and shells that lie among grass blades and scurry for the underside of these shelters when chased. In the subtropics in winter, when drift algae is most common, mud crabs can be especially abundant in clumps of drift algae. Mud crabs are most at home feeding along the bottom and hide at the base of grass blades or burrow into the soft bottom when chased. They usually make more of an effort hiding than defending themselves with showy slashing of claws.

While conducting research in grass beds in southern Florida one winter, I found numerous large (1 inch across) female mud crabs with eggs hiding in drift algae. Perhaps this is one reason why I later found red drum feeding so intently in patches of drift algae in another location. The red drum's intense feeding behavior is yet another example of why, when casting to tailing red drum, I try to cast the fly so it just about hits them on the head to be certain that they see the fly. It seems that they can become so focused on a particular prey that they are oblivious to everything around them.

Although seagrass beds in the tropics, subtropics, and warm-temperate areas have different species of walking crabs, the crabs have some similar characteristics that you can apply to your fly fishing strategy. First, your choice of color can be simplified to green and tan. Second, the action you give to the fly should be minimal—all species of walking crabs remain close to shelter (whether under a rock, among seagrass blades or algae, or burrowed into the bottom) and don't scurry over long stretches of open bottom. You may want to give the fly a couple of twitches to get the gamefish's attention and then let the fly sit still or move it ever so slowly so that you maintain a straight line to the fly. If you give too much action to the fly, the gamefish will know something is amiss and move on.

### *Shrimp*

Just as with crabs, the species of shrimp you find in seagrass habitats will vary depending upon location, but most species are similar enough to be imitated with a couple of good patterns. Shrimp will often take on the coloration of their surroundings, so it's worth carrying multiple color variations of your favorite shrimp fly patterns. Some species of grass shrimp are mostly clear, so they blend into any background color. Larger shrimp are too large to be translucent and thus usually take on coloration to blend into their surroundings. In an area with a mixture of seagrass and open bottom you are more likely to find shrimp that are almost clear or have a sand tint. In grass beds with dense seagrass, you are likely to find shrimp with a green cast to their shells.

### *Common Shrimp*

The most familiar shrimp found in seagrass beds are members of four families. Common shrimp (family Peneidae), which are the familiar commercially caught species, are found in all three regions. The shrimp eaten in restaurants are in this family. These shrimp often use seagrass beds as juveniles and migrate to deeper water as adults, although you can find some large individuals in seagrass as well. These shrimp are usually found in seagrass beds with soft sediments and are usually a shade of either tan or green depending on the type of bottom where they are living. In areas of mixed seagrass and open bottom, tan is the more common coloration. Generally, common shrimp are buried just under the mud surface or at the base of grass blades during the day and emerge at night to feed.

### *Mantis Shrimp*

Mantis shrimp (family Squillidae) live in holes among coral rubble or shells and in burrows in sand-bottomed seagrass beds and are also present in all three regions. Mantis shrimp are similar in appearance to the praying mantis land insect (thus the name) and are usually tan (when living among sparse seagrass with coral rubble or open sand bottom) or green (when living in dense seagrass). The claws of the mantis shrimp are incredibly powerful and come in two basic types: a club and a slicer. With the club type of claw, a mantis shrimp will knock its prey (including small fish) unconscious with a lightning-fast blow. With the slicing claw, a mantis shrimp can quickly and mortally wound prey. Mantis shrimp range in size from 1 inch or so in length to well over 6 inches. As you might guess from the power in their claws, only the smaller mantis shrimp are eaten by gamefish.

Mantis shrimp usually don't venture far from their burrows and scurry back into their burrows if approached. Species of mantis shrimp that do venture from their burrows in search of prey are most active at night. When snorkeling, you can sometimes see the eyestalks of mantis shrimp peering out from these burrows. Permit and bonefish readily eat small mantis shrimp that have ventured too far from their burrows or are caught while unaware of the approaching fish. When chased, mantis shrimp can swim rapidly backward with a flip of their tail or walk quickly along the bottom. Their defense posture is to turn and face their adversary while retreating backward.

The slicing and punching abilities of mantis shrimp are known by permit, bonefish, and other gamefish that eat them. Probably for this reason, gamefish make a quick decision about mantis shrimp flies and either bolt in another direction or quickly engulf the fly and crunch it with the bony plates that are in their mouth (bonefish) or throat (permit). There is usually not much hesitation in either case. This aggressive predation behavior is one reason why I like mantis shrimp patterns when fishing for bonefish and permit.

### *Snapping Shrimp*

Depending on the species, snapping shrimp (family Alpheidae) found in grass beds are associated with rubble or shells or live in burrows in areas of mixed seagrass and open bottom. Snapping shrimp are high on the menu of bonefish, red drum, permit, and speckled trout. Snapping shrimp found in grass beds are usually green to brown in color and range in length from less than 1 inch to 2 inches. They move slowly along the bottom, if they move at all, and retreat into shelter when they see a predator approaching.

Although snapping shrimp have an enlarged claw, I don't know that gamefish note the difference in snapping shrimp fly patterns with and without claws. The success of the impressionistic Fernandez Snapping Shrimp attests to this theory. Although many anglers attach rattles to their snapping shrimp flies to attract gamefish, I'm not sure this strategy is really effective. It is likely that the rattle emits sound at a frequency that is too high for most gamefish to hear (most fish hear in lower frequencies). This theory is certainly something that should be tested. On the other hand, if using a rattle makes an angler more confident in a fly pattern, I say go with it because I don't think it hurts.

### *Grass Shrimp*

Although often the most abundant shrimp in seagrass habitats, grass shrimp (family Palaemonidae) are often overlooked because of their small size (less than 1 inch). Grass shrimp live on and among the grass blades and, depending upon the species and their habitat, will burrow into the sediments, hide among the bases of the grass blades, or grab onto seagrass blades and try to become "part of the seagrass" to escape predators.

Grass shrimp are a major prey item for speckled seatrout, although other gamefish feed on grass shrimp as well. Grass shrimp are present in grass beds throughout the year, yet their abundance changes seasonally; they are most abundant in spring and summer and least abundant in winter. What's more, you will find many of the females with eggs attached to their undersides in late winter/early spring, so you might want to tie a few of your grass shrimp fly patterns to reflect the presence of eggs on grass shrimp. There are times when spotted seatrout and red drum won't take larger shrimp flies, preferring smaller flies imitating grass shrimp. Striped bass can show a similar preference for grass shrimp in spring, gorging on them exclusively. Shrimp patterns in size 4 or 6 are worth trying in these situations.

## Final Thoughts

A nice thing about crustaceans is that most gamefish will take the opportunity to feed on shrimp or crabs if given the chance. Crustaceans arguably pack the greatest reward for the effort for gamefish because they are very high in caloric content for their size. For this reason, even in areas where crustaceans might not be the most common food item, such as on St. Croix where clams are a favorite for permit, flies imitating crabs and shrimp are high on my list of go-to flies.

Crustaceans can be imitated with a fly and can be effective either weighted or unweighted to match a given situation. For example, when fishing for red drum, permit, or bonefish in areas of dense seagrass, an unweighted, weedless shrimp pattern is probably the best choice. When fishing with a floating line, you can allow the fly to sink slowly toward the bottom, using occasional strips to pull the fly back toward the surface. This method allows you to keep the fly in a very small area for a long time and gives the fish a better chance of finding the fly. In areas of sparse seagrass, open patches, or deeper water, a weighted pattern will be best for getting the fly down to the bottom in a hurry. After the fly is on the bottom you might give a couple of short, quick strips to get the fish's attention and then let the fly rest on the bottom or move it ever so slowly. You don't have to worry about snagging the fly on grass, and you will be able to quickly put the fly into the fish's area of vision on the bottom and keep it there. This is especially crucial when casting to fish on the move.

## RESIDENT PREY FISHES

Any particular seagrass bed can be home to dozens of species of fish. For example, in a recent survey of a seagrass bed in the Caribbean, ninety-one species of fish were recorded. Some of these species are present year around and thus are considered residents. This group includes gobies (family Gobiidae), blennies (family Blenniidae), and some species of wrasse (family Labridae) and parrotfish (family Scaridae). Most resident fishes are relatively small (generally less than 4 inches) and thus are potential prey items for many gamefish. In warm-temperate areas, the total number of species is typically lower than in the tropics, and small fishes are most abundant in warmer months.

Nonresident fishes of seagrass beds that are potential gamefish prey are usually seasonal, dominated by juveniles in spring and summer. When these nonresidents are in low abundance, resident prey species become even more important in the diets of gamefish.

## Gobies and Blennies

Gobies and blennies live on the bottom and are present in all three regions. They are common in most grass beds but are unseen to all except the most observant angler. They live among the grass blades, in drift algae, and in shells. Gobies and blennies rest on the bottom, their heads propped above the bottom by modified fins when they aren't feeding, and dart about with short, rapid movements—either to feed or to chase a competitor from their territory. Although the pattern and tone of coloration varies for each species and among locations, green and brown dominate.

All species of gamefish found in seagrass habitats will eat gobies and blennies if given a chance. If a gamefish can get the jump on a blenny or goby, the gamefish will likely take advantage. Gobies are shaped somewhat like a pencil, with a larger head tapering to a more slender tail, and are usually only 1–2 inches long. Blennies tend to be larger and are more heavily bodied—both taller and wider. One of my favorite flies for imitating these prey fish is a muddler minnow-style fly: brown deer-hair head, gold body, and brown marabou tail. I use a weighted and unweighted version depending upon the conditions, and fish it with short, quick strips to give the fly a darting-and-resting motion.

## Killifishes

Killifish (family Fundulidae) can be found year-round in the subtropics in shallow areas of dense seagrass close to shore. Their abundance in seagrass beds may increase during the wet season and decrease during the dry season because they are changing location in relation to changes in salinity. Small (1 inch) and dark in color (brassy olive), killifish fall prey to snook, red drum, speckled seatrout, jacks, striped bass, and other gamefish as they venture onto the shallow grass flats on a rising tide. However, killifishes are especially important prey in salt-marsh and mangrove habitats and thus will be discussed in detail in those chapters.

## Wrasses and Parrotfishes

Parrotfishes are limited to the tropics (wrasses are mostly in the tropics, but a few species are farther north) and swim among and just above the grass blades. When threatened, they may flee across the tips of the grass blades in a zigzag pattern or dive into the seagrass for shelter. The most common wrasses in Caribbean seagrass beds are the slippery dick (*Halichoeres bivittatus*)—tan to tan/green in color with a thin black line along its midbody from head to tail—and the black-ear wrasse (*Halichoeres poeyi*)—medium to bright green in color. Both species are generally cigar shaped and are a few inches in length. I like to cast a tan-and-white or chartreuse-and-white Clouser Minnow over grass beds that are a few feet deep and strip the fly so that it swims erratically over the grass. Barjacks, yellow jacks, blue runner, and barracuda will cruise over grass beds looking for an opportunity to eat a wrasse that doesn't see them coming in time and are likely candidates to grab your fly. You might also hook up with a bonefish or snapper.

Only one species of parrotfish is consistently found in seagrass beds in the Caribbean. The bucktooth parrotfish (*Sparisoma radians*) often swims in small schools along the tops of the grass blades and feeds on blades of turtle grass, leaving crescent-shaped cutouts in the blades. Shaped like a stereotypical fish, these small parrotfish (a few inches long) are usually grass green in color and are of a size and shape best imitated by a deceiver or bendback pattern. Because the bucktooth is generally in seagrass beds of 2 feet or deeper, weighted flies and sinking or intermediate lines are best. Larger jacks, barracuda, and occasional tarpon and snook are your most likely catches with this approach.

# IMITATING BEHAVIOR OF RESIDENT PREY

An important component of using a fly to imitate small fish in grass beds is the fishes' behavior. It is well worth the time and effort to snorkel the grass beds to get a fish-eye view of how the prey species use the habitat. Observation by snorkeling will give you an idea of how pinfish and mojarras zigzag through the grass blades. If you snorkel over a seagrass bed, you may see fishes swimming just above the tips of the grass blades. As you approach these fish, they will either dive into the grass blades for cover or speed quickly away, skimming the tips of the grass blades as they flee in a zigzag pattern. The latter behavior is one that is most amenable to imitation in the design and fishing of flies in these areas.

Snorkeling in grass beds will also give you insight into how crabs and shrimp move among the grass blades and on open bottom. Your observations will undoubtedly give you ideas for new fly patterns and strategies for how to fish these new flies. For example, one of the toughest aspects of sight-fishing with shrimp and crab patterns is that an angler's first instinct is to strip the fly when the fish approaches. However, as you will see when you snorkel a grass bed, the first response of shrimp and crabs to being chased by a predator is to hide among the grass blades or burrow into the bottom. If that fails, a shrimp or swimming crab might try to make a run for it but probably not. This means that when you cast a shrimp or crab fly to a tailing red drum, bonefish, or permit, after the fish sees the fly it is best to leave the fly motionless on the bottom.

## SEASONAL PREY FISHES

Juvenile fishes are seasonal residents of grass beds that are also potential prey for gamefish. These may be juvenile gamefish, such as snapper, grouper, and speckled trout, or juveniles of nongamefish species. Often, these species occur in grass beds only as juveniles, and the adults live in other habitats. The seasonality in presence of juvenile fish is due to the life cycles of these species, as outlined in Chapter 1. And although the seasonality of these species in seagrass beds is similar in all three regions (generally more juveniles in summer), the species vary from the tropics to subtropics to warm-temperate zones.

During summer months in the tropics, juvenile fishes can be important food items for gamefish that feed in grass beds.

Most species of coral reef fish spawn in spring and summer, so the larvae and juveniles are most abundant from May through October. Juveniles of some coral reef fish species use seagrass habitats before moving to coral reefs as young adults. Grunts (family Pomadasyidae) are perhaps the most common juvenile coral reef fish in seagrass habitats in summer. When small, most grunts are similar in appearance and have a basic yellow-and-white or silver coloration with various striping patterns. Yellow-and-white Clouser Minnows or small yellow-and-white deceivers are my standard patterns.

Juvenile snappers (family Lutjanidae) are also seasonal residents of shallow grass beds in the tropics. Most common are juvenile yellowtail snapper (*Ocyurus chrysurus*) of 2–3 inches. A yellow-and-white fly of 3 inches or so, fished just above the grass blades, is a good way to imitate these juvenile fish. Juvenile mangrove, lane, and mahogany snappers also use grass beds, mostly in summer.

In subtropical and warm-temperate areas, a somewhat different group of juveniles invades seagrass beds. The majority appear in spring and summer. For example, juvenile croaker and mojarra first appear in shallow areas, including grass beds and areas of mixed seagrass and open bottom, in spring. Juveniles of both species are almost all silver and can be imitated with small (1–3 inches) white deceivers or similar patterns. Both species feed on organisms in the bottom and thus are most often found in areas of sparse seagrass or open areas within seagrass beds. Larger croaker are usually found in deeper areas of open bottom. Depending on the species, larger mojarras (3–4 inches) can be found in open bottoms intermixed with seagrass throughout the summer or along mangrove shorelines.

Juvenile speckled trout also make an appearance in seagrass habitats in spring and summer. The juveniles look like miniature versions of adults and are most common in areas of dense and continuous seagrass. As they feed on small shrimp and fish found among the grass blades, they can fall prey to larger fish, including adult speckled trout. Juvenile speckled trout are generally longer than they are high or wide, so white-and-silver flies with long profiles are good imitations.

One of the most interesting and important prey species in subtropical and warm-temperate seagrass beds is pinfish. Although briefly addressed in Chapter 1, pinfish are worth covering in detail here because of their extreme importance in subtropical and warm-temperate seagrass beds. Pinfish are an extremely important prey item for gamefish, including snook. David Blewett, a biologist with the Florida Fish and Wildlife Conservation Commission's Fish and Wildlife Research Institute, has conducted extensive research of snook diet in southwest Florida and has found that pinfish are seasonally a major part of snook diet.

Pinfish show distinct seasonality in size, abundance, and habitat use. Pinfish larvae enter estuaries and other shallow areas with seagrass in the winter months. These larvae then transform into juveniles that are less than 1 inch long and look like miniature versions of adult pinfish. When given a choice, these small juvenile pinfish prefer seagrass beds that contain drift algae, probably because the drift algae provides the necessary food and shelter.

Pinfish grow very quickly, so a fish that was less than 1 inch in March will be a few inches long by summer. As pinfish grow, they change their diet and behavior, lose their association with drift algae, and forage throughout the seagrass beds. So, you will see a change in the average size of pinfish in seagrass beds: a lot of small fish in winter, a mixture of small to medium fish in late winter, medium to larger fish in late spring/summer, and the largest fish in early autumn before many of the adults migrate to deeper water for winter. This seasonal change in size parallels a change in habitat use—from drift algae in seagrass beds for the smallest pinfish to seagrass beds and even deeper habitats for the larger pinfish.

David Blewett's research shows that snook seem to select a particular size of pinfish as prey. Although he found pinfish from ½ inch to 5 inches in the snook stomachs he examined, most pinfish were between 1½ and 3 inches long. Even more interesting is that the size of pinfish Dave caught while sampling using seines was dominated by smaller pinfish between ½ and 2 inches. In other words, snook selected a certain size pinfish from what they had available. Given what we know about seasonality and size of pinfish, you'd expect the size of pinfish preferred by snook to be available mostly during summer. And Dave's data reflect this. Although the total number of pinfish Dave caught during sampling with a seine was highest in spring, the spring pinfish were small. In contrast, although there were fewer total pinfish in summer, the pinfish in summer were in the preferred size range for snook. So, although snook ate pinfish in all but the winter months, summer is when pinfish flies are best for snook.

Your fly selection should include a range of sizes of flies to imitate pinfish through the seasons. I like yellow-and-white deceivers of 1–2 inches for winter, 1–3 inches for spring, 3–5 inches for summer and autumn. Ken Bay of Ormond Beach, Florida, has come up with a fantastic pinfish imitation made entirely with artificial materials. For juvenile pinfish, I like to strip the fly so it swims just above the drift algae and seagrass, using short, quick strips to give the fly a darting motion. For larger pinfish, I like to cast over seagrass and along edges of grass beds and use longer, slower strips.

## Midwater Baitfish

Another group of small fishes in seagrass beds remains in the middle and upper levels of the water column. The numerous species of herrings (family Clupeidae—includes herring, sardine, menhaden, shad), anchovies (family Engraulidae), and silversides (family Atherinidae) are what most people picture when they think of baitfish. In the tropics and subtropics, seagrass lagoons are attractive to these species because these areas are relatively shallow, sheltered, and calm. These baitfish species tend to school during the day and disperse at night to feed.

In lagoons with mangrove shorelines, schools of baitfish can often be found along the mangroves, seeking shelter among the mangrove roots. In warm-temperate areas during summer, large schools of baitfish are common over deep seagrass beds and to a lesser extent over shallow seagrass beds.

## Herring Family (Family Clupeidae)

The abundance of baitfish varies seasonally. In the subtropical and warm-temperate regions, baitfish are in lowest abundance in winter. This is especially true for the species in the herring family, many of which migrate to offshore waters during late autumn and winter. Warming waters of spring prompt the return of many of these migrating adults as well as the appearance of juveniles. The larvae enter the shallows in spring and early summer and grow throughout the summer. By autumn, you will find the greatest numbers of baitfish in grass beds, and that is when you are most likely to experience a feeding blitz in the shallows, when schools of marauding gamefish corral schools of baitfish and thrash the water to a froth with their feeding.

Although the species in this family are mostly silver, they can take on a range of colors on their dorsal surface, most notably a green hue when in grass beds. The number of herring species you might encounter over grass beds is lengthy, but the shape and coloration of the different species are similar. In estuaries with tannins, the baitfish may have a brassy sheen to them. In clear tropical waters, even minor splashes of color (such as yellow ventral fins) become more prominent. Your selection of flies should incorporate the local color variations.

My favorite fly patterns for species of herring are deceivers with color variations to match local baitfish and variations of Dave Skok's Mushmouth. For both patterns I begin with a base body of white and vary the color of the back of the fly. Colors I use for the back include dark green, black, green and brown for stained or darker waters, and chartreuse or blue for clear tropical waters. I carry a range of sizes to match the baitfish that are most common at a particular place or time: smaller patterns (2 inches) early in the spring and summer when the juveniles first make their appearance and larger patterns (3–5 inches or more) in late summer and autumn.

## Silversides and Anchovies

Silversides and anchovies are year-round residents of grass beds but show a seasonality in abundance similar to that of herrings. They are most abundant in summer and least abundant in winter. Small juvenile silversides are too small to adequately imitate with a fly and are mostly eaten by small species we generally don't target, such as needlefish, or by very small juvenile gamefish. For this reason, I use only flies that imitate adult silversides. Most anchovies and silversides will range from 3 to 4 inches, but some, like the tidewater silverside (*Menidia peninsulae*), can reach 6 inches.

Numerous species of silversides inhabit grass beds, but all are similar enough in appearance that a single pattern is adequate. Members of both families have long, slender bodies and a silver stripe on the side and are typically bland in color, and some are almost colorless. The silver-lined gut and relatively large eyes are prominent features in these species. Most fly pattern books are full of silverside and anchovy imitations (often called glass minnows).

## Mullet

Mullet are present in all three regions but show distinct differences in seasonality in each region. For example, adult striped mullet in the subtropics will spawn in winter, and not long after you can find small juvenile mullet in shallow areas, including grass beds. In late winter/early spring, these juvenile mullet will be small, but by midspring into summer, when tarpon and snook can be found on the flats, the juvenile mullet will be in the medium-size class (4–8 inches long), so a medium-size mullet fly is a good choice in late spring and summer. In the autumn, small schools of finger mullet crisscross grass beds and are favorites of red drum. Often, even tailing red drum will take notice of a surface fly that imitates juvenile mullet (aka finger mullet) in autumn. In addition to snook, tarpon, and red drum, crevalle jacks, spotted trout, and cobia will feed on these juvenile mullet in the grass beds.

If you've witnessed the spectacle of large gamefish feeding on mullet in shallow grass beds, it is not something you will forget.

It's a spectacular sight: Schools of mullet erupt from the water en masse and splash back into the water like a giant hailstorm; tarpon or snook or red drum crash through the tightly packed schools of mullet, their large backs and tails spray water and send wakes rolling across the surface. These feeding frenzies are easy to see and easy to fish. Often, all it takes is a well-placed cast with an approximate imitation to hook a large fish. In other instances, there can be so many mullet (or other baitfish of the moment) that your fly gets lost in the crowd. When this happens, I often switch to a fly that will stand out from the crowd—one with more flash or a brighter color or even a popper.

During these frenzies, try to overcome the temptation to cast into the middle of the school of mullet or other baitfish. A better strategy is to cast to the sides of the school of bait and move your fly along the edge of the school and away. When the grass bed is shallow, the gamefish work the bait from the edges of the school. In this scenario, a fly cast along the edge of a school of bait is more likely to be found by a gamefish as it moves in to feed on the panicked baitfish.

## Applying What You've Learned

### Seasonal Strategies for Gamefish in Grass Beds

Just like their prey, gamefish undergo seasonal changes in use of seagrass habitat, even in the tropics. For example, tarpon are most abundant in subtropical seagrass habitats from spring through autumn.

Bonefish prefer a limited temperature range and thus can be difficult to find if the water is either too warm (during August in Florida or the Bahamas, for example) or when the water is too cold (after a winter cold front passes through south Florida). During warm-water times, bonefish may switch to a dawn-and-dusk feeding pattern. Bonefish often retreat to deeper water during cold spells and return to the shallows after the water has warmed. In general, the changes in water temperature in the Caribbean are more moderate and thus don't get as cold or as warm as in Florida. Accordingly, I've never tracked water temperature while fishing for bonefish in the Caribbean, especially in locations where the flats receive new ocean water with each tide.

In the subtropics, through the warmer months snook may be found in patches of open bottom in grass beds—either in potholes or in smaller openings in the seagrass. During winter, snook often migrate into freshwater creeks or find deep holes in estuaries to seek refuge from cold temperatures. Seagrass flats adjacent to mangrove-lined creeks that empty onto the flat can be good places to fish during warm spells in winter because snook will venture out of the creeks during warmer weather and sun themselves on the shallow, dark bottom of the seagrass bed. These flats are also good places to fish in the spring when snook first start to migrate out of the creeks onto flats and toward their summer habitats.

When I fish grass flats adjacent to creeks, I prefer to anchor the boat and wade. I start by fishing the deep hole that usually occurs at the end of the creek and the inner edge of the flat. I then fish my way along the shallow shoreline to either side of the creek, or I pole the boat along a track parallel to the mangroves looking for snook sunning themselves in the open patches in the seagrass.

In the subtropics and northern Gulf of Mexico, although red drum can be caught in seagrass throughout the year, the sight of redfish tailing in grass beds is most common in winter during midday or early and late on summer days. In winter, low tides occur during midday, and red drum will enter the shallows to feed as the tide turns and floods. They also seem more energetic as the sun warms the water. In summer, lowest low tides occur mostly at dusk or dawn, and the warm water of summer is coolest during these times.

Speckled trout are present in grass beds throughout the year, but they may change locations and depth depending on temperature, tide, availability of prey, and spawning (speckled trout spawn during summer). You'll want to fish deeper edges of grass beds at low tides and the middle and shallow portions of grass beds at high tide.

Warmer temperatures of spring and summer bring a host of other gamefish onto grass beds in search of a meal. In the subtropics and northern Gulf of Mexico, crevalle jacks, tarpon, and cobia will cruise the grass beds in search of prey. Tarpon will likely stay in deeper grass beds or along deeper edges of shallow grass beds but will occasionally venture into the shallows. I have seen large cobia feeding on blue crabs on a seagrass flat that was so shallow that the cobias' backs were out of the water.

Seasonal changes in warm-temperate grass beds are more extreme, with most species migrating to warmer water either offshore or to the south during winter. However, when these gamefish return to the grass beds in the spring, they are hungry after a long winter and want to refill their lost fat reserves. In the autumn, these same gamefish take advantage of the abundance of prey to fatten up for the long winter.

# 5
# Mangroves

Mangroves are tropical trees that grow along marine and estuarine shorelines in the tropics, subtropics, and some locations in warm-temperate portions of the Gulf of Mexico. Like seagrasses, they play several important ecological roles in the coastal environments where they occur and are also essential habitat for gamefish and their prey. Mangroves filter sediments from land that would otherwise smother seagrasses and corals, stabilize shorelines against erosion, and are an important component in the nutrient cycle that forms the base of the food web of the coastal environment. In short, mangroves are an essential part of a healthy coastal ecosystem.

Mangroves provide seasonal habitat for juvenile fish (including gamefish) and invertebrates (like spiny lobster) as well as for a resident community of fish and invertebrates that spends almost its entire life cycle within the mangrove ecosystem. Many of these species are important prey for gamefish that live or feed in mangrove habitats.

Mangroves are better able to tolerate large fluctuations in salinity than are seagrasses but require a marine or estuarine environment to survive. In salty environments, mangroves have an advantage over other plants because they are able to process and excrete the salt that kills most other land plants.

Mangroves present a different challenge to gamefish than do seagrass habitats. They exist on the edge of the marine environment and provide a habitat that transitions from the marine to terrestrial. The habitat provided by mangroves that is directly important to gamefish and their prey comes from the mangrove roots, not the branches that tower above the water.

The trees that tower above the mangrove root habitat, however, are indirectly important to gamefish and their prey because they create shade, which helps regulate water temperature and provide hiding places. The shade also gives gamefish an advantage in pursuing prey. Gamefish resting in the shadow of mangroves are less likely to be detected by baitfish swimming by in sunny areas, so an ambush-style predator like the snook is able to get closer to its prey before striking. This ambush advantage is analogous to a person standing in the darkness outside a house at night and being able to see into a lighted room, whereas a person inside the lighted room is unable to see outside into the darkness.

For all the advantages, in areas where mangroves are growing in intertidal zones (areas alternately covered and exposed at high and low tide, respectively), the shelter they provide can be fleeting. At high tide, the mangrove roots are partially or completely submerged, so they provide ample shelter for gamefish and their prey. But at low tide, the mangrove roots along shallow shorelines may be high and dry, leaving gamefish and prey no place to hide. This is why my favorite time to fish for snook, small tarpon, red drum, and other gamefish along mangrove edges is at low tide, when they and their prey are forced from the shelter of the overhanging mangrove branches and can often be found resting along the outer edge of the mangrove roots waiting for the tide to rise. This is when they are most accessible to fly anglers.

Learning how to read these and other nuances of mangrove habitats is important to successfully fishing these areas with a fly rod. Although the general ecology of mangrove habitats is similar wherever mangroves are found, the species of gamefish and prey that fill each ecological role often differ among regions. In this chapter I will present information on the general ecology of mangroves and their importance to gamefish and region-specific examples of mangrove habitats and prey.

## MANGROVE SPECIES AND THEIR ECOLOGICAL ATTRIBUTES

Sixty-five mangrove species exist worldwide, but only two species in our coverage area are considered fish habitat: red mangrove (*Rhizophora mangle*) and black mangrove (*Avicennia germinans*). Both species of mangroves are unique in their ability to tolerate sea water due to a variety of special physiological and physical adaptations (particularly their ability to exclude or excrete salt, which would otherwise kill the plants). Throughout their range, mangroves are found in similar conditions, along low-energy shorelines. Shorelines that are consistently buffeted by high energy from waves and strong currents are not suitable for these plants. In the tropics, this means you will find mangroves on lee sides of islands, in lagoons, on flats where the large expanse of shallows protects the mangroves from wave energy, along shorelines that are protected from waves by coral reefs, and in estuaries. In the subtropics of south Florida and from southwestern Texas southward, mangroves are most common in estuaries and lagoons, on the landward side of barrier islands, and in locations like Florida Bay, which is an expansive, low-wave-energy, shallow area.

The red mangrove's northern limit is central Florida and southernmost Texas. Black mangroves are found as far north as some portions of the warm-temperate northern Gulf of Mexico, but northern outposts of black mangroves are often temporary because especially cold winters can kill them.

### Red Mangroves

When fishing, you will most often encounter the red mangrove. One of the most important adaptations of red mangroves is the support structures, called prop roots, that elevate most of the plants above the water. Because the prop roots support most of the plants above the water, red mangroves are able to take advantage of submerged areas that other land-based plants can't. And because many of these areas are exposed at low tides, they aren't suitable areas for seagrass to grow, so mangroves are the only source of shelter and food for gamefish. From an angler's point of view, the most important feature of red mangroves is that prop roots create a complex labyrinth of habitat for a large, near-shore community of gamefish and their prey that is accessible to fly anglers.

Red mangroves are an important part of the food web in coastal environments. The combination of sediments trapped by the mangrove prop roots, the continual dropping of leaves from the mangrove trees, and byproducts of organisms within the mangroves forms the detritus that is the center of the food web in mangrove habitats. Bacteria and fungi, and even some fishes, such as mojarras, feed on the detritus. An extensive community of algae, sponges, barnacles, oysters, clams, mussels, and other organisms grow directly on the prop roots (often referred to as the fouling community). In turn, small organisms, such as shrimp, crabs, worms, and fish, feed on the detritus and on organisms in the fouling community and are then preyed upon by larger organisms. The structure of the mangrove prop roots and the abundant food combine to make these great habitats for small fish and invertebrates, which in turn attract gamefish.

## Prop Root Fouling Communities in the Tropics

In the tropics, a large variety of organisms, including numerous species of barnacles, mangrove oysters, algae, mussels, sponges, and anemones, competes for space on the mangrove prop roots.

The species of the fouling community tend to grow at different locations on the prop roots, resulting in a changing suite of species from the top to the bottom of the root. You can use knowledge of where different species grow to your advantage. The top of the fouling community is dominated by barnacles because they can tolerate exposure to air on every tidal cycle. The barnacles at the top of the prop roots are dry at just about every low tide. A smaller species of barnacle is usually at the top, followed by a larger species just below. But the barnacles must be under water for a significant portion of the tidal cycle. So barnacles mark the typical high tide line. Mangrove oysters are usually next—they can tolerate some time out of the water but not as frequently or for as long a time as barnacles, so they grow in the midtide range that is exposed for only shorter periods at low tide or only during spring tides. The fouling community on the portions of the prop roots covered by water during all but the lowest tides will be dominated by mussels and algae. Sponges and anemones can tolerate only occasional exposure to air, if at all, and thus are lowest on the prop roots.

Even if you have a tide chart, the direction, strength, and duration of wind and changes in barometric pressure can have significant effects on water level that result in higher or lower water than predicted by the tide charts (see Chapter 2 on tides). Although these differences may seem minor to us, they can influence gamefish behavior. For example, numerous days of strong, onshore winds can make high tides higher than predicted and will prevent low tides from dropping as low as predicted. Offshore winds will have the opposite effect—both high and low tides will be lower than predicted. If you are very familiar with an area, you will know what the "normal" tide levels should be and can adjust your fishing strategy according to wind effects. However, if you are new to or visiting an area, if you are fishing in an area without reliable tide charts, if you left the tide charts on the kitchen table back home, or if you aren't quite sure of the effect of wind on the local tides, you can examine the prop root fouling community to determine what the normal water levels should be and then adjust your strategy if necessary.

Now that you know the types of areas that provide the best conditions for red mangroves, and you are able to interpret clues to determine how water level may be affecting the gamefish you are pursuing, it's time to put this information into a fishing scenario and to learn from my mistakes.

## Applying What You've Learned

### Bonefish along the Mangroves

While living in the Caribbean, I had a favorite bonefish fishing location—a mangrove shoreline on a small island. It was a great spot to find tailing bonefish on an evening high tide. It wasn't an easy place to get to, so it was important to make the trip only when there was a good chance of finding feeding bonefish, typically on the late rising tide. Even for such a remote location, with practice I was able to predict the tides. Unfortunately, I couldn't predict the winds.

An hour before dusk I was wading the mangrove shoreline in search of tailing bonefish. It was late in the incoming tide, and I expected to find bonefish riding the flooding tide into the mangrove prop roots to feed on crabs. Although I was fishing on the lee side of the island, I could hear a decent breeze whistling over the tops of the mangrove trees and could see whitecaps dancing over the deeper water in the distance. These strong winds were not predicted by the most recent weather forecast.

I'd been wading the shoreline for thirty minutes and had not seen a tail, mud, or wake, and I hadn't heard the telltale swashing of a bonefish tailing within the flooded prop roots. In a forehead-slapping moment, I noticed that the water barely covered the mangrove oysters growing on the prop roots, despite the tide being nearly high. The strong wind had kept water off the flat, which caused a lower-than-expected high tide. The bonefish I was searching for had this figured out long before I did. In what was left of daylight I waded away from the mangroves and out onto the flat to try to save the evening's trip and was able to find a few cruising fish in deeper water.

What I experienced wasn't a huge difference in water depth, and it would have been difficult to predict even with tide charts and an accurate weather forecast. But it was enough of a difference to keep the bonefish in deeper water and away from what I expected to be an evening casting to fish feeding along the shoreline. Seeing the barnacles high and dry was the information I needed to change my strategy for the evening.

## Prop Root Fouling Communities in the Subtropics

In the subtropics, you are likely to find several species of oysters growing on prop roots, and these oysters dominate the fouling community. Here, it is the oysters that create complexity in the prop root community that provides habitat for numerous small prey species. Because oysters can cover the entire submerged portion of a prop root, they give fewer clues on water level because there is no transition in species like you'll find in the tropics. However, there are some clues. The upper end of the oyster clusters growing on prop roots will be at the upper portion of the intertidal range. Oysters can tolerate exposure to air (they close their shells and wait for water to cover them again before opening) but need to be in water for the majority of the tidal cycle and thus will grow only as high on the prop roots as most midlevel tides will cover.

In contrast, mangrove leaves can't tolerate being submerged in salt water on a regular basis, such as at every high tide. If you examine a mangrove shoreline, you will notice that the lowest leaf-covered branches hang in a line that is parallel to the water. This leaf line indicates the level of the typical high tide. The water will reach the leaf line only on the strongest high tides.

The differences in requirements of oysters and mangrove leaves result in a gap between the uppermost oysters and the lowest mangrove branches. When water fills the gap between the oysters and mangrove branches or is as high as the mangrove branches, you know you are experiencing an especially high tide. A typical high tide will cover the uppermost oysters. A typical low tide will expose the upper two-thirds of an oyster-encrusted prop root. You can use the water depth in relation to the oyster growth on prop roots and the height of mangrove branches as a rough

*At low tide, the entire red mangrove prop root system is exposed, revealing oysters, barnacles, and other indicators that anglers can use to their advantage.*

guide to water level and how the water levels you observe on a particular day might relate to what is "typical" for that area.

## Black Mangroves

Black mangroves are also ecologically important in coastal environments but are limited to areas closer to the high-tide line than are red mangroves. Instead of prop roots, black mangroves have pencil-sized aerial roots (pneumatophores) that stick up vertically from the mud bottom. You can recognize black mangroves because they have tens or hundreds of these sticklike pneumatophores surrounding the area around the base of the tree. This structure allows the black mangrove roots to exchanges gases with the air while living in sediment that is naturally hypoxic (low in oxygen) or anoxic (no oxygen) and full of sulfur (the rotten egg smell of marsh muds).

Although pneumatophores are very successful adaptations that allow black mangroves to thrive in tough environments, they can't tolerate long periods under water as well as can the prop roots of red mangroves. This means that black mangroves are rather good indicators of the high tide line. Where they occur together, black mangroves are generally behind (on the inland side of) red mangroves or in backwaters with a relatively minor tide range, thus ensuring that the pneumatophores can be exposed to air for at least some of the tidal cycle.

In the Caribbean, where the tidal range is narrow, black mangroves are often found in shallow, soft-bottom backwaters that are not as frequently encountered by fly anglers in pursuit of bonefish, permit, and the like. These are often areas that tend to be too shallow for gamefish most of the time. But black mangroves also fringe the edges of flats that are dotted with small red mangroves and are great places to find bonefish feeding on spring tides.

In the subtropics, where tidal range is often wider, black mangroves are most often found in two types of locations: inland of red mangroves in shallower water closer to the high-tide line and along shallow, often muddy shorelines, such as the protected backwaters and creeks of an estuary or lagoon. Both of these locations are frequented by gamefish like red drum.

Because black mangroves don't have large prop roots like red mangroves, they provide a different type of habitat that is smaller in scale and less complex than that of prop roots. There is no fouling community on black mangrove roots. Instead, the marine community associated with black mangroves revolves around the mud and sand bottom, and sometimes oyster bars, around the pneumatophores. Fiddler crabs, marsh crabs, mud crabs, and small fishes that feed on the bottom detritus are the most common gamefish prey found in black mangrove habitats.

In addition, because the pneumatophores are near the high-tide line and often are submerged for only part of the tidal cycle, they provide only temporary shelter to the small fishes found along these shorelines. The areas adjacent to black mangroves are usually open bottom—either muddy or sandy sediment—which also don't provide much shelter for prey. Gamefish know all about the habitat limitations of black mangroves and take advantage of

*Black mangrove pneumatophores require exposure to air for at least part of the tidal cycle and thus are good indicators of the typical high-tide zone.*

the limited shelter this habitat provides to their prey. A section of deeper water adjacent to a black mangrove shoreline is a good place to look for gamefish feeding on small baitfish or crabs huddled along the muddy shoreline at low tide. And closer to high tide, look for gamefish to search for crabs among the pneumatophores.

## Applying What You've Learned

### Black Mangrove Shorelines

The knowledge you've now gained about the interaction between tides, mangroves, and the organisms living among the mangrove roots can be incorporated into a fishing strategy. During the high water associated with spring high tides, red drum and other gamefish will ride the higher water well into the black mangrove root habitat to feed on fiddler crabs and other crabs. Fiddler crab burrows are usually near the high tide within the intertidal zone and thus are mixed in with the black mangrove pneumatophores. Although fiddler crabs are usually most active at low tide, when they can be found feeding on detritus and debris left by the previous high tide, red drum and other gamefish will still take advantage of high tides to search for fiddler crabs that might venture outside the safety of their burrows during high water. The following example may give you some ideas for finding and targeting red drum feeding in these areas.

I paddled my canoe along a mangrove shoreline at high tide, hoping to find snook cruising the outer edge of the red mangrove prop roots. I heard a soft splash way up in the mangrove forest—not the *slurp-POP* of a feeding snook but rather a much softer sound. I heard the sound again and was able to figure a direction, so I poked the bow of the canoe into the mangroves to take a look. As my eyes adjusted to the dim light in the mangrove forest, I turned my head as I heard the soft splashing again just in time to see a red drum tail waving among the flooded pneumatophores of black mangroves.

It's impossible to get a fly to these fish way back in the mangroves, but it's worth exploring these areas to find small openings in the mangroves that are close to areas with flooded black mangroves or close to a spot where you can see or hear a red drum feeding. If you are lucky, you might be able to intercept the fish as it moves along the shoreline. Or, if you can figure out the avenues the red drum are using to access the mangroves on the rising tide, you may be able to intercept some fish as they come out of the mangroves with the ebbing tide.

## GAMEFISH PREY IN THE MANGROVES

The communities of fish and invertebrates that inhabit mangroves are generally made up of two components: resident species and seasonal species. Resident species are present throughout the year and are usually the most common. Seasonal species are present for only a portion of the year and are fewer in number except during seasonal peaks in abundance, when they can dominate mangrove communities for short periods. This occurs, for example, during pulses of juveniles during summer, which frequently draws the interest of gamefish.

## Crustaceans

Among the most common gamefish prey in mangrove habitats amenable to imitation with a fly are crabs and shrimps.

### *Crabs*

Crabs are very important prey items for gamefish feeding in mangrove habitats. Fortunately for anglers faced with choosing a crab fly pattern, although there are at least three families (and perhaps a dozen species) of crabs that live in mangrove habitats and are preyed on by gamefish, most of these crabs are similar in color and come in only three general body shapes.

#### *Swimming Crabs*

Although not as important as prey items as in seagrass habitats, swimming crabs (family Portunidae)—blue crabs (*Callinectes sapidus*) and related species—are important prey in mangrove habitats. Swimming crabs will usually be olive to tan depending upon bottom coloration, are able to swim sideways using their rearmost legs, and are wider (side to side) than they are long (front to back), with pointed ends on their shells. When cornered by a gamefish, swimming crabs use one or more of three escape strategies. A first strategy is to swim rapidly sideways through the water out of the gamefish's field of view. If pursued, a swimming crab will often dive to the bottom (the second strategy) and quickly bury in the sediment in areas where the bottom is soft enough. But in some areas the bottom is not soft enough for rapid burying, so flight is the only option for these crabs. As a last resort, the crab may spread its claws in a defensive posture and snap at anything that comes close. Such behaviors explain why the best strategy for fishing a fly that imitates a swimming crab is to move the fly until the fish sees it, then let the fly rest still on the bottom, and then scoot it slowly across the bottom so it kicks up sediment like it is trying to bury.

The proximity of mangroves and seagrass provides a great situation for juvenile blue crabs. They do well in the shelter of thick seagrass when they are especially small and can forage among the mangroves after they are larger. Juvenile blue crabs are most abundant in late spring and summer. In contrast, mangroves with mud adjacent will likely harbor fewer juvenile blue crabs, although adults may be present. Connections between habitats such as this are important for anglers to notice because juvenile blue crabs are on the menu of numerous gamefish found in the subtropics, including snook and red drum. Given an opportunity to sight-fish for red drum along a mangrove shoreline lined by seagrass, I will often use my imitation of a juvenile blue crab.

### *Mangrove and Marsh Crabs*

Bonefish, permit, red drum, and even snook and tarpon will feed on mangrove crabs and marsh crabs (family Grapsidae). Mangrove crabs live on prop roots and branches of red mangroves above the waterline and feed on mangrove leaves. Marsh crabs live in burrows in mud around mangrove branches. These crabs have square bodies and are relatively small—most species are 1 or 2 inches across. They are dark colored (dark purple, olive, brown, or reddish-brown) and are often mottled. These crabs are not able to swim and scurry among mangrove prop roots and branches or on the shoreline above the low-tide line. When threatened, these crabs will flee into the water—either running from shore or dropping from mangrove branches. These crabs either scurry just below the water surface or drop to the bottom and move toward shore but are not nearly as adept at moving through the water as the swimming crabs. A gamefish that hears or sees one of these crabs drop into the water will take advantage of the relatively easy meal of a crab that doesn't move very well in the water. A number of floating crab patterns are productive when cast to mangrove shorelines with a loud landing.

### *Fiddler Crabs*

Fiddler crabs (family Ocypodidae) live in burrows in the sediment near the high-tide line, often in the intertidal zone between high and low tide lines of mangrove shorelines. Because of this trait, they are common among black mangrove pneumatophores or at the most-landward portion of a red mangrove stand. Fiddler crabs usually retreat into their burrows during high tide and come out to feed during low tides. But the burrows may be shallow enough or some fiddler crabs may remain active enough at high tide that red drum and bonefish enter these areas to search for fiddler crabs at high tide. Although the enlarged claw is the most notable characteristic of fiddler crabs, it is not a necessary component of a fiddler crab fly. Only the males have this appendage, which is associated with territorial and courtship displays. Females do not have an oversized claw, so when tying flies to imitate fiddler crabs, I suggest you concentrate more on matching the general color, size, and shape of fiddler crabs than on imitating the oversized claw. The homage I pay to the enlarged claw in my fiddler crab fly patterns is typically just a tuft of marabou and flash.

You may encounter five or more species of fiddler crabs in the mangroves in the tropics and subtropics. All of these species are in the genus *Uca*. Burger's fiddler crab (*Uca burgesi*) and the Caribbean fiddler crab (*Uca rapax*) are the most common species on sheltered mud flats near mangroves in the Caribbean, whereas Ive's fiddler crab (*Uca speciosa*) is perhaps the most common in the upper intertidal zone from south Florida to Mississippi and again from eastern Mexico to Cuba in the Gulf of Mexico. The lavender fiddler Crab (*Uca vocator*) is common in mud bottoms partially shaded by mangroves and is a common fiddler along the Texas-Mexico coast. Each species prefers a different type of sediment and salinity, so you will encounter different species depending on where you are fishing.

Fiddler crabs have a squarish body and come in a wide range of colors, including olive, brown, mottled brown, tan, orange-brown, and purple, and most have white-tipped claws. Typical body sizes for fiddler crabs range from ½ to almost 1 inch.

To find out if fiddler crabs are potential prey for gamefish where you are fishing, explore an area at low tide to determine if fiddler crabs are abundant. If fiddler crabs are abundant, you will see their burrows scattered throughout the intertidal zone and may even see some crabs scurrying across the ground.

### *Mud Crabs*

A few species of mud crabs (family Xanthidae) live in mangrove swamps and are on the menu of bonefish, permit, and red drum. The mud crabs you will find in mangrove areas are dark colored—reddish, grayish, brownish-green, black, or dark—often have white-tipped claws, and will be from ¼ to 1¼ inches across.

Although gamefish feeding in mangrove habitats have many species of crabs to choose from, the similarities of these crabs will allow you to get away with just a few fly patterns. Most of your crab flies should be small (less than 1 inch across), earth-tone colors, and perhaps have a white tip on the claws. The greatest difference will be in the way you fish the flies—you can give more action to a fly that imitates a swimming crab, whereas a fly that imitates one of the walking crabs should be given minimal motion and then only enough to imitate a crab moving slightly on the bottom.

## ***Shrimp***

Among the shrimps, the common shrimp (family Penaeidae—the shrimp we eat are in this family, and all have a similar appearance) can be abundant as juveniles in mangrove habitats. These shrimp tend to be somewhat translucent with shades of brown and green to match the surroundings. When searching among red mangrove prop roots, I've found these types of shrimp to be most abundant in areas where seagrass is nearby, although they also occur seasonally in mangrove creeks.

Snapping shrimp (family Alpheidae) can also be abundant in mangrove habitats, especially among oysters growing on prop roots or among oyster shells on the bottom under the mangroves. *Alpheus armillatus*, *Alpheus heterochaelis*, and *Alpheus viridis* are the most likely species. Size 2 or 1, long-shank shrimp flies in olive green to brown with one enlarged claw are a suitable imitation of snapping shrimp in mangroves. The fly should be fished with minimal movement on the bottom because snapping shrimp are not fast walkers or swimmers.

#### *Juvenile Lobsters*

Juvenile spiny lobsters (*Panulirus argus*) also live among mangrove prop roots but are only seasonally abundant. These small lobsters are like candy for mutton snapper and permit that cruise the edge of the mangrove roots. In fact, a large mutton snapper will engulf an adult lobster given the chance, so juveniles are easy targets. Juvenile spiny lobster will remain hidden among the prop roots during the day and venture out to feed on the bottom adjacent to mangroves at night. Lobster-imitating flies tied on long-shank hooks, sizes 1 and 1/0, are appropriate for sight-casting to mutton snapper and permit that cruise mangrove shorelines. Although juvenile lobsters might be present in mangrove habitats at any time of year, it seems that late spring and summer are peak times of juvenile lobster abundance.

### Insects

Surprisingly, insects, which are an important component of the above-water mangrove community, can also be an important part of the diet of juvenile tarpon. The presence of insects in the stomachs of juvenile tarpon living in mangrove-lined estuaries may help explain why small poppers work so well for these small tarpon in the backcountry.

## RESIDENT PREY FISHES

The core group of resident prey fishes is going to be important prey items for gamefish throughout the year, so you should be familiar with these prey species. Important families of fish in this group include herring (family Clupeidae), silversides (family Atherinidae), anchovies (family Engraulidae), mojarras (family Gerreidae), mullet (family Mugilidae), killifish (family Cyprinodontidae), gobies (family Gobiidae), and blennies (family Blenniidae).

## Gobies and Blennies

Gobies and blennies are found among the mangrove roots and on the nearby bottom. The species of gobies and blennies will vary, but they all have a similar appearance and behavior. Just like their relatives in grass beds, these fish are generally small, brown to dark green, and alternate between resting on the bottom or on prop root fouling growth and darting about to grab food or chase off intruders. Gobies and blennies never make the top five prey items found in the stomachs of gamefish because they remain hidden in or near the bottom, are often well camouflaged to hide in their surroundings, and are not highly abundant like silversides. Given the chance, however, gamefish will take advantage of an opportunity to make a meal out of these small fish. I have counted numerous gobies in the stomachs of red drum that were feeding along mangrove shorelines, and flies that imitate gobies have been productive for bonefish feeding in this habitat as well. Appropriately colored Clouser Minnows work well as goby imitations.

## Killifishes

Numerous species of small fishes—(family Fundulidae—sheepshead minnow, *Cyprinodon variegates,* rainwater killifish, *Lucania parva,* Gulf killifish, *Fundulus grandis,* and many other species; family Poeciliidae—sailfin molly, *Poecilia latipinna,* and mosquitofish, *Gambusia holbrooki*)—are common along quiet mangrove shorelines in backwaters and creeks. These species are especially abundant in brackish areas in the subtropical and warm-temperate backwaters. All of these species are similar in color—brassy to dark brown/olive (some have bars, stripes, or other markings)—generally blunt-nosed, and somewhat cigar-shaped. Earth-colored streamers of 2 to 3 inches with gold flash, such as the Mangrove Muddler or a bendback, are good for imitating these species.

### Mojarras

Mojarras (family Gerreidae) are important prey for many gamefish. Mojarras are very common along mangrove shorelines and over mud and seagrass areas next to mangroves. They feed on the small invertebrates or detritus on the bottom. They alternate between hovering over the bottom and darting to the bottom to take mouthfuls of detritus. The many species of mojarras are silver to silvery tan in color, have a large eye, and are generally high-bodied. Among the more-common species are silver jenny (*Eucinostomus gula*), slender mojarra (*Eucinostomus jonesi*), spotfin mojarra (*Eucinostomus argenteus*), and yellowfin mojarra (*Gerres cinereus*). Some of the species have faint vertical bars, striping, or mottling on their sides. The color and patterns vary depending upon the area where the mojarra is living. For example, a mojarra will have a more tannish hue in backwaters stained by tannins from mangroves, whereas a fish in clear water will be mostly silver. The mojarras you will encounter in or near mangrove habitats will range from 3 to almost 16 inches depending on the species. Deceivers and similarly shaped flies make good imitations of mojarras.

## SEASONAL PREY FISHES

The second part of the community of fishes and invertebrates found in mangroves is made up of the species that use these habitats on a seasonal basis. These species are most often represented by juveniles using the mangrove habitat as a nursery area and then migrating to different habitats as they grow larger. These species are usually in highest abundance from late summer through autumn and are either absent or in low abundance at other times of the year.

These small juveniles are a good seasonal source of food for gamefish. The fact that most fish don't make it past the juvenile stage because predation is so high indicates that gamefish and other predators feed heavily on these small fish. Including in your fly selection flies that imitate small fishes in this vulnerable life stage is a good strategy.

Many of the species that use seagrass habitats as nursery areas are also found in mangroves in the same seasons, which should help to keep your fly selection a reasonable size. There are, however, some species whose juveniles are more abundant in mangroves. Fortunately, many juveniles are similar enough in appearance that they can be imitated with the same flies.

## Grunts

Grunts (family Pomadasyidae) are most abundant in the tropics, with French grunts (*Haemulon flavolineatum*), white grunts (*Haemulon plumieri*), bluestriped grunts (*Haemulon sciurus*), and sailor's choice (*Haemulon parrai*) the most common depending upon location. Juvenile grunts all have a yellow-and-white background coloration, with minor dark lines or markings that differ for each species. A yellow-over-white Clouser (size 1 or 2) or yellow-and-white deceiver (size 1) cast along the mangrove edge makes for a decent imitation of juvenile grunts. Because the majority of grunt larvae enter the mangrove habitat during summer, it is best to use smaller flies during summer and larger flies in autumn. Often the juvenile grunts will migrate away from mangrove habitats to adult habitats on reefs by winter, but this is not always the case. Sometimes larger grunts (more than 4 inches) can be found along the mangroves throughout the year and are popular prey items for barracuda.

## Snappers

Snappers (family Lutjanidae) can also be abundant among mangrove prop roots. Like grunts, juvenile snapper are most abundant during summer and migrate to adult habitats in autumn or winter. However, in areas where mangroves are along a steep shoreline or next to a channel, you might find some large snappers year-round. Species that are represented by a lot of juveniles during summer in the tropics are schoolmaster snapper (*Lutjanus apodus*), yellowtail snapper (*Ocyurus chrysurus*), and gray (mangrove) snapper (*Lutjanus griseus*). In the subtropics, gray snapper is probably the most abundant species. In the tropics, you may find larger schoolmaster and gray snappers among mangrove prop roots in deeper water, whereas adult yellowtail snappers are found in deeper reef areas. Lefty's deceivers in white with dark-colored backs are good snapper imitations.

## Other Juveniles

Juvenile parrotfish (family Scaridae) can also be found among mangrove prop roots, mostly during summer. Juveniles of most species found among mangrove prop roots are light in color, have a typical fish shape, and often have longitudinal stripes. White Clousers, Seaducers, and muddlers are good imitations.

Juvenile jacks (family Carangidae) will occupy mangrove prop roots in loosely associated schools before moving to other habitats as they grow larger. Many juvenile jacks have vertical barring over silvery sides, are similar in shape to adults, and can be imitated with a 3-inch all-white deceiver. The vertical bars on juvenile jacks and the mottled patterns on some mojarras may explain the success of the Glades Deceiver along mangrove shorelines.

You'll recall my experience of finding bonefish feeding on juvenile grunts that I related in Chapter 1. That experience is a great example of gamefish focusing on seasonal residents. As I explained in that story, such occurrences are hard to predict but are situations you should be ready for during the summer juvenile season. Different locations may have different collections of juveniles, so it may take a little investigation on your part to determine which flies are most appropriate. The extra investigation is likely to pay off.

## MIDWATER BAITFISH

### Herring (Family Clupeidae)

The Clupeidae (herring) family includes larger, schooling baitfish that are best imitated with 2- to 7-inch-long deceivers. In the tropics these species are present year-round, whereas in the subtropics they are seasonal. The species in this family that you are most likely to encounter near mangrove shorelines and mangrove lagoons include red-ear sardine (*Harengula humeralis*), scaled sardine (*Harengula jaguana*), and species of similar coloration and shape: They have silver sides and gray to green-shaded backs, with a high body profile. Their size will vary seasonally, especially in the subtropics. For example, juvenile scaled sardines found in seagrass beds near mangrove shorelines are most abundant in late spring and grow to adult sizes by summer. Mangrove lagoons with moderate depths, large areas of open water, and decent water clarity are where you will most often find schools of herrings in association with mangrove habitats.

In the tropics, groups of barjacks (*Caranx ruber*), blue runner (*Caranx crysos*), and horse-eye jacks (*Caranx latus*) will often strafe schools of small herring in the open water sections of these mangrove lagoons, whereas crevalle jacks (*Caranx hippos*) are the primary marauders in the subtropics. Tarpon, snook, red drum, spotted seatrout, ladyfish, barracuda, and even the occasional large bonefish will also feed heavily on herrings found near mangrove habitats. It is quite a sight to watch tarpon herd a school of herring along a mangrove shoreline and take turns charging open-mouthed through the panicked baitfish.

### Silversides and Anchovies

Silversides and anchovies can spend all or a significant portion of their lives in the vicinity of mangroves. You will most often encounter silversides among the mangrove prop roots and anchovies in more open waters. Species from these families are often collectively referred to as glass minnows and always occur in schools. Fortunately for anglers, the similarities in size and coloration of anchovies and silversides mean we can imitate these prey with the same flies.

Silversides and anchovies have large eyes relative to their body size. A silver stripe runs the length of their body. Their lower half is generally pale, and the distinct silver of the abdominal cavity lining shows through the pale flesh. Their dorsal (top) half is a darker shade of tan to olive. Anchovies and silversides can grow as long as 4 to 6 inches but are typically found in smaller sizes. Species of silversides you will most likely encounter are inland silverside (*Menidia beryllina*) and tidewater silverside (*Menidia peninsulae*). Common anchovies include striped anchovy (*Anchoa hepsetus*), dusky anchovy (*Anchoa lyolepis*), bay anchovy (*Anchoa mitchilli*), and Cuban anchovy (*Anchoa cubana*).

While fishing in the Caribbean, I've often watched barracuda suspended in the shadows among the mangrove prop roots suddenly dart out and engulf a mouthful of silversides from a school as it passed along the outer edge of the mangroves. In the subtropics, snook lie in wait and are the prime consumer of glass minnows among the mangrove prop roots. Small tarpon can be found feeding on large schools of these baitfish in backwaters of both the tropics and subtropics.

## Mullet

You will potentially encounter as many as six species of mullet along mangrove shorelines and shallows adjacent to mangroves and in mangrove lagoons. Fortunately, all of the mullet species are similar in shape and coloration and thus can be imitated with any generalized mullet pattern. Mullet are bullet-shaped, with a silvery-gray coloration, lighter on the belly with darker shades on their backs. In the subtropics and warm-temperate areas you are most likely to encounter the striped mullet (*Mugil cephalis*), although white mullet (*Mugil curema*) can be found in the same areas but usually in lower abundance. In the tropics, liza (*Mugil liza*) replaces striped mullet, and white mullet is often the most abundant species. Fantail mullet (*Mugil gyrans*) are most abundant in the tropics. Although adult mullet can reach 2 feet in length, it is the juveniles that are best imitated with a fly and are often targeted by gamefish in mangrove habitats. In general, juvenile mullet will occupy the shallow water near mangrove roots, whereas adults will venture farther from the shoreline and use a wider variety of habitats.

## LOCATION MATTERS

The composition of fish and invertebrate communities depends in large part on three factors: where the mangroves are located (in semienclosed lagoons, on shorelines exposed to open sea, on flats, along a backwater estuary, or along a creek); what habitats are adjacent to the mangroves (seagrass, sand, or mud); and the depth of water near the mangroves. Although there is natural variation even among similar habitats, some generalizations can be made about prey species most likely to be found in these different areas.

Mangroves adjacent to creeks often have more total species and a greater number of individuals of resident and seasonal species than do shallow areas. In part this is because many species will follow the flooding tide into the mangroves to feed on the rich and diverse communities in these intertidal areas and then retreat as ebbing tides drain the mangroves. The creek provides a deep-water refuge close to the food source for these species.

In turn, the greater number of organisms and the behavior of the species that utilize this strategy attract gamefish, which can often be found at the edges of these creeks opportunistically feeding on prey that is washed out of the mangroves with the dropping tide. The spring tides that are associated with new and full moons are especially good for fishing the edges of mangrove creeks because increased volumes of water being moved by these tides create stronger currents that force more prey from the mangrove shallows to the creeks.

Areas with seagrass adjacent to mangroves generally support more species than do areas with mud or sand. Small juvenile fishes prefer locations with seagrass adjacent to mangroves, but as they grow juveniles often move to areas where open bottom is adjacent to mangroves. This change in habitat occurs because larger juveniles are able to avoid more predators, feeding opportunities are better for their changing diets, and shelter of mangrove prop roots is nearby as protection from larger predators. Again, you may want to vary the size of your flies with the habitats you are fishing—smaller flies for seagrass and larger flies for areas of open bottom next to mangroves.

However, fishing for large gamefish, like snook and red drum, is often best along shorelines where no seagrass grows into the prop root habitats. Areas with open bottom next to mangroves are easier places for gamefish to find and capture prey and easier for you to see the gamefish. In addition, a deep open bottom may hold more large fish than a shallow open bottom because gamefish can wait in the shadows of the mangroves and ambush passing prey more easily. Sight-fishing for snook, red drum, tarpon, and bonefish on open bottom adjacent to mangroves, whether they are cruising or laid up, can be fantastic.

In the tropics, mangroves that are exposed to open water are likely to harbor high numbers of juveniles of the same coral reef fishes found in seagrass beds that surround coral reefs (see Chapter 4). In contrast, mangroves that are more removed from the ocean (such as lagoons that are connected to the ocean by only a narrow channel) or are deep within estuaries will be dominated by the core group of resident species that is primarily associated with mangrove habitats, with considerably fewer seasonal juveniles.

This pattern also holds in the subtropics. In general, mangroves closer to the ocean environment will have more marine species and more seasonal species. The farther upstream you go in a tidal mangrove creek, the fewer seasonal fish you will find, and the communities of baitfish (like tidewater silversides and killifish) and other prey (such as fiddler crabs) will be dominated by residents. Numerous gamefish, such as tarpon and snook, are able to travel from salty ocean areas to mangrove habitats that are almost fresh water. So in the upstream locations a brown-with-gold flash fly that imitates killifish is a good choice, whereas a white-and-yellow deceiver is a good choice for the oceanside mangrove shoreline.

## DAY VERSUS NIGHT

Many species of fish use mangrove prop roots as shelter during the day and then venture out at night to feed in adjacent open areas of seagrass, sand, or mud. This is especially common for juvenile grunts of 2 to 5 inches. Grunts will form large schools along the edges of mangrove prop roots just prior to dusk and will venture out into lagoon feeding areas after darkness falls, often following the same routes each evening. This period, which is from sunset to approximately thirty minutes after sunset, has been termed the quiet period because there is little activity relative to daytime. Most fishes have either retreated to nighttime shelters or are waiting to venture out under cover of darkness. But this is somewhat of a misnomer because it is also a time of peak predatory activity. Large mutton snappers (*Lutjanus analis*), barracuda (*Sphyraena barracuda*), and other species lie in wait along these movement routes as the grunts begin to move out into adjacent habitats. If you find a section of mangroves that harbors a large number of grunts during the day, you may want to make a mental note and return just prior to dusk. There are no guarantees, of course, but you may find yourself witness to a flurry of feeding by large predators. Yellow-over-white deceivers are suitable imitations of these small grunts.

Anglers who have witnessed the sudden surge in feeding activity by snook in estuarine mangroves also know the potential of the dusk feeding period to provide great fishing. Snook have an advantage over their prey at dusk (they can see and detect the prey better) and thus tend to be more aggressive in their feeding behavior. Snook might also feel less threatened by potential predators under cover of low light and thus may wander farther from their prop root shelters. In any case, snook that might have been tentative toward a fly during the day will be more likely to have shifted into feeding mode at dusk.

## SEASONS IN THE MANGROVES

Although not as drastic as in temperate latitudes, seasons do occur in the tropics and subtropics, and these seasons influence gamefish and their prey living in mangrove habitats.

The tropics and subtropics experience two major seasons: The wet season is generally from May or June through October or November, and the dry season is from November or December to April or May. The actual months vary somewhat among locations. And some regions, like the Caribbean coast of Costa Rica, might receive heavy rains through much of the year. In contrast, some islands in the Caribbean, such as Curacao, don't receive much rain at any time of year. The extent to which gamefish respond to changes due to wet and dry seasons varies depending on how much seasonal variation there is in their area.

During the dry season, less fresh water is flowing down rivers into the estuaries, so the salinity of the estuaries increases. In some years, the salinity can be nearly the level of the open ocean far into the estuaries and river mouths. For example, during a dry winter period in south Florida, jacks, red drum, and other gamefish might be found much farther up into an estuary than you would normally find them in summer or might be more abundant in areas where you might not normally find them. One recent winter I found large red drum in a river mouth at the head of an estuary as far from the ocean as they could be before entering the river. Part of the reason why these large adult red drum were exploring this area was because the salinity was higher than normal—25 ppt (the Gulf of Mexico is typically 30–35 ppt).

In the wet season, salinity in the rivers and estuaries drops as more fresh water flowing from rivers and creeks mixes with salt water from the ocean. The same area where I found the large red drum in winter had a salinity of less than 10 ppt the following summer wet season, and these large red drum had left for higher-salinity waters lower in the estuary or offshore.

Knowing how wet and dry seasons influence salinity and clarity of water in mangrove estuaries can help you create a strategy for where and when to fish and what type of flies might be best. For example, during the wet season you are more likely to find large red drum in areas with medium to high salinity, so you should concentrate your efforts where salinity is higher. The amount of high-salinity area is smaller during the wet season, so you have a reduced search area. In contrast, during the dry season red drum will be more widely dispersed and may be farther into the upper portions of the estuary, so you may have to expand your search area.

Snook provide another example of the effect of wet and dry seasons. Snook spawn in summer, and in order to spawn successfully snook need salinities greater than about 25 ppt. As the amount of fresh water coming out of rivers and creeks increases during the summer wet season, larger mature snook migrate to areas closer to open ocean to spawn. This may cause a sudden decrease in the number of large snook you see along a mangrove shoreline near the head of an estuary as the wet season progresses. This means that the best place to find large snook during spawning season is near the passes or along the beaches. However, after spawning some of these big snook return to the mangrove creeks, and learning when these fish begin to return to the backcountry can bring big rewards.

Seasonal changes in temperature also influence gamefish and thus can influence when and how they use mangrove habitats. This is particularly true in the subtropics. In winter, mangrove creeks (especially creeks with deep holes) are some of the best places to find snook. Snook, a tropical species, is near the northern extent of its range in the subtropics and can't tolerate cold temperatures. Snook find refuge in deeper waters of creeks sheltered from cold winter winds, and these are great places to find hungry snook in winter. Many of these winter refuge areas also have a source of fresh water, which may provide a more-consistent temperature during winter than do many open-water marine locations. As the water warms in spring and into summer, snook will move out of the creeks and will feed along mangrove shorelines and adjacent flats.

Warm spells in winter can trigger a brief change in the distribution of snook and other gamefish in the subtropics and tropics. Shallow, muddy bottoms near creeks used by snook as winter refuge areas can be good places to fish in the afternoon during warm spells. The shallow water over dark bottom will be warmed considerably by the sun. Snook will move to these areas in midday and afternoon, when the water is warmest, to warm up (much like a snake basking in the midday sun). Because snook generally feed less during winter they are usually hungry, so these basking fish can be pretty aggressive toward a well-cast fly. Similarly, red drum will move onto shallow, dark flats to warm up in the same fashion. A sunny day and rising tide are the perfect combination to find snook, redfish, and other gamefish warming up on the flats during winter.

Red drum are also a great example of how seasonal changes influence gamefish use of mangrove habitats. As summarized in Chapter 4 on seagrass, winter is probably the best time to fish for tailing red drum in subtropical grass beds. In contrast, during summer days, red drum feed in the shade of mangroves. I can think of two possible explanations for why red drum habitat use changes seasonally. First, on average, in much of red drum subtropical range, daytime tides are generally lower in winter than in summer (when lowest tides tend to be at night), so access to mangroves is more limited than in summer. Second, in winter the water is cooler, and the sun-warmed flats are a more amenable temperature for red drum. Because red drum, like other fishes, are cold-blooded, the warmer waters of the shallow flats are more desirable for them in winter. During summer, the water warms considerably, and although red drum can be found tailing in grass beds (typically in the morning and evening), you will find more red drum feeding in mangrove habitats. The high daytime tides of summer in much of the red drum subtropical range help them in several ways. Red drum use the shade of the mangroves to find cooler water during summer, and the high daytime tides allow red drum access farther back into the red mangrove prop roots and even into the flooded roots of black mangroves to feed on marsh and fiddler crabs. The shade of the mangrove branches is also a great place to look for snook and even spotted seatrout and crevalle jacks during hot summer days.

The gamefish you find along mangrove shorelines in summer will be ready to pounce on flies that imitate any of the small baitfish that can be abundant during this time of year. Small mojarras in the tropics and subtropics and pinfish in the subtropics can be especially abundant along mangrove shorelines in summer.

Seasonal changes in temperature can also affect tropical gamefish, such as bonefish and permit. This is especially true in the northernmost portions of their range, where seasonal changes in temperature are greatest, such as in the Florida Keys and even the northern Bahamas. For example, in Florida it seems that bonefish are most abundant in Florida Bay during warm months but move to the Atlantic side of the Florida Keys during winter. Florida Bay is very shallow, and shallow waters can be cooled or warmed more rapidly by the air than can deeper water, making them more susceptible to dropping temperatures brought on by cold fronts in winter. In contrast, the Atlantic side of the Keys has water temperatures that are more stable, and bonefish have quicker access to warmer, deeper waters as a refuge from dropping temperatures that are associated with cold fronts.

## Applying What You've Learned

### Gamefish in the Mangroves

I prefer two approaches to fishing red mangrove shorelines. The standard approach is to wade or to pole a boat some distance from the mangroves and cast into the shadows. "Some distance" means as far away as you can comfortably cast. It is important to stay away from the mangroves to remain unseen and unheard by the fish. A weedless fly is a must because you need to cast the fly as far up under the overhanging mangrove branches as you can. If you don't occasionally snag a mangrove branch or prop root, then you aren't casting close enough to the shoreline. For this approach I generally use weedless streamer patterns like bendbacks, Muddler Minnows, and Seaducers. Snook are ambush predators, which means they are sitting in the shadows of the mangroves waiting for an unsuspecting prey fish to swim by or for a school of resident silversides to move within striking distance. This ambush strategy and their body shape are probably why some people call snook saltwater pike. Red drum will also lie in wait and take advantage of an unsuspecting fish, and crevalle jacks will cruise the mangrove edges chasing just about any small fish they can find.

Low tide is my favorite time to fish along mangrove edges. Near high tide, snook, redfish, tarpon, and other game-fish can hide way up under the mangrove branches, but as the water drops they are forced to leave the shelter of the mangrove overhang. Often, during low tide a fish will remain as close to its preferred mangrove hideout as water depth will allow, often lying motionless on the bottom. Believe it or not, it takes some practice to pick out the motionless form of a snook lying perpendicular to the shoreline, sometimes so shallow that the top of its tail or dorsal fin is exposed. If you miss spotting a laid-up snook as you pole along a shallow shoreline, you'll learn soon enough as it explodes out of the shallows because you poled too close. It's important to cast to these laid-up fish from far enough away that the fish can't see you or your fly line on your false cast. A sidearm cast is a good idea. A quiet boat is also important as you pole along the shoreline—any noises out of the ordinary will put the fish on alert or send them to deeper water—so take your time as you pole these shorelines.

A second approach is to wade or pole close to the mangroves and look for fish either cruising or resting in the strip of open bottom that is often between the mangrove shoreline and seagrass bed or in open-bottom potholes in seagrass adjacent to the mangroves. You can use this strategy from low to midtide levels. It is important that you see the fish from a long way off because they are especially wary because they are lying on exposed bottom. A long cast, soft landing, and patient presentation are also helpful. Resting fish may seem like they are asleep, so it may take a few casts—each one closer than the last—to move the fish.

You should expect numerous break-offs while fishing mangrove habitats because hooked fish will often head into mangrove prop roots and cut your line on oysters, barnacles, mussels, or other sharp edges. A heavy bite tippet is a good idea for these conditions. I like a relatively short leader (7 feet) with twenty-pound or higher tippet. After a fish is hooked, the main goal is to keep the fish from swimming into the mangrove prop roots. If the fish does make it into the prop roots, loosen the drag—when the tension is released on the line, the fish will often stop. Then you can weave your way through the mangroves to disentangle the line and resume the fight.

One of my greatest frustrations in fishing mangrove shorelines is trying to track and cast to fish that are feeding far into the mangrove forest at high tides. These fish can be snook, tarpon, red drum, or bonefish. Except for bonefish, I've had occasional success casting small poppers along the outer edge of the mangroves. I think the feeding fish hear the popper and come out of the mangroves to investigate.

My favorite flies for casting into mangrove shadows are flies that hover. This is because I want the fly to remain in the strike zone among the mangrove prop roots as long as possible, but I still want to be able to give action to the fly with short strips. Two favorite patterns for this are the Seaducer in red and grizzly and Mangrove Muddler in brown (with gold flash) or olive (with green flash). Additional choices include deceivers, glass minnow imitations such as bendbacks, and divers.

When fishing for bonefish feeding within the mangroves at high tide, listen for the telltale swashing sounds a bonefish makes when feeding in the flooded mangrove forest. It is worth your time to pinpoint the location of the feeding fish and to find indentations in the mangrove shoreline where you might intersect the bonefish as it moves through the mangroves. Often, a fish will zigzag in and out of the mangroves as it moves along in search of food, and you can sneak a cast to the fish as it briefly moves out of the mangroves. If you are able to intersect these hungry fish, you have a good chance of hooking up. The not-so-elegant catch I describe below proves it's worth tracking bonefish feeding in mangroves.

A friend and I waded along a flooded mangrove shoreline at dawn. High tide had pushed water well into the mangrove forest. A good distance ahead of us we heard a ruckus deep within the mangroves. A feeding bonefish? We worked our way slowly along the mangrove edge toward where we thought the fish was feeding, listening for more signs of the feeding fish. We heard nothing, but as we reached the spot where the noise had come from, a bonefish tailed halfway between us.

I made a quick roll cast in case the fish hadn't already spooked, and as the fly dropped toward the bottom I stripped twice. A wake appeared as the fish bolted toward the fly. The wake bulged as the fish turned on the fly, the fly line jumped, and I set the hook.

Catching that bonefish was pure luck. It tailed between two anglers who were only 30 feet apart and then ate the fly. But we were in the right place at the right time because we made the effort to find the fish we heard feeding deep within the mangroves and lucked upon the fish as it worked its way out onto the flat.

Numerous species of jacks will cruise the edges of mangrove prop roots at high speed picking off unwary glass minnows as they go. Even if you can't see the jacks, you can sometimes follow their path by watching for the telltale sign of schools of glass minnows jumping from the water to escape. When jacks are in this rapid-fire mode, be sure to cast ahead of where you think they might be rather than at the spot where you just saw glass minnows jump out of the water. By the time you cast to the spot where you saw the action, the jacks will probably be another 10 feet or more farther along the shoreline.

Snook that ambush glass minnows along mangrove shorelines will also give their location away due to glass minnows' escape behavior. A shower of glass minnows along the edge of mangrove prop roots, along with the "slurPOP" of air being sucked in with a mouthful of water and glass minnows, is a sure sign of a feeding snook.

The largest snapper you will find feeding along mangrove prop roots is the mutton snapper *(Lutjanus analis)*. Large adult mutton snapper will forage along the mangroves much like a permit or bonefish, feeding on crabs, lobsters, and fish. As mentioned earlier, a large mutton snapper will eat an adult spiny lobster, so the juvenile spiny lobster found among the prop roots must seem like buttered popcorn to a mutton snapper. More important, because mutton snapper will feed on the same prey as bonefish and permit, the same shrimp, crab, and juvenile lobster flies are appropriate for all three species. However, unlike bonefish and permit, mutton and other snappers that live among mangrove prop roots in deeper water will also chase poppers. So, if you find yourself in a lagoon or creek with water too deep to sight-fish, don't despair—it's worth some casts of a popper along the mangrove edge. If not snappers (possibly mutton, mangrove [aka gray], schoolmaster, lane, or others), then maybe jacks, snook, or small tarpon will strike the fly.

Finally, fishing around mangroves requires caution for two reasons. First, because the roots of mangroves trap sediments and dampen currents, the bottom in and around mangroves can be rather soft. This is not always the case (there are some great hard-bottom wading opportunities along mangrove shorelines), but this is a possibility an angler should take into consideration when fishing an area for the first time. Wade with caution! Some areas are so soft you can become permanently stuck. Second, because mangroves provide protection from wind and are home to many insects, the mosquitoes and no-see-ums can be brutal and can sour an otherwise productive day of fishing. So be sure to take some strong bug repellent.

# 6
# Oyster Bars

My favorite series of oyster bars lies in knee-deep water along the deep edge of a large, shallow grass bed. The oyster bars protect the grass bed from waves that build under south winds whipping across 2 miles of open water. These disconnected patches of oyster bar also break up incoming tidal currents whose diversions have carved small sand potholes, about 5 feet across, at the ends of the bars. Baitfish will temporarily congregate in the shelter provided by the oyster bars, taking refuge from the forceful currents and seeking escape from foraging gamefish.

Unfortunately for the schooling baitfish, the oyster bars render a false haven. At low tide the shallow oyster bars provide shelter from gamefish, but the baitfish are at the mercy of wading birds like blue heron. At high tide, when water covers the bars, this is an easy place for gamefish to corral and feed on the baitfish because of the bars' proximity to deeper water. I have witnessed snook, tarpon, red drum, and spotted seatrout feeding on sardines, mullet, and anchovies that have sought shelter in the shadows of these oyster bars. When the baitfish and gamefish are both present, an appropriately sized streamer cast into the mix almost always results in a strike.

A whole community of potential gamefish prey lives permanently among the oyster shells and takes advantage of food and shelter provided by oyster bars' many crevices. These residents seem to live a less-frantic existence than the baitfish. When gamefish feed on the resident prey their feeding is more methodical, and your fly-fishing approach must follow suit. This chapter will introduce you to the intricacies of oyster bars so you can interpret how these habitats are used by gamefish and devise strategies for fishing these habitats at different tides, locations, and times of year.

Oysters can grow in many locations—on mangrove prop roots, pier pilings, rocky shorelines, and many other surfaces that are suitable for attachment by the oysters. The communities of organisms that live among these oysters can attract feeding gamefish. But oysters growing on prop roots, pilings, or rocks are merely components of the habitats where they are growing. In contrast, oysters also occur at a scale large enough to constitute a different and unique type of habitat all their own—oyster bars.

Some people make a distinction between oyster bars and oyster reefs, with *bar* denoting a smaller structure than *reef*. It seems to me too subjective a definition—what constitutes a bar in a location with extensive oyster growth may be considered a reef in an area with relatively minor oyster coverage. In addition, many local nuances on oyster habitats tend to further confuse the issue. Therefore, throughout this chapter I use *bar* and *reef* interchangeably to describe natural structures made entirely of oysters and standardize the definitions of some of the different configurations of oyster bars. A fly angler might encounter six species of oyster while in pursuit of gamefish in coastal habitats, yet only one species forms oyster bars or oyster reefs—the eastern oyster, *Crossastrea virginica*. Other oyster species grow only on mangrove prop roots or rocky shores and don't form reefs or occur in very low abundance on oyster bars composed almost entirely of eastern oysters. In the tropics, oysters are mostly found growing on mangrove prop roots and rarely, if ever, as oyster reefs because in most locations there isn't enough plankton to support large reefs. In the subtropics and warm-temperate climates, however, where the eastern oyster is abundant, oyster bars are common and important estuarine habitats that are used as feeding areas by gamefish.

Even in subtropical and warm-temperate environments, the importance of oyster bars to gamefish varies. In areas with abundant seagrass or mangrove habitats, oyster bars are just one of

*Low spring tides are good times to explore oyster bar habitats. In this photo, the small channel between two bars is evident. Later, as the tide rises, this will be a good spot to focus efforts for fish using the channel to enter this habitat.*

three major habitats where gamefish find prey and shelter. But in areas with no mangroves and little or no seagrass, oyster bars are very important habitats because they provide the best habitat and shelter for gamefish prey.

What gamefish are you most likely to find around oyster bars? The short answer is any gamefish worth catching. For example, in North Carolina you will commonly find gulf flounder, red drum, spotted seatrout, black drum, weakfish, bluefish, gray snapper, and juvenile gag. In the subtropics, gamefish that are common on or near oyster reefs include red drum, spotted seatrout, snook, ladyfish, and gray snapper. Tarpon, cobia, and crevalle jacks occasionally show up around reefs near deep water.

## ECOLOGICAL REQUIREMENTS FOR OYSTER BARS

Oysters follow a life cycle typical of many marine organisms—they employ the broadcast spawning process similar to that described in Chapter 1 (eggs and sperm are ejected into the open water). After hatching, the larvae float as plankton for a few days before they must find a good place to settle. The oyster larvae require a hard surface to settle, with oyster shell the most preferred surface. The time period for settlement is short, so if oyster larvae don't find a hard substrate in a few days, they will die. After they are settled, the tiny oysters (called spat) cement themselves to the hard surface and begin to grow. Thus, oyster bars are generations of oysters built one upon the other—a true connection among generations. How an oyster bar gets started in a soft-bottom estuary is anyone's guess, but after it is established the subsequent generations are able to build upon that initial success and provide valuable habitat for gamefish and their prey.

Because their life requirements limit where they can grow successfully, oyster bars won't form in just any location. Oysters need a constant source of new water to survive. Oysters are filter feeders (they filter plankton and particles out of the water they pump through their gills) and thus need a constant supply of new water to bring them food. This is why oyster bars grow in areas where new water arrives with each rising tide or where tidal currents or flows from creeks and rivers continually bring new food for the filter-feeding oysters.

The filter feeding of oysters is an essential component to the health of the estuaries where oysters grow. Individual oysters are able to filter plankton and organic particles from as much as fifty gallons of water per day, and as you'll remember from Chapter 4, the clearer the water, the better the conditions for growth of seagrass. Plus, the more water that oysters can filter, the less likely are the plankton blooms that have such negative effects on the ecology of the estuaries, including fish kills.

Currents are essential for carrying food to the oysters, and oysters are efficient filter feeders, but it is essential that currents don't carry too much sediment. Too much sediment will smother and kill the oysters, resulting in a dead reef. Over time, a heavy sediment load will entirely cover a once-living oyster reef, and because oyster larvae need a hard surface to settle, the habitat is buried forever.

Currents can also help to mix surface and bottom water, and areas with a lot of mixing can produce healthier oyster bars. This is because in deep areas bottom water can become low in oxygen, which can slow the growth of—or, in severe conditions, kill—oysters living at the bottom of oyster bars in deeper water. These low-oxygen conditions are most common during summer months and are worsened by high nutrients from farms, lawns, and urban areas. In general, the upper portions of oyster bars in deep water will have the healthiest oysters. This is important to gamefish because healthier oyster bars host larger prey communities.

Oyster bars tend to grow across the prevailing currents, with a higher mound forming in the middle and the reef tapering at each end, often into deeper water. In areas with optimal growing conditions, oyster bars can form massive reefs and can deflect and reroute currents. In less-than-perfect growing conditions, scattered oyster clumps or patchy bars form instead. These patchy oyster bars have a less-dramatic effect on currents but can provide great gamefish habitat. And like the advantage that gamefish get from feeding in open patches in seagrass or along the outer edge of mangroves, gamefish feeding along the edges of oyster bars have a better chance of capturing prey than gamefish pursuing prey hiding among the oyster shells, so patchy reefs have their advantages.

## TYPES OF OYSTER BARS

Oyster reefs can be entirely subtidal (always submerged, even at low tide) or intertidal (exposed at low tide and submerged at high tide). In general, intertidal and shallow subtidal reefs are the most important to fly anglers because they occur in shallow water that makes gamefish more accessible. Regardless of whether reefs are intertidal or subtidal, for our purposes we will define three environments where oyster bars are found.

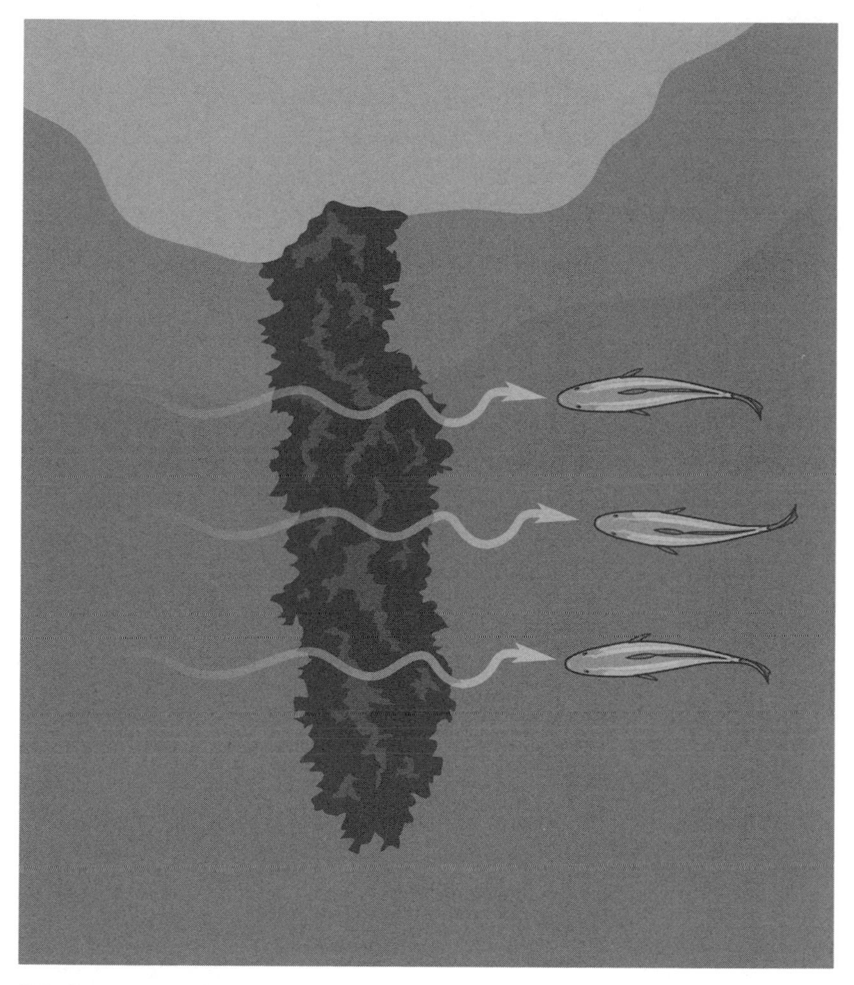

*Point bar*

One type of oyster bar (I call it a point bar) begins at the shoreline (often a point on the edge of a marsh) and extends outward over open bottom into current-swept waters. The growth of these reefs occurs on their outer ends that extend into the currents because the outer part of the reef receives the most plankton-filled water. Over time these reefs can get very large, and the seaward growth may choke off currents to the landward part of the reef. Over time, the inner portion of the reef is often colonized by marsh plants or mangroves, creating more wetland.

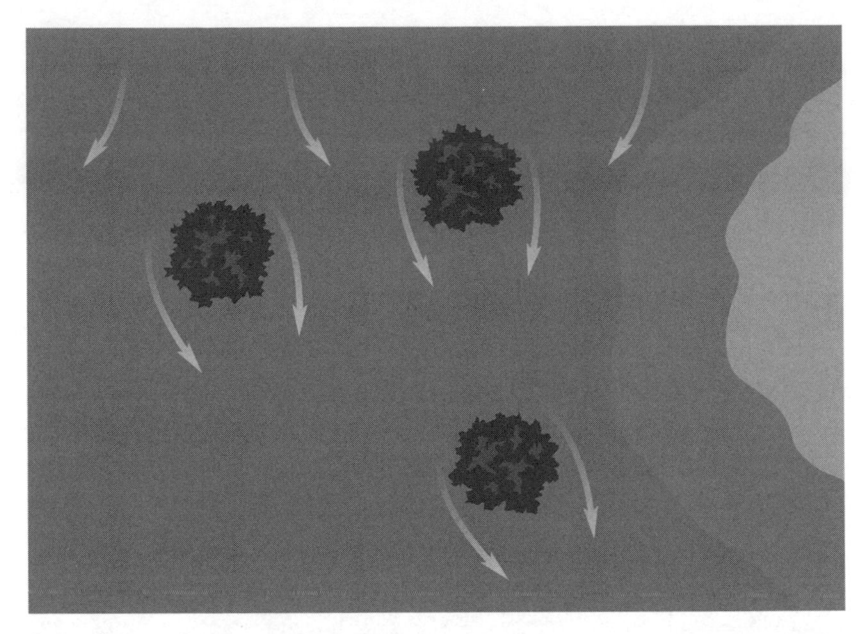

*Isolated bar*

A second type of oyster bar, an isolated bar, grows on sandy or muddy bottom without any association to land or marsh habitats. Isolated oyster bars often form on a large expanse of open bottom. Sometimes the reef will be surrounded by a ring of open bottom separating the oyster bar from seagrass, though on occasion seagrass will grow right to the edge of the oyster bar. Over time, some intertidal bars will be colonized by mangroves or marsh plants, but the tidal range is often too great or currents too strong for mangroves or marsh plants to become established.

A fringing oyster bar grows along a shoreline or marsh fringe (bounded by land, marsh, or mangroves), with seagrass or open bottom on the outer edge. Fringing oyster bars are especially important at stabilizing shorelines, and the deeper edges provide refuge for many marsh organisms at low tide. Fringing oyster bars provide complex habitat to an otherwise open, muddy, marsh bottom, which results in a concentration of gamefish prey seeking shelter among the oyster shells.

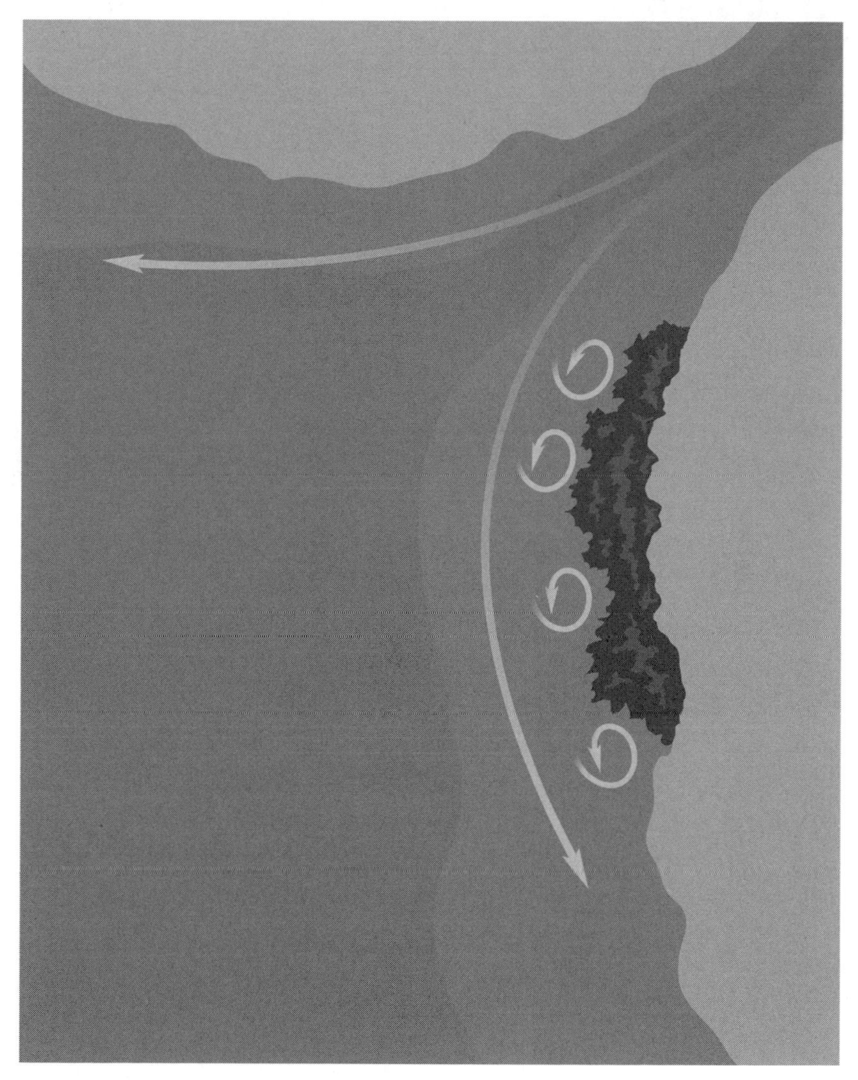

*Fringing bar*

## CURRENTS

Now that the types and general requirements of oyster bars have been established, we can explore how oyster bars influence currents and how changes in currents affect gamefish. Because they are solid structures rising off the bottom, all oyster bars that are exposed to currents will influence those currents. Depending on their size and orientation, oyster bars might produce small eddies, concentrate water flow through narrow channels, or completely deflect currents onto a different path. In each case, the resulting water movement affects the species living on or near the oyster bar. Whether this influences gamefish is partly a matter of scale. At one extreme, large bars can influence the course of large volumes of water (diverting the flow of creeks draining a marsh, for example), which can have notable effects on distributions of gamefish. At the other extreme, small oyster bars will influence only their immediate surroundings, much like a rock in a stream, and influences on marine gamefish will be less dramatic.

Regardless of the type of oyster bar (point, isolated, or fringing), when large bars block currents they often create an area of slow water on the upcurrent side of the bar. Upcurrent still waters are usually areas of slow, swirling water, and baitfish drifting downstream often get confused by these slowly whirling currents and collect in these eddies. Upcurrent still waters that hold baitfish will often also hold gamefish.

More common, and easier to fish than upcurrent still waters, are downcurrent eddies. Large point oyster bars that extend far from shore can significantly impact currents, even to the detriment of the oysters growing closest to shore. Large bars can deflect currents so that most water passes over the outer, growing end of the bar, leaving only a very slow, downcurrent eddy near shore. As you might expect, the very slow currents at the shoreline end of the bar bring little food, so these areas often have few live oysters and tend to hold fewer prey for gamefish. However, this is not always the case. Some of these backwaters can be good collecting places for baitfish and may hold concentrations of killifish and sheepshead minnows and thus are worth checking out.

On point bars extending from shore the strongest currents will flow over and around the outer portions of the bar. These are usually the best spots for fishing. At low tide, the majority of the bar may be exposed, so any moving water will pass over the bar's outer edge. At high tide, much or all of the bar might be covered, so currents may sweep over most of the bar. Where the strongest currents occur will depend on the shape of the bar and the orientation of the bar to the current. In addition, some bars experience best flows for fishing during an incoming tide, others on an outgoing tide. For example, during an incoming tide, the best fishing in the early part of the tide will likely be at the outer edge of the bar, but as the tide rises you should shift your position shoreward, and by high tide you might be fishing where the bar meets shore. Follow the reverse path when fishing during a dropping tide—start at the shoreward end and work your way toward the outer edge of the bar. It will take some observation and experimentation on your part to figure out which tide is best for each bar.

Spots with the strongest currents are most likely to harbor sleek gamefish—species built for speed. Crevalle jack, bluefish, ladyfish, and Spanish mackerel all have small scales, a streamlined body shape, and a forked tail—characteristics that decrease drag so these species can feed in faster flows. Species that aren't as hydrodynamic, like weakfish, spotted trout, red drum, and snook, will be more abundant in the slower flow and will either dart from behind an obstruction into the faster current to pick up wayward prey or wait in the slower water for prey to come to them.

Isolated, intertidal oyster bars situated in currents will have water racing around the ends of the bars (except near high tide when the whole bar is covered), whereas subtidal isolated bars will have currents around the sides and over the top of the bars throughout the tidal cycle. In either case, currents may dislodge and wash away sediments from around the edge of a bar, creating deeper holes that are attractive to gamefish. The best locations to look for deeper holes will depend on the depth of water where the bar is located and on the bar's configuration. On bars that have little water flow over the top, you are likely to find deeper holes on the ends of the bar or in the cuts between adjacent bars. These holes aren't necessarily large, but they don't have to be to hold fish. Oyster bars that have strong water flow over the top will often have deep holes on the downcurrent side of the bar. These holes are best fished when water is flowing strongly enough to sweep small fish and other prey over the top of the bar. This includes prey that are being swept downstream, such as silversides, and prey that live on the oyster bar, such as shrimp, crabs, and gobies, and that are dislodged by strong currents.

Fringing oyster bars experience currents that run parallel to the shoreline and thus tend not to produce large eddies and deflections of currents. However, clumps of oysters and individual shells protrude into the currents and thus create small-scale turbulence along the surface of the oyster bar—miniature eddies that are used as shelter from current by small fish, crabs, shrimp, and other prey. Gamefish will often forage just above or just adjacent to fringing bars, hoping to find prey that gets dislodged from these small eddies.

## TIDAL RANGE

Oyster bars are three-dimensional structures, so they add complexity to the bottoms where they grow. Even in areas with slower currents, the holes that form next to and between oyster bars often hold gamefish because gamefish that forage on the edges of oyster bars at high tide wait out the low tides in the deeper holes. As the tide turns and begins to rise again, these fish become more active and renew their search for food along the edges of the oyster bars.

Many of the small, mobile species associated with oyster bars move with tides to feed and find refuge. These species (crabs, shrimp, and especially small fish) move up and down the slope of an intertidal oyster bar in order to remain in shallow water. Given the mobility of prey in relation to tides, you might expect gamefish to use tides to their feeding advantage, and they do. This is one reason why the best locations for searching for gamefish are along edges rather than on top of oyster reefs.

## SALINITY

Salinity is also an important component in the formation of oyster bars. Oysters can tolerate a wide salinity range, but overall they do best in the brackish waters of estuaries. It's all about growth and predation.

On one hand, oysters grow fastest in higher-salinity water and grow most slowly in low-salinity water, and they will die if exposed to fresh water for more than twelve days or so. On the other hand, the oysters in high-salinity water fall victim to predators and disease to a much greater degree than oysters in low salinity. For example, a major oyster predator, the oyster drill (a type of snail) is found mostly in high-salinity water and can really do a number on oysters. The oyster drill is aptly named—it actually drills a hole in the oyster's shell and digests the oyster while the oyster is still in its shell. In addition, diseases that affect oysters are active only at higher salinities.

So, the trade-off is that oyster growth rate is higher in saltier water, but so is the oyster death rate, whereas oysters in low-salinity water don't grow as fast but are less likely to die from predation or disease. The best of both worlds seems to be medium-salinity water. Fortunately, the planktonic oyster larvae from adults in medium- and low-salinity areas are able to recolonize reefs in high-salinity areas where predators or disease have reduced the numbers of live oysters and thus maintain the oyster bar habitat throughout the estuary. This is why you will often find that high-salinity areas are dominated by younger, small oysters and that the largest oysters are in mid-salinity areas.

Salinity also influences the organisms that live on oyster bars. In general, there are more total organisms on upstream than downstream oyster bars, but the total number of species is higher downstream. So gamefish feeding on oyster bars have fewer choices of prey upstream, but if they like to eat what they find on upstream bars, they are in luck because prey abundance may be higher.

## Applying What You've Learned

### Exploring Oyster Bars

When you put the ecological requirements of oysters together, you get a good idea of where you will find the healthiest oyster bars and what types of fishing situations you are likely to encounter. The first locations to eliminate when searching for large, healthy oyster bars are areas that are either completely fresh water or have full-ocean salinity throughout the year. In contrast, locations that are medium salinity or experience fluctuations in salinity that reduce the occurrence of predators and disease while not killing oysters with low salinity should have the best oyster bar habitats. Backwater areas that receive little flushing are also poor locations for oyster bars, whereas locations that receive frequent tidal flushing or are regularly exposed to currents—either from tides or rivers—are your best bets for finding healthy oyster bars.

So, if you come across healthy oyster bars while exploring new waters, you can be sure the location receives current and/or significant tidal flushing and is in a portion of the estuary that receives a good mix of fresh and salt water. In other words, this is good gamefish habitat.

Exploration of a new area at low tide will show you where the intertidal oyster bars are located. Looking for eddies and changes in current direction during incoming or outgoing tides will help you pinpoint the locations of shallow, subtidal oyster bars or intertidal bars covered at high tide. Large point oyster bars will probably give you the most-varied fishing conditions in a single location—from slack water near shore to strong currents near the end of the bar, and the location of the best currents for fishing will change with the tide.

Fringing oyster bars will provide the best conditions for casting along the shoreline for gamefish feeding along the confluence of marsh, oyster bar, and open bottom. Depending on the depth, fringing bars can provide good fishing at different tidal stages—shallow areas will be best at high water, and deeper areas may hold gamefish at low water. Fringing bars offer great opportunities to cast flies right to the edge of the shoreline and fish the fly from the marsh edge down the slope of the oyster bar. In many ways it is similar to casting streamers along rocky shorelines for smallmouth bass.

Sometimes fringing bars will grow out from the shoreline, or perhaps the shoreline will erode, leaving a shallow lagoon between the fringing bar and shore. Such a lagoon is often used as shelter by small fishes and even by large mullet. Gamefish will sometimes venture into these areas to feed, making quick charges into the lagoon before heading back to deeper water. Even if you can't catch up to a fish you see feeding in the shallows, you'll likely be able to intercept it as it moves back into the deeper water along the outer edge of the bar.

Isolated oyster bars, my favorite, often present opportunities to fish upcurrent or downcurrent eddies during moving tides and holes between bars during low tides. It may take a little investigation to figure out whether an isolated bar is best on an incoming or outgoing tide and on which side the deepest holes are located. But after you find an isolated bar that is productive on a particular tide, it should be productive under similar conditions much of the time.

It's worth exploring networks of isolated bars to chart where the best holes between bars are located. Sometimes you will find that bars are separated only by shallow mud that would never hold a gamefish at low tide. But you will sometimes find at least a few spots where isolated bars are separated by open bottom deep enough to hold gamefish at all but the lowest tides. I explore these areas in two ways depending upon how much time I want to invest. The strategy that takes the most time but can also yield fish is to methodically work my way from spot to spot, casting to areas between oyster bars that might have deep holes. A sudden swirl and a tight line are the rewards for taking this patient approach. If I am in more of an exploratory mood, rather than fish the area, I will move from spot to spot and examine each to determine if it is deep enough to hold gamefish. Although I sometimes spook gamefish holding in the deeper holes, this is an efficient method for scouting areas that I can later return to and fish effectively.

## Applying What You've Learned

### Basic Fishing Tactics

So far in this chapter you've learned where you are likely to find the largest and healthiest oyster reefs, what types of reefs to expect in different locations, what conditions to expect for different types of oyster bars in different locations, how the health of the reef influences the number and types of prey, and how the habitats adjacent to oyster bars influence gamefish and their prey. So, now we'll take a break and apply this information to a few fishing situations.

The first consideration is currents. I like to approach upcurrent still waters from the upstream side and cast streamers to the edges of the eddy where the swirling water meets the downstream flowing current. I always cast to these upcurrent still waters from as far away as possible because an approach that is too close can alert any gamefish to my presence. I prefer to angle the cast across the current and let the fly swing into the slow water of the eddy.

I cast from a distance because I've found that while holding on upcurrent sides of bars, gamefish are more wary of approaching anglers than are their counterparts on the downcurrent sides of bars. My sometimes-less-than-stealthy approach from the upstream side of an oyster bar has resulted in more than a few large wakes made by gamefish heading off to safer waters. Perhaps the fish on the downcurrent sides of bars can't see or hear anglers approaching from upstream, whereas the fish on the upcurrent side of the bar can.

After you've fished the edges of the eddy to your satisfaction, it's worth a few casts with a sinking fly (such as a

Clouser Minnow) to the slower water right along the front of the bar. This area often contains the deepest hole (scoured by currents) and can hold large fish in its depths. I've pulled some large spotted seatrout from these deep spots.

In areas with strong currents, you should take the time to fish the holes on the ends and backside of the oyster bar just as you would rocks in a stream. Cast across and just upcurrent from the bar and let the fly wash over the bar and swing through the deeper water of the hole. Start by casting to the area nearest to you and make your casts progressively longer until you've sufficiently covered the hole.

The strength of the currents, the size of the hole and eddy, and the feeding activity level of the fish can help you determine the best fly to use. For example, a strong current that sweeps into a large hole probably requires a sinking fly, such as a Clouser Minnow. With a slow current, a shallower hole, or fish actively feeding on the surface, I prefer an unweighted streamer or even a popper.

In areas with slow currents, you are likely to find gamefish feeding along the edges of the bars on a rising tide and resting in the deeper holes next to, between, and behind oyster bars at low tide. Red drum, for example, will take advantage of higher tides to feed along oyster bars that are not accessible for much of the tidal cycle and then either rest or continue feeding in the deeper holes around the bars during low tides.

The holes between oyster bars and the deep water behind bars are good places to find red drum and spotted seatrout in warm-temperate areas like Louisiana. In these murky water areas, it is often difficult to see where the deeper holes are, and any fish resting in these murky holes will be impossible to see. Making a couple of casts into each of the spots where you suspect holes are located is your best strategy in this situation. In such conditions, flies that can be heard or detected by a gamefish's lateral line system can be productive. In holes that might have snags on the bottom, a fly that pulsates and sends out vibrations but stays in midwater, such as a Seaducer, is a good bet.

After you've covered the water to your satisfaction, head in for a closer look. You might find that the holes weren't oriented quite like you thought or that fish were holding differently than you anticipated. Or you might find that there were no holes decent enough to hold fish. In any case, you can learn from what you find and file it away for future use.

So, now that you have a short list of the most likely locations to find oyster bars, the types of oyster bars, and some general fishing strategies for each, you are ready to learn about the structure of oyster bars and how the mix of oyster bars and other habitats is perceived by gamefish and their prey.

## COMPLEX HABITATS

Oyster bars provide complex habitat for many small organisms that are prey for gamefish. In the tropics, gamefish and their prey can choose from seagrass, mangroves, coral reefs, rocky shorelines, and other coastal habitats that provide shelter and places to feed. In the subtropics, seagrass and mangroves are still available, but coral reefs are not, and rocky shorelines are rare (human-made jetties are an exception in some areas), so oyster bars are an important component of coastal habitats. In warm-temperate latitudes, mangroves are no longer present (replaced by salt marshes), and seagrass occurs less frequently than in the subtropics (in many areas, seagrass is completely absent), so gamefish and their prey are even more reliant on the shelter provided by oyster bars.

Oysters provide a complex, three-dimensional habitat that is full of crevices—perfect hiding and feeding locations for small fish, crabs, shrimp, worms, and a host of other organisms that seek shelter between shells or within empty oyster shells. In addition, many organisms, including mussels, sponges, and anemones, attach directly to the shells. Although not directly important to most gamefish, these attached organisms are food for the organisms that gamefish prey upon. More importantly, they add to the three-dimensional structure of the oyster shell habitat, so an oyster reef with more attached organisms can support more gamefish prey. And some fish that feed directly on organisms like mussels, such as sheepshead (*Archosargus probatocephalis*), are potential fly rod targets. Sheepshead are a challenging quarry on fly, but anglers who use crab and shrimp flies and are persistent can reap the rewards of sheepshead on fly.

At first glance, all oyster bars might look the same. But like grass beds and mangroves, not all oyster bars provide habitats of equal quality. Even oyster bars that are close to one another can differ in the quality of habitat they offer to their inhabitants, and these differences can impact how oyster bars are used by gamefish. Two of the major factors that determine these differences are how healthy the oyster reef is and where the oyster reef is located in relation to other habitats.

By "healthy" I mean that the proportion of living oysters and attached organisms is high. Oyster bars composed of live oysters tend to house more prey than oyster reefs with few live oysters. Although still home to more prey than open bottom, a dead-shell oyster bar is not as good a habitat as a live bar. In general, the healthier the oyster reef, the more prey will be available to gamefish.

As I discussed in previous chapters, more-complex habitats provide better shelter and hiding places for gamefish and prey, and the complex habitat provided by oysters is no exception. In general, live oyster bars provide more complex habitat than dead bars. Similar to what occurs in complex seagrass and mangrove habitats, gamefish can have a hard time catching prey that remain within the small crevices of the oyster reef. This is one reason why gamefish will often feed along the edges of oyster bars rather than search for prey within the oyster bar.

The habitats that surround an oyster reef help determine the amount and types of prey a gamefish will encounter and influence where gamefish are likely to feed. First, let's consider an oyster bar surrounded by open bottom. In this scenario, oyster bars provide the most complex habitat for gamefish prey and thus hold more prey than the open bottom, and thus the diets of gamefish are often dominated by prey associated with oyster bars in these areas.

In contrast, when an oyster bar is surrounded by seagrass or is adjacent to marsh, gamefish diets tend to be a more even mix of prey from the oyster bar and the adjacent habitats. This is because gamefish are able to feed among a variety of habitats over a large area rather than have to focus on a single habitat (an oyster bar) surrounded by bare bottom. This means that their feeding efforts will likely be more evenly distributed among the available habitats than when they are feeding on an oyster bar on open bottom.

Interesting research in southern North Carolina provides some insight into the extent that gamefish diets reflect where a gamefish has been feeding—on the oyster reef or on nearby habitats like seagrass, open bottom, or marsh. Although the following examples are from North Carolina, the general patterns are true of gamefish in other locations as well. Some gamefish, such as gulf and southern flounder, appear to have little variety in their diets, regardless of where they feed. The flounders examined in the North Carolina study fed mostly on small fish, regardless of whether they were caught on an oyster reef or in another habitat. Similarly, spotted seatrout ate mostly fish, whether on the oyster reef or another habitat, but were also opportunistic and ate shrimp and polychaetes (worms). In contrast, red drum varied their diets depending upon where they had been feeding. When they were feeding on or near oyster reefs, crabs and shrimp were common in their stomachs, whereas fish were the most common prey for red drum feeding on nonreef habitats. Surprisingly, although bluefish ate mostly fish (as their reputation would suggest), bluefish feeding on oyster reefs also ate shrimp and crabs. At the very least, this stomach content data should emphasize that many gamefish will vary their diet according to the habitat where they are feeding and that the diet differences should be reflected in your fishing strategies.

Regardless of the surrounding habitat, an oyster reef can be a crowded place, and many organisms venture away from the reef in search of food. When small fish, shrimp, and crabs venture from the shelter of oyster bars onto open bottom in search of food, they are easier targets for gamefish. Gamefish are aware of the abundance of prey living in oyster reefs, and they are also aware that many of these potential prey venture onto open bottom surrounding the reef. Often, rather than try to capture prey hiding among the oyster shells, gamefish such as red drum, black drum, weakfish, and spotted seatrout will cruise along the edge of a reef hoping to surprise a crab, shrimp, or fish that is out over open bottom.

Many oyster bar inhabitants use oyster bars as shelter during the day and venture into the surrounding habitats to feed at night. This is especially true for oyster bars on open bottom, where abundance of fish and crabs on the bottom surrounding the oyster bar is low during the day and increases dramatically at night. As you learned in the chapter on mangroves, many of the species that hide during the day and feed at night start their movements around dusk and return around dawn. This is one of the reasons why my favorite times for fishing for tailing red drum around oyster bars are dawn and dusk.

## SEASONALITY

Because oyster bars occur in subtropical and warm-temperate climates, the associated communities display a rather distinct seasonality. For example, in warm-temperate areas, juvenile fish are most abundant from late spring to summer, peaking in June–July. Timing is similar in the subtropics, but juveniles of some species (such as pinfish) arrive in late winter, and juveniles of other species (such as some mojarras, mullet, and ladyfish) arrive in autumn and winter.

Other species also show seasonal changes in abundance. In southern North Carolina, for example, peak abundance of fishes (juveniles and adults combined) associated with oyster bars occurs in late summer to early autumn, with medium abundances in late spring and late autumn. As you might expect, lowest abundances occur in winter when water temperatures are lowest. Patterns in abundance of small fishes are similar in the northern Gulf of Mexico.

Gamefish also show seasonal changes in their association with oyster bars. For example, in South Carolina oyster bars are good places to find large schools of red drum in winter. Because of the low number of prey species that remain through the winter, flies that imitate the mummichog (aka mud minnow) are your best bet. Trout, which prefer cooler (but not cold) water, also hang in deep holes around oyster bars in winter.

In the subtropics, seasonal changes in abundance tend to be less dramatic than in warm-temperate latitudes. Declines in fish abundance usually occur later in the autumn, and increases occur earlier in the spring than in warm-temperate climates. Crabs and shrimp show similar regional differences in seasonality, with more-dramatic seasonal differences in warm-temperate than in subtropical areas. Further details on seasonality of gamefish prey are provided in the following section on gamefish prey.

## GAMEFISH PREY OF OYSTER BARS

As in previous chapters, I've split the prey that a gamefish will encounter into two groups—residents and transients. A gamefish that forages around oyster bars can depend upon the resident prey species throughout the year, especially during periods when seasonal or transient prey are absent, but may switch diet almost entirely to take advantage of temporary abundances of seasonal and transient prey species. Because a gamefish's behavior will differ depending on the prey it is pursuing, this information is an essential component of any strategy for fly fishing oyster bar habitats.

## Crustaceans

### *Crabs*

#### *Mud Crabs*

As in seagrass beds and mangrove habitats, a large portion of the resident community of gamefish prey is made up of crabs and shrimp. One of the most abundant groups of potential prey on subtropical and warm-temperate oyster bars is mud crabs. In fact, mud crabs usually outnumber shrimp and other crustaceans on oyster bars by a sizeable margin, so crab flies should be a staple in your fly selection for fishing oyster bars.

In many cases, the species of mud crabs you find on oyster bars are also found in seagrass beds. Fortunately, even when the species are different between habitats, they are similar in appearance, so the same crab patterns you used in seagrass beds may be applicable on oyster bars. And because of the many potential snags on oyster bars, the weed-guards you tied into your mud crab fly patterns for seagrass are just as necessary here.

We are fortunate that the most-common species of mud crabs are similar on subtropical and warm-temperate oyster bars. For example, studies in North Carolina found that common mud crab (*Panopeus herbstii*), Say's mud crab (*Neopanope sayi*), depressed mud crab (*Eurypanopeus depressus*), and juveniles of the closely related and similar-in-appearance stone crab (*Menippe mercenaria*) were the most common species. Say's mud crab is replaced by the Texas mud crab (*Neopanope texana*) in the northern Gulf of Mexico, but both species are similar in appearance. Studies in the subtropics found that depressed mud crab, numerous species in the *Panopeus* genus of mud crabs, and juvenile stone crabs were the most abundant crab species.

The colors of mud crab carapace (the top shell) range from brown to olive and are often mottled, and all of the species listed here share a prominent feature—black tips on their large claws. Behind the black tip, the dorsal (top side) portion of their claws is similar in color to their carapace, whereas the ventral (underside) portion is pale or white. Most mud crabs range from ½ to 2 inches across, with the common mud crab growing the largest of the species listed here. The typical size of mud crabs I have found in red drum stomachs in southwest Florida is ½ to 1 inch across. Stone crabs grow much larger than mud crabs, but the juveniles found on oyster reefs are similar in size to mud crabs. As they grow, stone crabs move to other habitats.

Mud crabs on oyster bars, like mud crabs in seagrass beds, tend to hide during the day and venture out at night to feed. However, the habitats—oyster bar versus seagrass—force a different feeding behavior by gamefish in search of a mud crab meal. In seagrass red drum can move slowly with their snouts in the bottom and push aside the grass blades and push their snouts into the bottom to capture the crabs. I have examined the stomach contents of many red drum caught while they were tailing in seagrass beds, and most were dominated by mud crabs.

In contrast, oyster shells provide mud crabs a solid shelter that is not easily breached by red drum or other gamefish. The edges of oyster shells are sharp and thus deter much grubbing by gamefish in search of prey. And because many of the oyster shells are cemented together to form clumps, even if the shells weren't sharp, the clumps would be too heavy for a fish to move.

However, only so many crabs can feed on an oyster bar, so many crabs that emerge from hiding at the end of the day to feed venture onto the surrounding bottom. Even those that remain on the oyster bar to feed are often on the edge of the bar rather than hiding in the crevices that extend deep beneath the shells. Thus, once again, the edges of oyster bars are the best areas to find feeding gamefish.

Finally, you might find a couple of mud crab species living in burrows between the high and low tide lines in the marsh mud adjacent to fringing oyster bars. Harris' mud crab (*Rithropanopeus harrisii*) is brown, grows to 2 inches wide, and is most active at low tide. The mangrove mud crab (*Eurytium limosum*) grows to 1 inch wide, is dark in color—from dark gray to black—and is most active at high tide.

### *Other Crab Species*

Although mud crabs are usually the most abundant type of crabs, many other species of crabs inhabit oyster bars. For example, in addition to the four species of crabs listed earlier, research in North Carolina found seven other species of crabs, with blue crabs and spider crabs (*Libinia dubia*) the most common of these other species. Blue crabs and spider crabs are also found on subtropical oyster bars, as are hermit crabs. In general, blue crabs are more abundant in the habitats surrounding the oyster bar than on the oyster bar itself. So, once again, oyster bar edges are important feeding areas for gamefish and their prey.

## **Shrimp**

### *Common Shrimp and Grass Shrimp*

Although not as abundant as crabs, numerous species of shrimp inhabit oyster bars and are important prey for gamefish. Brown, pink, or white shrimp, from the family Penaeidae (the type of shrimp that people generally eat), are present on oyster bars and nearby marsh habitats as juveniles. Grass shrimp (mostly the genus *Palaemonetes*) are also common in these habitats and are very similar in appearance to small juvenile brown, pink, and white shrimp but reach a maximum size of only 2 inches. Each of these shrimps is mostly clear or may take on a translucent tan or gray coloration to blend into its surroundings. Grass shrimp are residents, but the juvenile brown, pink, and white shrimp move away from the oyster habitats as they grow.

### *Snapping Shrimp*

Snapping shrimp are also common oyster bar residents, especially in the subtropics. The most ubiquitous species is the common snapping shrimp (*Alpheus heterochaelis*), which can grow to approximately 1½ inches long, is slow moving, and is usually dark green with pale (often reddish) legs and an orange-fringed uropod (tail fan). In a study on South Carolina oyster bars, the striped snapping shrimp (*Alpheus formosus*) was also abundant. Snapping shrimp are common prey for red drum on subtropical and warm-temperate oyster reefs but are also eaten by spotted seatrout and weakfish.

### *Seasonality*

Despite their almost-constant presence, crabs and shrimp do undergo seasonal changes in abundance. For example, mud crabs are present in similar numbers throughout the year, whereas blue crabs show seasonal pulses of juveniles in late spring and summer. Peak crab abundance is from late spring to late summer, with more dramatic seasonal differences in warm-temperate than in subtropical areas. Similar seasonality occurs for juvenile shrimp, with differences among regions. For example, pink shrimp (*Penaeus duorarum*) juveniles are present throughout the year in subtropical estuaries but are most abundant from summer through autumn. In warm-temperate regions, juveniles are present in both autumn and spring but are most abundant in autumn. In the western Gulf of Mexico, juvenile brown shrimp (*Penaeus aztecus*) are dominant. I provide some additional information on juvenile common shrimp in the following chapter on salt marshes.

## Brittle Stars

Oyster bar residents that are often overlooked as gamefish prey suitable for imitating with a fly are brittle stars. Among the species you might find on oyster bars are the smooth brittle star (*Ophioderma brevispinum*) and the angular brittle star (*Ophiothrix angulata*). Brittle stars have a round, flat body (called a disc) that is shaped like a coin. Radiating from the body are five long arms that are either smooth or covered in short spines and taper to a point. Unlike the stereotypical sea star, brittle stars can move rather quickly, using their arms like a spider to crawl across the bottom. Brittle stars found on oyster bars are usually green to tan and may be mottled or striped, and their central body disc is about 2 inches across with arms extending five or more disc widths from the body. Although never the most abundant prey item in gamefish stomachs, brittle stars are eaten by numerous gamefish, particularly red drum in the northern Gulf of Mexico.

## Applying What You've Learned

### Good Times and Strategies for Fishing Oyster Bars

Like mud crabs, many oyster bar resident crabs, shrimp, and brittle stars hide during the day and are most active at night. Fortunately, you don't have to fish at night to take advantage of this behavior. Instead, fish the transfer times between night and day.

First, by fishing at dusk you will catch the beginning of nighttime feeding activity by these prey species. The timing is very similar to the dusk "quiet period" for small fishes in mangrove prop root habitats. As dusk approaches, the resident crabs, shrimp, and brittle stars become active as they ready for a night of feeding. If the tide is right, you may find gamefish cruising along the edges of oyster bars or in the surrounding habitats in search of prey that have emerged from their daytime shelter. Many times I have fished through dusk and into darkness, casting to tailing red drum and spotted trout in the fading light. In the early minutes of dusk, flies with a lot of flash attract the attention of feeding gamefish. As light fades, flies that create vibrations in the water that can be detected by the gamefish tend to work best.

Second, limit the parts of an oyster bar that you fish. A major mistake that many fly anglers make when fishing oyster bar habitat is casting to the middle of the bar. The middle (or top) of the oyster bar is not where you are likely to find gamefish. And when you do find gamefish feeding over the top of an oyster bar, flies imitating crabs or other bottom-dwelling prey are not the best choice. When a weighted fly falls into the crevices between oyster shells, it is out of view of the gamefish. And to fish these flies naturally, you have to get the fly onto the bottom, which can result in hooking oysters rather than fish. You can combat this somewhat with a weed-guard, but there are so many nooks and crannies for a fly to hang in that it is easy to get frustrated. So, if you must fish on the oyster bar, use an unweighted streamer or popper instead.

Instead of becoming frustrated by casting to an area of an oyster bar that is full of snags and mostly devoid of gamefish, focus on the gamefish that will be cruising the edge of the oyster bars in search of crabs, shrimp, and other prey that have left the shelter of the bar to feed. You don't have to limit this strategy to dusk. Although mud crabs will be most abundant at night, there will always be a few that dare to venture out during the day. This is especially true on a rising tide. Often, crabs will follow the rising water as it covers the bar, and you will sometimes find gamefish following suit, hoping to catch crabs that linger too long along the deeper edges of the bar.

Third, focus your efforts on the best tides. My favorite time for chasing tailing red drum along oyster bars is the first hour or so of incoming tide. I think the best time is as soon as the tide has raised the water level enough to allow the red drum to come in to feed. Focus on the deeper holes between or near oyster bars in case red drum have been waiting out the low tide in these deep spots. As the water rises, these fish will move to the oyster bars in search of prey.

In the event you don't find red drum tailing on a rising tide, don't hesitate to do some blind-casting along the edges of oyster bars. Bouncing a small (size 2 or 1), dark-colored, olive or brown crab fly or similarly colored Clouser Minnow across mud bottom next to oyster bars might catch the attention of gamefish you didn't spot, including red drum, spotted seatrout, weakfish, or gray snapper. Better yet, try the old standby Seaducer worked slowly along the edge. Regardless of the fly you choose, it doesn't get much better than when it all comes together—an early incoming tide at dusk or dawn, with hungry gamefish prowling the edges of an oyster bar.

## RESIDENT PREY FISHES

### Gobies, Blennies, and Toadfishes

A typical oyster bar in a subtropical or warm-temperate estuary will have a dozen or more resident species of small fishes. Species from four families—gobies (family Gobiidae), clingfishes (family Gobiesocidae), toadfishes (family Batrachoididae), and blennies (family Blenniidae)—rest on oyster shell or on the bottom and dart out to capture prey or ward off competitors. Most of these species are medium to dark brown, but some are olive, with mottling and markings on their sides. If you pick up enough oyster shell from a shallow oyster reef, you will eventually find some of these fishes. Because these species are closely associated with the bottom, your flies should be also, and because of all the possible snags your flies should be weedless.

Common species of goby include the frillfin goby *(Bathygobius soporator)*, code goby *(Gobiosoma robustum)*, and naked goby *(Gobiosoma bosci)*, each around 2 inches long. They are found in the subtropics and into the warm-temperate northern Gulf of Mexico. These species can also be found in nearby seagrass and mangrove habitats. The skilletfish *(Gobiesox strumosus)*, a clingfish that grows to 3 inches, is found on oyster reefs throughout the warm-temperate and subtropical regions. You will find the gulf toadfish *(Opsanus beta)* in subtropical waters, and the similar-looking oyster toadfish *(Opsanus tau)* in warm-temperate waters. Both species can grow quite large (12 inches or more), but the smaller juveniles are common prey for gamefish on oyster reefs. Among the blennies, the Florida blenny *(Chasmodes saburrae)* inhabit oyster reefs throughout Florida and into the northern Gulf of Mexico, whereas the feather blenny *(Hypsoblennius hentzi)* and crested blenny *(Hypleurochilus germinatus)* reside on oyster reefs throughout subtropical and warm-temperate climates. Both blennies grow to 4 inches long.

Fortunately, within each family, the species listed here and other related species not listed look similar enough that one or two fly patterns should be sufficient for a decent imitation. Gobies are round-bodied, their body tapering from a large head to a pointed tail. My favorite fly for imitating gobies is a muddler minnow variation: size 4 long-shank hook, a head of spun brown or tan deer hair, trimmed short, a body of gold braid wrapped around the hook shank, and a tail of brown buck-tail tips—uneven so they taper to a point. I tie in a small cone ahead of the deer-hair head for deeper reefs and tie in a weed-guard for both weighted and unweighted versions.

The skilletfish and toadfish are similar in shape—large, wide heads and a body that tapers to the tail, much like a sculpin you'd find in fresh water. The late Brock Apfel of Punta Gorda, Florida, showed me a small (size 2 or 4), brown, dahlberg-diver variation (brown head, tan, artificial material tail with vertical bars) that is a reasonable imitation of these bottom-dwelling, troll-like fishes. I have done well with this pattern—weedless and either unweighted or weighted with a conehead—for red drum on oyster bars.

Like gobies, skilletfish, and toadfishes, blennies have a large head and tapered body. However, blennies are higher-bodied than they are wide and thus have a larger profile from a side view. They have steeply sloped foreheads and thus are almost square-fronted when viewed from the side. The dorsal fin runs the length of the body and the anal fin from midbody to the tail. Flies imitating blennies require a higher profile than flies imitating gobies, skilletfish, and toadfishes.

## Killifishes

A handful of species from two families—killifishes (family Cyprinodontidae) and mollies (family Poecilidae)—is found above and around oyster reefs in shallow areas near shore. These species are mostly associated with oyster reefs that are in or near marshes and mangroves. Among the most common killifishes associated with oyster bars are the gulf killifish *(Fundulus grandis)*, goldspot killifish *(Floridichthys carpio)*, mummichog *(Fundulus heteroclitus)*, striped killifish *(Fundulus majalis)*, and sheepshead minnow

*(Cyprinodon variegatus).* The sailfin molly *(Poecilia latipinna)* is the most common molly near oyster reefs. Mosquitofish *(Gambusia holbrooki)* will inhabit oyster reefs in protected backwaters. The gulf killifish is mostly limited to medium- to low-salinity waters, whereas the other five species listed are present across a wide range of salinities.

Fortunately, killifish and mollies are similar in size and shape, so even though species may vary among locations, the same flies should work throughout. In fact, many of the species are similar enough that anglers confuse them and lump them all together as "mummichogs." In general, killifish and mollies are small (from 1 inch to as much as 7 inches long, though most are on the smaller side of the size range) and tan to medium brown in color. A good standard imitation for these species is a Muddler Minnow variation or a brown-over-tan Clouser Minnow or bendback.

Killifish and mollies are among the most abundant and important fishes in subtropical and warm-temperate marshes. Because killifish and mollies are such integral parts of marshes, I will save some of the specifics on these fishes for the chapter on salt marshes.

## Other Resident Fishes

A species of fish you might not think of as typical gamefish prey is the blackcheek tonguefish *(Symphurus plagiusa).* The tonguefishes (family Cynoglossidae) are flatfishes that are similar to small, elongated flounder with a teardrop shape. The blackcheek tonguefish is dark to medium brown and grows to 7 inches long. Tonguefish inhabit soft or sandy bottoms that surround oyster reefs and thus are worth mentioning here. Tonguefish have been found in stomachs of red drum and spotted seatrout, among others.

Finally, mojarras (family Gerreidae) are everywhere. I mentioned mojarras as prey fish in grass beds and mangrove shorelines and now again in association with oyster habitats. In the subtropics, the most common species near oyster reefs are the silver jenny *(Eucinostomus gula)* and tidewater mojarra *(Eucinostomus harengulus).*

Both species are silver but often have mottled gray sides, and the tidewater mojarra has a slightly higher body profile. Both species grow to 7 inches but are usually much shorter and are associated with soft or sandy open bottoms around oyster bars. Three-inch white deceivers are good imitations of these two species.

## SEASONAL PREY FISHES

Just as in seagrass and mangrove habitats, many gamefish prey use oyster bars only on a seasonal basis. Some of these species use oyster bar habitats only as juveniles, whereas others migrate from oyster bars to deeper habitats due to cold water temperatures in winter. Gamefish may change their feeding behavior to take advantage of seasonal changes in prey, so knowing what changes may occur in your area should be an important part of your fishing strategy.

A large pulse of juveniles arrives on oyster reefs in spring and early summer in both subtropical and warm-temperate estuaries. Among the species with juveniles on oyster reefs that are appropriate for imitating with a fly are pinfish, pigfish, spot, croaker, spottail pinfish, mojarra, and gray and lane snapper. In general, abundance of these juveniles peaks in midsummer (June and July). As the summer progresses, and as the juveniles grow, they move away from the reefs onto other habitats.

Although not as abundant on oyster reefs as in seagrass, juvenile pinfish in some areas can be among the most abundant prey fish on oyster reefs. This is especially true in areas that have little or no seagrass. As in subtropical grass beds, juvenile pinfish arrive in late winter through early spring and grow throughout the summer before migrating to deeper water in late autumn. This puts the arrival of pinfish slightly earlier than the other species mentioned earlier, so early-season gamefish may concentrate their feeding efforts on juvenile pinfish.

Pigfish are present during summer and are similar to pinfish in coloration and size and thus can be imitated with the same patterns.

Spot, croaker, spottail pinfish, and mojarras vary somewhat in shape, but all are silvery-white and are well imitated with white deceivers, light-colored Clouser Minnows, and similar patterns.

The biggest challenge when imitating these juveniles is matching their size. Because many larvae will enter the estuaries at the same time, you will find large groups of similar-sized juveniles, which eases your burden in selecting the right size fly. But because pulses of larvae may arrive weeks or months apart, you may have a wide range of juvenile sizes to choose from, so it might not be the case that "one fly fits all." Instead, it's worth becoming familiar with the sizes and species of juvenile fishes that are common in the areas you fish. Because fish larvae ride currents into estuaries (see Chapter 1), and these currents vary, different oyster bars may receive different numbers of fish larvae of different species at different times. This means that the size of juvenile fishes may vary among different locations in the estuary.

## Midwater Baitfish

Transient prey species can be found near oyster bars occasionally, but they are not present throughout the year, and although they might be common at certain tides, their presence can be unpredictable. This group of species is generally what we are imitating when we cast baitfish imitations into currents that sweep past and over bars. Silversides (family Atherinidae), anchovies (family Engraulidae), and herrings (family Clupeidae) are the most common members of this group. The baitfish species that gamefish key on varies with location and time of year, but within each family the species are similar enough to be imitated with a couple of basic patterns. Clouser Minnows, bucktail streamers, and deceivers are the classic imitations of these baitfishes.

In my experience, the best time of year to cast and swing baitfish imitations across sandbars and oyster bars is from midsummer through autumn. Mid- to late summer is when many of these species are in greatest abundance, and autumn is when the migratory baitfish species begin to collect in larger schools and leave the estuaries to migrate to winter locations. The abundance and migration of baitfish combine to make these species a common diet item for gamefish in late summer and autumn. This is one reason why, when you drift a size 1 chartreuse-and-white Clouser Minnow over an oyster bar on an outgoing tide, the weakfish that sees the fly might mistake it for a silverside lost in the currents. Drifting flies into the holes around sandbars and oyster bars can bring in a grab bag of gamefish, including crevalle jack, speckled trout, and red drum, on successive casts.

Finally, several species of mullet can also be found near oyster bars. This is probably due to the association of mullet with shallow, protected areas and the presence of oyster reefs in these same shallow areas rather than an association with oyster reefs. Mullet feed on detritus and algae and thus don't feed in oyster reefs but rather likely feed on the surrounding bottom. However, when pursued by gamefish, mullet will seek shelter in the shallows that surround oyster bars.

## Applying What You've Learned

### Fly Selection

Spotted seatrout and a host of other gamefish will hide in the current shadows and eddies of oyster bars and dart out to pick off prey caught in the currents washing over or around the bar. In winter, spotted seatrout and small red drum may be the only gamefish feeding in the currents. During winter, the selection of prey washing over the bar will be slim, with killifishes (often the mummichog) the dominant prey. Because so few prey are available, fly selection is easy during winter.

In summer, ladyfish, bluefish, and jacks often join the fray, and so do a whole host of baitfish, including mullet, juvenile menhaden, anchovies, silversides, juvenile spot, and juvenile croaker. Although any streamer may be the right fly on some days, on other days the fish will be focused on one particular species of baitfish, so keep an eye out for which baitfish are dominant on any particular day. In addition, as the summer progresses the baitfish will grow larger, and this increase in size should be reflected in your fly selection. Finally, it is true that larger gamefish eat larger prey, so although smaller flies will likely result in more fish, every once in a while it's worth starting out with a large fly just in case that big fish is lurking behind the oyster bar.

## Applying What You've Learned

### Be Ready for Baitfish

I prefer floating lines for fishing oyster bars because a sinking line can get snagged on the shallow part of the bar. A floating line also allows me to drift an unweighted fly over the far side of a bar without worrying about hanging the fly line on the bar during the drift. If I am fishing a deeper hole next to an oyster bar, I prefer to use a sinking fly such as a Clouser Minnow and a slow retrieve to get the fly deeper. Because many of the baitfish associated with oyster bars are also found in seagrass beds and along mangrove shorelines, they can be imitated with the same flies, but the transient nature of their association with oyster bars means you have to be on the lookout for when these baitfish are present. One August day my strategy of keeping a second rod rigged with a white deceiver while I cast a Muddler Minnow into holes between bars paid off.

The small creeks I was fishing drained a large marsh, and on outgoing tides moderate currents flowed out of the creeks onto grass beds that stretched across the creek mouths. Snook often waited at ambush points where the creeks narrowed and picked off small silversides that were caught in the currents. Situated near the mouths of the creeks, and spilling over into the seagrass, were scattered isolated oyster bars. I began the day fishing the mangrove creeks early in the falling tide and then switched my attention to the oyster bars as the tops of the bars became exposed. I had limited success finding small snook in the creeks and caught only an occasional spotted trout in the holes next to the oyster bars.

As I poled to the next in a series of small oyster bars, I noticed plumes of white spray erupting from the water about ½ mile down the shoreline. My first thought, that a group of brown pelicans had just hit the water en masse, was immediately negated because the eruption continued. Because it was late summer, my second thought, that it was marauding crevalle jacks, seemed a reasonable explanation. Ready for some fast action, I stowed the push pole and motored the boat toward the chaos.

As I made my way along the shoreline I could see that the school of feeding fish was moving toward me. I shut down the engine and pulled out the rod rigged with a white deceiver. Whatever the gamefish were, I knew what they were feeding on. Scaled sardines *(Harengula jaguana),* an abundant baitfish (family Clupeidae) in the subtropics in late summer, erupted from the surface as large fish chased from below. The school of gamefish was easy to spot by the large wake they pushed ahead of themselves as they moved through the grass bed from oyster bar to oyster bar. As the marauding school came upon each small oyster bar, its pace quickened and its bow wake became larger and more pronounced. I watched as the fish sped toward the oyster bar in front of me, the water exploding as they attacked sardines that were trying to hide in the shallow water surrounding the bars. I caught my first glimpse of color as a large fish broke the surface and rolled through the panicked sardines. The copper hue told me these were big red drum.

I threw a cast into the mix, and as the fly darted forward with my second strip of the line, the water boiled with the ferocious charge of a red drum. The fish fought with an energy born from the bedlam of a marauding school in the midst of a feeding frenzy. As I fought the fish the school passed me and continued its plunder along the line of disconnected oyster bars.

I was able to get in front of the school of red drum two more times, hooking three large fish and landing two, before a line of strong thunderstorms came through and sent all of us packing. All three fish were caught on a 4-inch white deceiver. It didn't take much more than my being in the right place at the right time, knowing that gamefish might be keying on the sardines that were hiding among the oyster bars, and being ready with a rod rigged with a white deceiver just in case.

# 7
# Salt Marshes

In the tropics and subtropics, mangroves are the dominant wetland vegetation, providing crucial habitat for gamefish and their prey, protecting shorelines from erosion, and serving many other valuable functions. In temperate regions, salt marshes fill these vital roles. Although they do occur (rarely) in the tropics and are a bit more common in northern subtropical areas, salt marshes become the dominant type of wetland from mid-Florida north and thus are important gamefish habitats for the entire warm-temperate region. In the Gulf of Mexico, salt-marsh habitats are dominant north of Cedar Key, Florida, on the east and Port Isabel, Texas, on the west. On the Atlantic coast, salt marshes dominate north of Cape Canaveral, Florida.

Salt marshes are vital gamefish habitats in temperate regions because they are host to a suite of resident organisms and visiting juveniles that is prey for larger gamefish. In addition, many gamefish juveniles use the protection provided by salt marshes, so these habitats are important nurseries. Like mangroves to the south, salt marshes stabilize shorelines, filter sediments from land that would otherwise smother other nearby habitats and their organisms (such as oyster bars), and form the base of the food chain that supports many gamefish.

Salt marshes form in intertidal zones of temperate climates with abundant rainfall and in locations where mud and silt can accumulate. The most common sites for salt marshes are along the shorelines of estuaries that lie on the coastal plain, on the back sides of bars or barrier islands that separate an estuary from the open ocean, and on coastal shores that are protected from wave energy. The first step in the development of a salt marsh is the deposition of fine-grained sediments by slow-moving currents. Salt-tolerant marsh grasses then take root in these areas, and as the grasses grow they baffle the currents, much like seagrass. This causes more sediment to be deposited, which is soon mixed with the remains of dead marsh plants. The original colonizing grasses spread outward via an underground root system, and if these plants are able to spread fast enough to keep pace with sediment deposition, a salt marsh is established. The spreading plants stabilize the surrounding sediments and cause more sediments to be deposited, slowly expanding the marsh.

Stabilization of sediments is an important function of salt-marsh plants. Without stabilizing marsh plants, sediments would be constantly displaced and relocated by runoff from rains, storm waves, and even strong tides. Such an unstable habitat would not support many prey or many gamefish. For example, the stable sediments allow burrowing organisms like fiddler crabs and polychaetes (worms) to live in the marsh, and these types of organisms are important prey for salt-marsh gamefish. Eventually, enough silt and plant material accumulates to raise the portions of the marsh surface above sea level, which allows plants less tolerant of salt water to become established. In the meantime, sediment deposition often continues on the outer edge of the marsh, allowing seaward migration of the intertidal portion of the marsh.

As you might guess from the fine-grained, soft sediments that dominate a salt marsh, salt marshes are found only in areas protected from strong waves and currents. Despite the stabilizing effect of marsh grasses, salt-marsh sediments are easily eroded in high-energy areas because the marsh grass root systems are not strong enough to hold the sediments in place. The protected nature of salt marshes makes them especially nice places to fly fish on windy days when more-exposed areas might be unfishable. An added bonus is that gamefish also know the value of protected salt marshes during windy periods with rough seas and will often take shelter in these areas.

Because salt marshes are intertidal, they are inundated by high tide and drain on the dropping tide. The rising water of an incoming tide comes onto the marsh via creeks as well as slow inundation of the wider marsh surface. On the outgoing tide, especially in the later stages of the tide, much of the water flows out of the marsh through the creeks that crisscross the marsh. The creeks are also important for draining the fresh water that runs onto the upper marsh from land.

Sediments stabilized by marsh grass are essential to the formation of the creeks that drain the marsh. In a new marsh, areas that were naturally low soon become collecting areas for water draining the marsh, and bit by bit creeks and drainage channels are born. Stable sediments held together by the roots of marsh grasses form the walls of the creeks, and after it is established, the course of a creek is slow to change. Another bonus is that the creeks also allow more water to enter the marsh with a rising tide, which helps to maintain good tidal flushing essential to sustaining a healthy marsh.

Because sea level has been rising since the last ice age, estuarine salt marshes that are nearer the coast are older than salt marshes near the head of the estuary. When sea level was lower, salt water encroached only on the outermost coastal areas; so, this is where salt marshes first formed. As sea level has risen, salt water has intruded farther inland, allowing new salt marshes to become established. Why is this important? Mature salt marshes have deeper sediments and more intricate patterns of creeks and drainage channels, which often translates to more diverse prey communities and more gamefish.

How far inland salt water penetrates is also a factor influencing the type of marsh you will find as you travel from the ocean into the estuary. Marshes closest to the ocean or Gulf of Mexico will experience the highest salinities and thus will be dominated by salt-tolerant marsh grass. Farther inland, where tides mix with fresh water, the marsh will be dominated by brackish water species. Beyond the reaches of salt water you will find freshwater swamps. There is no set distance of saltwater influence, so how far inland you will find salt marshes varies with the location. In coastal Georgia, for example, the transition from salt water to fresh water occurs over a relatively short distance. In contrast, the saltwater influence travels farther inland along the Louisiana coast.

You can use the dominant species of marsh plants as a general guide to finding the inland boundary of salt marshes. Low-salinity marshes are dominated by waterhyssop *(Bocopa monniere)*, camphorweed *(Pluchea camphorata)*, and various species of the genus *Spartina*. In contrast, dominant marsh plants in salt and brackish areas are black needlerush *(Juncus roemerianus)*, smooth cordgrass *(Spartina alterniflora)*, seashore saltgrass *(Distichlis spicata)*, saltmeadow cordgrass *(Spartina patens)*, and other species in the genus *Spartina*. As you explore new areas, you can also use the distribution of marsh plants as clues regarding salinities and tides and focus your energies on the salt marshes most used by saltwater gamefish.

## ZONES OF A SALT MARSH

As you've probably surmised, tide, rainfall, and salinity are major structuring forces of a salt marsh. These forces result in the formation of two zones—a high marsh and a low marsh, each zone dominated by different marsh plants. We can use our knowledge of marsh zonation to figure out the most promising spots for finding gamefish.

### The High Marsh

The portion of the salt marsh that abuts land is called the high marsh. The high marsh is inundated by salt water only during spring high tides and does best with a mixture of runoff from rain and the occasional salt water from high tides. So, although rainfall probably doesn't come to mind when you think of a salt marsh, rainfall is an essential component of a healthy high marsh. High marsh is often dominated by saltmeadow cordgrass, but black needlerush can dominate high marsh in some areas, especially in brackish water, and seashore saltgrass is also common. Under most circumstances, tides won't be high enough in these areas to allow gamefish to enter (except, perhaps, on some spring tides, especially in summer). Recognizing where these species of marsh grass occur, however, will help you focus on the most-productive fishing areas of the marsh because a healthy high marsh often indicates an adjacent healthy low marsh, which is where you will find the gamefish.

The low marsh is fully intertidal and occupies the area between mean sea level and the mean high water mark. The low marsh is subject to daily incursions of the tides and thus is an area of high salinity, and the sediments remain wet. As you might expect, plants in the low marsh must have special adaptations enabling them to tolerate salt water—they are able to exclude salt water from their tissues and excrete salt from the water they do take in.

Rainfall influences the extent and robustness of salt marshes, especially the high marsh and upper portion of the low marsh. As a general rule, areas with low rainfall will have wetlands only in the portion of the intertidal zone that is frequently flooded by the tides. Such a salt marsh will mostly consist of only a narrow section of low marsh, with few, if any, high marsh plants present. In extremely arid areas, wetlands may be completely absent or will be very sparse. In contrast, wetlands will cover the entire intertidal zone in regions with high rainfall. However, even in wet regions you may find barren areas in normally healthy salt marshes during prolonged dry spells. In most instances, these open areas will be recolonized by marsh grasses after normal rains return.

But not all open spots in a salt marsh are caused by low rainfall. Even salt marshes that receive sufficient rainfall can have areas of open bottom. Large mats of floating dead plant material can be carried well into the low marsh, and even to the high marsh, by a rising tide. When the dead plant material isn't carried away by another high tide, it can smother the marsh grass that it covers, creating a bare spot in the marsh. Often, these bare spots become small depressions, lower than the surrounding marsh due to erosion, and salt water brought in by high tides can collect in these depressions. If high tide only occasionally reaches the bare spots, the evaporating water will leave behind salt deposits, which may inhibit the recolonization of marsh grasses. If, on the other hand, tides frequently flood these spots, small fishes may collect in these pools at low tide. These pools can be a feeding stop on the rounds of a gamefish that follows a rising tide into the low marsh.

## The Low Marsh

Sediments of the low marsh tend to be oxygen-poor. This would kill most plants because the roots need oxygen to survive. Because salt-marsh plants don't have prop roots (like red mangroves) or pneumatophores (like black mangroves) that are able to obtain oxygen from the air, they use a different process. Salt-marsh plants are able to transport to their roots some of the oxygen they assimilate through their leaves, so they can remain firmly rooted in the anoxic sediments. Healthy roots, in turn, help stabilize the sediments of the marsh, thus creating excellent gamefish habitat.

The species of marsh grass in our warm-temperate region that is best adapted to dealing with the stresses of full salt water, low-oxygen sediments, and daily inundation by tides is smooth cordgrass. Smooth cordgrass is so superior at handling these stresses that it is the overwhelmingly dominant plant species in low marshes with high salinity. In fact, in many locations it is the only plant in the low marsh. In areas of brackish water and low tidal range, like much of the northern Gulf of Mexico, black needlerush can be the dominant marsh grass. These grasses are good indicators of where in the salt marsh you will most likely find gamefish.

Although smooth cordgrass is best adapted to the low marsh, even it has limits, and some areas of the low marsh have better growing conditions than others. The varying qualities of growing areas are revealed by the height of the cordgrass. Better growing conditions result in taller smooth cordgrass, whereas less-than-optimal conditions produce shorter plants. Because the same factors that influence the growth of smooth cordgrass also affect gamefish and their prey, it's worth addressing some of these environmental factors because healthier portions of the marsh tend to attract more gamefish. Understanding why this is the case will help you to read a salt marsh in order to get the most out of your fishing time. For example, do you know during which stages of the tidal cycle gamefish will be most active in different areas of the marsh?

What are the best growing conditions for smooth cordgrass? First among them is tidal flushing. Sediments in areas of the low marsh that are frequently flushed by tides have a greater percolation rate, which bathes marsh grass roots with new water with each tidal cycle. This means the sediments are better aerated and thus have a higher oxygen content, which results in better plant growth. Although smooth cordgrass and black needlerush can tolerate sediments with low oxygen, they grow best in aerated sediments. A second factor contributing to growth of smooth cordgrass is the type of sediment. Fine-grained sediments are more densely packed and have higher nutrient levels than sandy soils, which result in better growth. Not coincidentally, tides help deposit fine-grained sediments in the low marsh, so once again areas with frequent tidal flushing are good. Finally, smooth cordgrass grows best in medium salinity, which relates back to the importance of rainfall to a healthy salt marsh and should start you thinking about where these advantageous conditions occur.

You will find the best growing conditions along the edges of creeks that receive frequent tidal flushing and perhaps some fresh water as well and the most-seaward portions of marsh that benefit from daily incursions of tides. Outer portions of the low marsh that abut deeper water are often better than those adjacent to expansive intertidal mud flats because much of the fine-grained sediments will be deposited on shallow mud flats before they reach the marsh grass. Mud flats are indicative of low-energy areas, so although they may be intertidal they don't experience the stronger tidal currents associated with creeks. In addition, deeper water provides safe holding places for gamefish to wait out low tide and quick access to the marsh after the tide begins to flood. Once again, stable sediments are key—they allow the growth of smooth cordgrass right to the edges of the creeks and the outer fringe of the low marsh and help to create great habitats for gamefish prey.

Some of the best salt marshes you will encounter while fishing for gamefish seem to go on forever. The low marsh extends along the shoreline as far as you can see and reaches far out into the estuary. Behind the low marsh, the high marsh rolls slowly landward into the distance. In other locations, a slender high marsh gives way to a low marsh that is only a narrow strip along the shoreline that drops abruptly at its seaward edge. Both types of marshes are in areas protected from waves and strong currents, so why are they different?

All other things being equal, the best explanation for the difference between these two marshes is that they differ in slope. A marsh that slopes gently from its landward edge to sea level will cover the greatest area and will have the widest high and low marsh zones. This is because the slope affects how far a tide can flood a salt marsh. The shallower the slope of a marsh, the farther a typical high tide will penetrate. These types of locations are also most likely to have more creeks crisscrossing the marsh, increasing the quality of the habitat for gamefish. In a shallow sloping marsh, even just a vertical foot of tide can flood a very large area of marsh. Because the low marsh is defined by the area between sea level and mean high water, the farther the high tide penetrates, the wider the low marsh zone. And because the high marsh often covers the area where the low marsh used to be, the high marsh also covers a wide, shallow-sloping terrain. In contrast, steeply sloping marshes don't provide much horizontal surface area for the tide to cover, so the low marsh is limited to a narrow zone. The high marsh is similarly narrow, if it exists at all.

## Applying What You've Learned

### Red Drum in the Marsh

It was late afternoon on a midsummer day under clear skies. The air hung heavy and still—a perfect day for fishing in the low-country salt marshes of South Carolina. The slick surface of dark backcountry water slid into a green sea of waist-high marsh grass. The bright green of early season growth was gone, and the grass stood strong to the horizon. As the flooding tide crept into the marsh, the pace of the fiddler crabs become more frantic as they hurried to finish their meal of mud and detritus before retreating into their burrows. Small blue crabs scurried about in preparation for the advancing tide. Some of the crabs abandoned the flight altogether and climbed the stalks of grass to sit out the high tide above the fray. The marsh was electric with anticipation of what the crabs hoped would not happen but what I was planning on—hungry red drum invading the shallow marsh with the rising tide.

I was standing in this spot because my friend Joe Cronley had brought me here. I was midway through an extended drive up the East Coast, from Florida to New England. I say "extended" because the drive could be made in three easy days, but I was stopping to fish along the way, and a three-day drive turned into two weeks. Joe was kind enough to take me in for a few days and guide me through the world of low country red drum.

Now, however, I was standing in this spot alone. I had followed Joe from his house, I in my truck, he in his, and after a few minutes' drive we parked along the side of the road. Joe waited while I grabbed my rod and gear bag, and then we walked off the road and into the marsh. As we walked through the marsh grass across the hard-packed mud, Joe pointed out where the tide first entered the flat and where the red drum might first appear. Although it was tough to see some of the spots because of the higher grass, I nodded my head in understanding. As I scanned the marsh to get my bearings, Joe bid me good luck and headed back to his truck. He had a full schedule that afternoon and evening that didn't include fishing.

*Marsh edges are good places to focus fishing effort near low tide and when water is draining off the marsh (carrying prey with it) on the ebbing tide.*

I don't think Joe had made it back to his car before I started seeing signs of red drum coming onto the marsh. The first sign was the parting of the grass, as if by an unseen hand. The red drum were forcing their way through the heavy grass without hesitation, and their paths were marked by the tips of grass swaying in the still air. The second sure sign of advancing fish was the telltale splashing of a red drum as it turned on a crab. Using the thick grass as cover, I was soon close enough to see the glint of bright copper as a red drum worked its way across the flat in water so shallow its back was partially exposed.

I had tied on a size 4, copper-and-brown yarn crab fly, which seemed a fair imitation of the local fiddler crabs. After a few false casts I sent the fly toward the feeding fish. Although the distance was right and the placement was good, the fish continued on, never seeing the fly. The fly never hit the water. The fly line and leader were draped across the rough-edged cordgrass, the fly hanging 10 inches above the water as the fish passed below. I cast again with the same result. I brought in the line and clipped my leader to 4 feet of twenty-pound test. Hadn't Joe said something about this?

It didn't take me long to find the fish again because it hadn't moved far. The fish was rooting in the bottom intently as it moved in a small circle searching for another crab. I made another cast, and although the fly line hung across the marsh grass, the short, stout leader slid through the grass to the water. The splat of the fly hitting the water caught the fish's attention. I barely had time to take the slack out of the line before the fish surged forward to investigate and slurp in the fly. I had no idea a red drum could move so quickly and so far through marsh grass that was so thick that it made for tough walking. Fortunately, the fish was well-hooked, and a red drum the color of a new penny eventually came to hand.

I was fortunate to capitalize on Joe's local knowledge, which put me in the right place at the right time. But my experience encapsulates many of the characteristics of salt marshes covered in this chapter. You can use these characteristics to your advantage when fly fishing in this productive habitat, whether you have local knowledge or not.

## Applying What You've Learned

### Seeing a Salt Marsh from a Gamefish's Perspective

Now that we've addressed the basics of salt marshes, it's time to take a break and summarize what we've covered. First, you learned the general environmental conditions required by salt marshes—low energy, protected areas with tidal flow, and fine-grained sediments. These requirements are perfect for fly fishing because they add up to great backwater locations that are out of the wind and are attractive to gamefish and their prey.

You also know that older, more-mature salt marshes are going to be closer to the ocean or Gulf. These older marshes tend to be firmly situated in the salinity range preferred by coastal gamefish and provide a transition from marine to brackish water realms. These older marshes also tend to be crisscrossed by creeks that create a diverse habitat that is rich in gamefish prey.

Within these marshes, the marsh grasses provide many clues that help narrow the list of best spots to find gamefish. Although the high marsh is unlikely to hold fish, except during spring high tides, recognizing the high marsh zone gives you your inland boundary in searching for gamefish. Lest you scoff at the likelihood of red drum traveling across the low marsh almost to the high marsh in their search for food, let me remind you of the story that you just read. Before that afternoon of fishing was over, I'd followed red drum through the low marsh and to the edge of the high marsh as they rode the flooding tide.

Now that you recognize the plants of the high and low marsh, a second look at a marsh that at first seemed a featureless sea of grass will show you how complex the marsh can be. You'll now note that the low marsh doesn't necessarily parallel the shore but rather tends to grow as a network of patches and gaps, so that the edge of the high and low marshes weaves in and out. Small embayments often interrupt the low marsh and may even graze the high marsh. When deep, these embayments may be good places to find gamefish waiting out the low tide. When shallow, these are great places to search for gamefish feeding along the marsh edge during rising and falling tides.

In situations where the low marsh stretches across wide areas from the water's edge to the high marsh, the most-inland reaches of the low marsh will probably never see a gamefish. But where creeks traverse the low marsh, gamefish will use the deeper of these creeks as avenues to gain access to the numerous species of prey that live well into the low marsh. And, of course, you can easily find these creeks amidst the endless grass because you know that it is along these creeks where the tallest grass grows.

Because the creeks drain the salt marsh, we also know that current is associated with marsh creeks. After reading about how gamefish use currents to their advantage in oyster bar habitats, you should already be connecting the dots—creeks with currents are great places to find gamefish on the dropping tide. The creeks with the strongest flows will usually have a deep hole at their mouth and may even have undercut banks at creek bends. This is because the currents are strong enough that fine-grained marsh sediments are swept away. You will often find that deeper holes and creek beds with strong currents are lined with shells or even live oysters. Spots where shells have been swept into a pile are favorite places for weakfish and spotted trout to wait for a meal to be delivered by currents. And, of course, because of frequent tidal flushing, mix of fresh and salt water, and good currents, these creeks are great places to find oyster bars.

In contrast, although gamefish feed over mud flats, mud flats don't receive the currents and exchange of water that the creeks do and thus tend to hold fewer prey. But remember the importance of adjacent habitats of different complexity that have been discussed in previous chapters—some of the prey species that live in marsh grass may venture onto adjacent mud flats in search of food, so mud flats next to healthy low marsh may be good places to look for gamefish that feed on these wandering marsh prey.

With a little exploration you will discover that some creeks lead to ponds hidden deep within the marsh. Some of the ponds are too small and shallow to hold fish, whereas others are large enough to be considered lakes. As long as these still-water areas are deep enough at low tide and are connected to open water through creeks, there is a decent chance they will hold fish when weather conditions are right. Louisiana is a great example of an area where these backcountry ponds and lakes can afford fantastic fishing in relative peace and quiet.

### Applying What You've Learned

#### Reexamining Red Drum in the Salt Marsh

With this new information under your belt, you should now be able to look back at the story about my low-country red drum and figure out the clues to why that flat was such a hot spot for red drum. The first clue is that the tide was incoming, so if red drum were going to feed on the flat that day they would be riding the rising tide into the marsh. Second, the tide was rising late in the day. As I've mentioned in previous chapters, the coincidence of a rising tide and dusk or dawn often translates into the best fishing of the day. This is especially true during the heat of summer when dawn and dusk offer the coolest temperatures of the day. Third, the presence of smooth cordgrass meant I was fishing in the low marsh, and because it was a frequently flushed intertidal area, fiddler crabs were in abundance. Fourth, Joe pointed out the areas in the low marsh where I would first see the rising tide flooding the flat and the best places to look for the first arriving red drum. These areas weren't actual creeks but rather were low-lying troughs that were just a little deeper than the surrounding marsh and thus were more frequently flushed by tides. These areas were lined by the tallest cordgrass and thus were easy to spot. Finally, the hard-packed sediments indicated this was a healthy marsh of long standing and thus was likely to have a diverse prey community. All of these factors combined to make this a good time and place to be fishing.

## TIDES

Tides are especially important factors to consider when devising a strategy for fishing a salt marsh. In a typical situation, fish will gather along edges of the low marsh or in holes near creek mouths during low tide. Often, you can cast to these fish in the hours around low tide, just as you would to fish holding in holes between oyster bars. Blind-casting to steep edges of the marsh, whether an outer marsh edge or the edge of a wide creek, especially edges lined with oysters, can be a productive way to fish during the hours around low tide. Many fish, shrimp, and other gamefish prey that reside in the low marsh in high water find themselves evicted from the marsh for the hour or two around low tide. These prey collect along the edges waiting for the rising tide to allow them back into the marsh. Although gamefish may seem inactive when they are waiting out the low tide in these deeper holes, they often will pounce onto a small fish or shrimp that ventures too far from the safety of the marsh edge.

As the tide begins to rise, the prey that have been waiting along the edges will be the first to head into the shelter of the marsh grass or across the shallows of the mud flats. Their arrival in the low marsh signals the arrival of a new tide to the fiddler crabs and marsh crabs that have been feeding on the exposed mud. If the tide is strong enough, gamefish will come into the marsh grass in search of crabs and shrimp. If the tide is weak, you may find gamefish mostly restricted to the edges and to creek beds.

Because of differences in tidal range, marsh slope, number of creeks, and other factors, each salt marsh will have optimum feeding times and zones for fish, so you may need to do some research to figure out each marsh. Salt marshes with wide-reaching low marsh but no creeks may see red drum venture only a short distance into the marsh because they don't want to get too far from the safety of deeper water. A similar-looking marsh, but with numerous creeks or shallow sloughs, may provide avenues for red drum to venture farther onto the flats in the same amount of time.

After the tide turns, you can again focus on the edges of the marsh and on the creeks. Some of the prey that were so eager to get into the marsh on the rising tide are swept off the marsh flats with the ebb, falling over the edges and into creeks. Red drum, spotted seatrout, weakfish, ladyfish, and bluefish are some of the gamefish that collect in these areas to pick off prey caught in the currents. Creeks with obstructions, such as oyster bars, that break up the flow are especially good places to find gamefish waiting for an easy meal. The same strategies that work for fishing oyster bars work in these situations.

## Applying What You've Learned

### Fishing the Tides

Creeks are important avenues that gamefish use to enter and exit salt marshes with the tides. Mouths of creeks are good spots on both rising and falling tides. On rising tides, gamefish that have been waiting out the low tide in the creek mouth or in deeper water nearby pass through the creek mouth on their way into the marsh. On falling tides, gamefish will stage at the creek mouth and pick off prey that is swept off the marsh and out of the creeks. Each creek will have its own variation on exact timing (because of depth, width, length, etc.), but in general early in the rising tide and late in the dropping tide are good bets. Fish that are eager to feed in the marsh will enter the creek early in the rising tide to get as far into the marsh as they can in the limited time before the tide turns. Gamefish feeding in the marsh will retreat into the creek as the tide begins to fall but may continue to feed as they move toward the creek mouth and may not take up a stationary feeding station until later in the tide. If, however, gamefish are not traveling into the marsh to feed but rather are remaining in the creek or in deeper water, as with a weak neap tide, early in the falling tide may be the best time to drift flies through the outgoing current at the creek mouth.

As the tide rises, the upper portions of the larger creeks that disappear into the low marsh are well worth exploring. Keep an eye out for small fish becoming airborne as they flee gamefish, for tails of red drum, black drum, or even spotted seatrout feeding in the marsh bottom for crabs, and for swirls and wakes from fish that you spook as you move silently up the creek. What to do when you see fleeing baitfish or a tailing drum is obvious—cast to it! But even the spooked fish are worth a cast. If they are not too badly spooked, a cast that leads a fish by 6 feet or more may prompt a strike. If not, no big loss. In all cases, it pays to be ready to make a cast quickly. Even if you spot no signs of fish, casting ahead of the boat—along both shorelines and in the middle of the creek—is worth the effort because gamefish don't always reveal themselves, even if they are feeding. Areas where smaller creeks dump into the large creek you are navigating are worth special attention because these junctures often have a deep hole that holds fish.

## DIFFERENCES BETWEEN GULF OF MEXICO AND ATLANTIC COASTAL SALT MARSHES

The ecological processes, dominant plants, and most of the gamefish and prey are the same in Atlantic and Gulf of Mexico salt marshes, but each coastline has some unique features that are worth examining. The differences mostly concern sediment type and marsh orientation, and because these factors influence gamefish and prey, knowing the differences will help you get the most out of fishing in each area.

In oceanographic terms, the continental shelf of the Atlantic is relatively wide and shallow, but it is not so wide and shallow that wave energy is dissipated before it reaches shore. This is why southeast Atlantic coasts are sandy beaches—there is too much wave energy to allow the deposition of the fine sediments necessary for marshes to become established, so Atlantic coast salt marshes are limited to estuaries or the back sides of barrier islands. In addition, the mixture of the ocean's energy and the runoff from land creates marsh sediments that are best described as muddy sand. This means that the sediments are relatively well aerated and that growth of marsh grasses is good. In North Carolina, salt marshes are limited to the edges of the sounds that lie behind the Outer Banks and the mouths of the rivers that feed them. In much of South Carolina and Georgia, the long string of barrier islands and the supply of new sediments from numerous rivers and creeks create good conditions for salt marshes along much of the coast. The salt marshes of northeastern Florida rest behind a series of mostly connected barrier islands that have melded with the coast in many locations, creating lagoons.

A consequence of the separation of the Atlantic Ocean from the estuaries by barrier islands is that salt water and brackish water are limited to narrow coastal areas. This is quite a contrast to the coast of the northern Gulf of Mexico, where salt marshes fringe much of the Gulf shoreline and spread far inland.

Another difference that contributes to the extensive coverage of salt marshes in the Gulf of Mexico is that the tidal range in the Gulf is very small. In the Atlantic, the large tidal range means that an area exposed at low tide might be under 4 to 6 feet of water at high tide. Many salt-marsh plants can't tolerate water that deep on a regular basis, so salt marshes are limited to the upper portion of the intertidal zone. In contrast, the combination of the Gulf's very shallow slope and the small tidal range means that large areas of coast are intertidal and thus exposed to salt water or brackish water and thus are suitable for salt-marsh plants. The salt marshes of Louisiana are a great example of such wide salt-marsh coverage.

Although atmospheric pressure and wind influence tides everywhere, the effects are especially notable in the Gulf of Mexico. The shallow continental shelf, shallow coastal bays and marshes, and small tidal range allow wind and atmospheric pressure to have a greater influence than they do in areas with deeper water and greater tidal range, such as the Atlantic coast. During periods of low pressure, there is less pressure from the atmosphere pressing down on the water, so tides can rise higher than predicted. When barometric pressure is high, more pressure on the water surface can prevent the water from rising as high as predicted. Wind can have similar effects. Strong onshore winds can make high tides higher than predicted and in extreme conditions can even prevent low tides from occurring—in effect creating a ghost tide. In contrast, offshore winds can make both high and low tides lower than predicted.

So, if nothing else, you should pay special attention to meteorological conditions when fishing the Gulf coast. And you can take advantage of typical weather patterns to plan the best times to fish different areas. For example, typical weather patterns combine with the spring and autumnal equinox to create periods of highest water levels of the year in April and May and again in September and October, with the best chance for low water from December through February. This occurs because typical onshore winds of spring, summer, and autumn combine with the spring tides to push water well into the shallow marshes and bays. During winter, strong offshore winds combine with the lowest tides of the year to drain many shallow marshes and bays, which may concentrate gamefish in deeper holes and sloughs. As you might expect, fish are keyed in to weather and tides and can change their behavior and distribution to take advantage of these periods. If you are in tune with the same conditions as the gamefish, you are more likely to be in the right place at the right time to catch more fish.

For our purposes we can divide the salt marshes of the Gulf of Mexico into four zones. The three zones from the Mississippi River delta east are dominated by sand, mud, and silt from the Mississippi River. In the first zone, from northern Florida to Mississippi, much of the coast is fringed by salt marshes. These marshes are protected by low-lying barrier islands or by extensive shallows that break up much of the wave energy long before it reaches shore. The second zone, the Mississippi delta, is famous for its extensive marshes, which extend far inland from the Gulf of Mexico. These marshes are relatively well protected by extensive mud shallows on their seaward edge, but the outer edges of these marshes are subject to forces of erosion during storms. The third zone, the western side of the Mississippi delta, boasts salt marshes that thrive on and lie behind low-lying, relatively stable, sandy islands called chenier islands. To the west of the Mississippi River, the salt marshes of the Texas coast are protected by extensive barrier islands that create the vast, shallow lagoons of the Texas coast. In fact, the barrier island that protects the Laguna Madre is the longest barrier island in the world. In addition to the seemingly endless shallow habitats of grass, mud, sand, and oyster bars in these lagoonal systems, the landward portions of these lagoons grade into extensive salt marshes and backcountry lakes that hold gamefish, especially from spring through autumn.

The shallow lagoonal marshes of Texas are especially vulnerable to influences of weather. They are so shallow and experience such a minor tide that portions of these lagoons can become unfishable when strong winds are from the right direction. Winter winds out of the north are especially bad—they push much of the water out of the marshes and pile it onto the backsides of the barrier islands. So, it pays to keep an eye on the weather when fishing the salt marshes and lagoons of Texas.

The small tides also mean that many of the inland ponds and lakes of Gulf coast marshes and the creeks that connect them to the Gulf hold fish throughout the tidal cycle. There just isn't enough tide relative to water depth to influence the behavior of fish. This is great news for anglers because these waters provide vast protected areas that are perfect for fly fishing. You'll often hear reliable reports of dozens of red drum on the fly in a day of fishing in these backcountry lakes.

In these backcountry salt-marsh habitats, weather and season are often more important than tide in finding gamefish. In general, you'll find the greatest numbers of gamefish in these backcountry areas beginning when water temperatures warm in spring and ending when temperatures start to drop in autumn. The exception is shallow areas that become too warm in the heat of summer. These locations are best in spring through early summer and later summer to autumn. During midsummer, many of the larger fish may move to deeper or more-open coastal habitats, such as beaches.

In late autumn and winter, the shallow waters in these areas can quickly drop in temperature when a strong cold front passes through, which can spell trouble for gamefish. In fact, every so often a particularly strong cold front passes through the Gulf coast, and the rapid drop in temperature kills fish that were trapped in the shallows. So, once again, locations that are very shallow are unlikely to hold fish during winter. During winter, marshes that are adjacent to deeper water or have deep holes where gamefish can wait out the cold periods will hold the most gamefish. But as the water warms, gamefish will quickly move back into the shallows.

## SALT-MARSH FOOD WEB

It's worth summarizing the food web in salt marshes because the richness of marshes supports so many gamefish and prey in the warm-temperate region. As you might guess from the toughness of salt-marsh grasses, few animals graze directly on marsh grass. Instead, nutrients from decaying marsh grass that has died and fallen to the ground helps fuel the salt-marsh food web. The fine-grained sediments and detritus from fallen marsh grass combine to make the perfect home for endless bacteria that cause the grass to decay. These nutrients are used by benthic diatoms (small, plankton-like algae that live on the sediment surface rather than in the water column like plankton) and algae that grow on marsh sediment surfaces. The benthic diatoms, algae, and detritus are then eaten by numerous marsh organisms, many of which are prey for gamefish.

Many species of worms eat the detritus, either by filter-feeding like oysters and mussels or by ingesting the detritus much like an earthworm ingests soil. Numerous species of fish—killifish and mullet among them—also eat the detritus, as do fiddler crabs, marsh crabs, shrimp, and other crustaceans. Fiddler crabs emerge from their burrows at low tide to scoop up morsels of mud and clean it of nutritional material. The small balls of mud you see around fiddler crabs' burrows are the crabs' way of setting aside the sediments they have already cleaned of food material. The next high tide will bring a fresh supply of detritus-laden sediment and diatoms to be gleaned for food.

In addition, nutrients resulting from decay of plant material support phytoplankton, which in turn supports zooplankton that can be abundant in waters around salt marshes, especially in summer. Oysters and mussels filter plankton and detritus particles that are swept into the water column and are in turn fed on by crabs and some fish. Numerous species of fish, including menhaden, sardines, and anchovies, also feed directly on zooplankton emanating from the salt marsh. What gamefish doesn't like to eat menhaden, sardines, anchovies, and their relatives, not to mention the crabs, fish, worms, and other organisms that feed directly on detritus or on smaller detritus-feeding organisms?

So, why is understanding the salt-marsh food web important to fly anglers? Because the same forces that influence growth of smooth cordgrass in the low marsh also influence the types and numbers of prey, which influences when and where you can find gamefish. For example, the process of bacterial decay of marsh plants uses oxygen and creates sulfur, so the amount of oxygen available to organisms living on and near the bottom can be a serious issue. But currents bring in oxygenated water, so the greater the tidal flushing, the greater the abundance of prey. This, in turn, creates more-hospitable conditions for marsh organisms that are gamefish prey. The changing tides also help deliver new detritus to organisms like fiddler crabs, which are able to take advantage of the intertidal zone by feeding on detritus delivered by each high tide. Finally, the three-dimensional structure provided by creek edges, bottoms, and associated mussel and oyster communities (which do best with moderate water exchange) provides more shelter to small organisms, which increases the number of gamefish prey.

## SALT MARSH RESIDENT PREY

Salt marshes in both the Atlantic and Gulf of Mexico host a variety of residents that are eaten by gamefish. Many of these species are also found in warm-temperate seagrass and oyster bar habitats, and most of the families are represented in tropical mangrove and seagrass habitats as well. Some of the species I have described in detail in previous chapters, so I will only mention them here and refer you back to those chapters for a complete description. Other prey species deserve a more-detailed description here because they are highest on the list of gamefish prey in the salt marshes.

## Crustaceans

### *Crabs*

#### *Fiddler Crabs*

Fiddler crabs are arguably the signature animals of warm-temperate salt marshes, where you may cross paths with as many as eight species. They are exceptionally adept at using the salt-marsh habitat to their advantage and seem to cover every square inch of marsh in some locations. I mentioned a few species of fiddler crabs in previous chapters, especially in the chapter on mangroves, but because they are so abundant in salt marshes I will build upon that information here.

Fiddler crabs are at the top of the menu of red drum in salt marshes. Fiddler crabs live in burrows in the intertidal zone of salt marshes and come out at low tide to feed on detritus and diatoms deposited by the previous high tide. A walk through the marsh at low tide will tell you where the biggest groups of fiddler crabs are located. You will likely hear them as they skitter across the marsh mud and will see the crabs retreating to their burrows as you approach. Fiddler crabs usually retreat into their burrows during high tide and come out to feed during low tides, but enough fiddler crabs remain active at high tide to be targeted by red drum. And although the enlarged claw is the most notable characteristic of fiddler crabs, it is not a necessary component of a fiddler crab fly because only the males have this appendage.

Like the species that inhabit mangrove habitats, each species of fiddler crab in salt marshes prefers a different type of habitat (sediment type, salinity, and portion of the intertidal zone), so you

*Although most fiddler crabs retreat into their burrows during high tide, some get stranded and spend the high tide clinging to marsh grass. When red drum bump marsh grass as they lumber through the marsh, they sometimes dislodge these fiddler crabs, which then fall into the water. This is likely why red drum swirl around in response to a fly that is plopped into the water.*

will encounter different species depending on where you are fishing. On one hand, because fiddler crabs are similar in size, you can use a couple of crab fly patterns of different colors to imitate them when fishing for red drum in the salt marshes. For example, typical body sizes for fiddler crabs range from ½ inch to almost 1 inch; they have a square carapace; and they come in a variety of earthy colors, including olive, green, brown, mottled brown, tan, and orange-brown. So, casting a fiddler crab fly of your choice to a red drum feeding in the low marsh is a good, simple strategy.

On the other hand, habitat preferences of different species of fiddler crabs tend to cause clumped distributions of fiddler crab colonies, so you will find that some areas of a low marsh are loaded with fiddler crabs, whereas other areas appear empty. You can be assured that the red drum know where the best areas are, so it is worth exploring an area at low tide to determine where fiddler crabs are most abundant to ensure that you are in these areas on the incoming tide and select fly colors that match these abundant species.

In addition, knowing what type of habitat each species of fiddler crab prefers will give you clues to the best locations to fish at different tides. For example, the red-jointed fiddler *(Uca minax)* lives mostly in brackish water in association with black needlerush marsh grass and is most common in Atlantic salt marshes. Because you know that black needlerush is mostly in the high marsh or in upper portions of a brackish-water low marsh, you also know that areas with red-jointed fiddlers will be accessible to gamefish only during spring high tides. If the high marsh is separated from open water or a creek by a wide, low marsh, it is unlikely that red drum or other gamefish will ever reach the spot. But if a creek provides close access, this spot may be worth checking during a spring high tide. Red-jointed fiddlers are dark-colored with red bands around their leg joints.

The red-jointed fiddler is largely replaced by the gulf freshwater fiddler *(Uca spinicarpa)* and Ive's fiddler *(Uca speciosa)* in much of the Gulf of Mexico. (The gulf freshwater fiddler is present only from the northern to the western Gulf.) As its name implies, the gulf freshwater fiddler prefers low-salinity areas, whereas Ive's fiddler prefers brackish water, both with tidal habitat requirements similar to those of the red-jointed fiddler.

Other common species of fiddler crabs living in salt marshes also provide clues for fishing in salt-marsh habitat. The mud fiddler crab *(Uca pugnax)* is widespread in mud flat areas of salt marshes, is brown to pale gray, has white-tipped claws, and often has a spot of turquoise between the eyes. The mud fiddler is common along the banks of intertidal marsh creeks. The front edge of the gulf mud fiddler *(Uca virens)* has a white fringe, and the front half of its carapace is green. It lives in habitats similar to those of the mud fiddler but is limited to the northern Gulf. The Caribbean fiddler *(Uca rapax)* is the most common fiddler crab in muddy bottoms of Texas marshes. The sand fiddler *(Uca pugilator)* is common on sheltered sandy shores of Atlantic salt marshes and is pale tan to white to match its surroundings. The panacea sand fiddler *(Uca panacea)* replaces the sand fiddler in the western Gulf, is found only from west Florida to Texas, and has a signature orange or red edge to its claw. The long-wave gulf fiddler *(Uca longisignalis)* is also limited to the western Gulf but lives in mud bottom and has a blue-green carapace.

### *Marsh and Mud Crabs*

Closely related to fiddler crabs, marsh crabs also live in salt marshes. Species you may encounter include purple marsh crab *(Sesarma reticulatum)* and gray marsh crab *(Sesarma cinereum)*. The purple marsh crab is common along the banks of intertidal marsh creeks and is dark purple, brown, or olive in color and reaches 1 inch across. Both the common and gray marsh crabs are light-colored, are less than 1 inch across, and live in the upper intertidal zone in burrows, often in association with layers of dead grass and detritus.

Mud crabs are common residents of the oyster reefs and mud flats that lie within salt marshes and are high on the menu of red drum, spotted seatrout, and weakfish. Mud crabs have been discussed in detail in previous chapters, so they will not be discussed further here.

One caveat to your selection of flies to imitate crabs in salt marshes and to your strategy for fishing these flies is that the waters of salt marshes are often rather murky. The fine-grained mud, clay, and sand that make up marsh sediments are easily disturbed by currents and waves and take a long time to settle back to the bottom, so the water of salt marshes is often turbid. During summer, plankton adds to the murkiness of the water. In these conditions, making exact imitations of different crabs is probably less important than getting the fish's attention with a reasonable facsimile, using colors that will be visible in these conditions, and giving the fly the appropriate action to imitate the real thing. In particularly murky water, flash, bright colors, and vibrations are useful factors in attracting the interest of a feeding gamefish. Appropriate for these conditions are flies with a lot of flash (I like a small, brown, bucktail bendback with copious copper flash), bright colors (orange, white, yellow, chartreuse, and white are good attractor colors), and materials that create waves in the water from their undulating motion (flies with palmered hackle or marabou move a lot of water). Sometimes you really have to splat the fly onto the water to get the fish's attention and then fish the fly slowly to allow the fish to find the fly. At other times the fish are wary of heavy-landing flies, so casting well beyond the fish and bringing the fly in front of the fish are the best approach. In either case, you'll know when the fish detects the fly because it will either suddenly surge toward the fly or turn and hightail it out of there.

### *Shrimp*

#### *Grass Shrimp*

Grass shrimp (usually *Palaemonetes pugio*) that occur in salt marshes are the same or similar to the species that occur in seagrass beds and oyster bars. In salt marshes, grass shrimp can be found feeding in shallow water among smooth cordgrass and along edges of creeks. Sometimes you will find large aggregations of grass shrimp trapped in small pools left by the falling tide. These can be hotspots after gamefish are able to reach these pools at high tide or when grass shrimp decide to leave pools on a dropping tide.

### *Mud and Ghost Shrimp*

Mud shrimp (*Upogebia affinis*) and ghost shrimp (*Callianassa atlantica, Callianassa major, Callianassa trilobata,* and *Callianassa jamaicense* depending on location) live in burrows on open bottom in the mid- to upper-intertidal zone within and near salt marshes. Each species prefers a different sediment type: Mud shrimp prefer the fine sediments of mud flats, whereas ghost shrimp are found only in clean sand. All of the species are pale to white and similar in size (2 to 4 inches).

## ***Hermit Crabs***

A few species of hermit crabs also live in salt marshes, often on open bottom flats, and are susceptible to gamefish when they are caught out of their shells. As hermit crabs grow, they have to find larger and larger shells, so they are always on the lookout for a new home. In fact, appropriately sized shells in good shape are rare enough that hermit crabs will often fight one another for a suitable shell. Gamefish occasionally surprise hermit crabs that are trying on a new shell or are homeless because they have lost their shell in a battle with another hermit crab. If the hermit crabs are in shells that are small enough, redfish may be able to slurp in the whole thing and crush it with their crusher plates. Common salt-marsh hermit crabs are long-clawed *(Pagurus longicarpus)* and green-striped *(Clibanarius vittatus)* in the Atlantic and flat-clawed *(Pagurus pollicaris)* in both the Atlantic and Gulf. The long-clawed hermit crab is small (¾ inch) and tan with white and brown markings. The flat-clawed hermit crab is also tan but grows to 3 inches, as does the green-striped, which has green and white stripes along its legs.

### Polychaetes (aka Worms)

Numerous species of worms live in salt marshes, and many species are eaten by gamefish. The most-common worms in the diets of gamefish are sandworms (family Nereidae). These segmented worms live in burrows in intertidal bottoms of mud and sand and feed along the bottom—picture earthworms with small jaws. The large sandworm *(Nereis succinea)* grows to 7 inches, and the small sandworm *(Nereis limbata)* grows to 6 inches, and both are earth-toned in color. Red drum are especially fond of these worms, but black drum and spotted seatrout also prey on worms when they can.

## RESIDENT PREY FISHES

### Mollies and Mosquitofish

Mollies and mosquitofish occur in shallow, low-energy areas of marsh that are protected from strong winds. Mollies are especially abundant in tidal creeks, mostly in subtropical salt marshes. They are pale to dark gray or brassy, with rows of fine dark spots so closely aligned they look like stripes running the length of their body. During the summer mating season, males become very colorful: The long, sail-like dorsal fin can be almost iridescent silver and black, and on some fish the fin has an orange fringe. Although mollies may reach 5 inches in length, 2–4 inches is the typical size in salt marshes. The related mosquitofish are brown to brassy in color, reach a maximum size of about 1½ inches, and prefer vegetated brackish areas with at least seasonal freshwater flow. Mosquitofish, and sometimes mollies, will move upstream to stay in brackish or nearly fresh water as freshwater flows decrease. This means that you need to say in tune with the conditions in the marsh to know when flies imitating these prey are appropriate.

### Killifishes

Killifishes are perhaps the most abundant group of resident fishes in warm-temperate salt marshes and thus are important prey for gamefish. (They are similarly important in subtropical mangrove wetlands and creeks, so much of what is presented here is applicable to mangrove wetland habitats as well.) Killifishes occur in loosely associated schools in shallow protected backwaters, flats, and creeks of salt marshes. Within the warm-temperate region you might come across eleven species of killifishes, each preferring a slightly different habitat or salinity. Fortunately, killifish are similar in size, shape, and color, so even though species may vary among locations, the same flies should work throughout. In general, killifish are small (from 1 to as much as 7 inches long, though most are between 1½ and 4 inches long), of classic "minnow" shape, and medium brown to dark brown in color.

Species you may encounter in both Gulf and Atlantic warm-temperate salt marshes are sheepshead minnow *(Cyprinodon variegatus),* marsh killifish *(Fundulus confluentus),* striped killifish *(Fundulus majalis),* and rainwater killifish *(Luciana parva).* Species mostly limited to the Gulf of Mexico include gulf killifish *(Fundulus grandis),* diamond killifish *(Adinia xenica),* salt-marsh topminnow *(Fundulus jenkinsi),* goldspot killifish *(Fundulus carpio),* and bayou killifish *(Fundulus pulvereus).* Species limited to the Atlantic are the mummichog *(Fundulus heteroclitus)* and spotfin killifish *(Fundulus luciae).*

Most killifish spawn in late spring or summer, and males of many species change coloration during spawning season. Whereas females retain the bland, earthy coloration, males display swaths of orange, yellow, or blue, accented by dark bands and spots. During the spawning season it seems that males can become so distracted during their mating displays that they completely forget about predators.

## Silversides

Finally, two species of silversides—inland silverside *(Menidia beryllina)* and tidewater silverside *(Menidia peninsulae)*—inhabit salt marshes. The inland silverside's range includes both Atlantic and Gulf salt marshes, whereas the tidewater silverside is found only in salt marshes of Florida and through much of the Gulf of Mexico. Both species reach about 4 inches in length. Silversides spawn in late spring or early summer, resulting in small juveniles (aka glass minnows) being abundant from summer through autumn.

## SEASONAL PREY

### Crustaceans

Blue crabs are abundant in salt marshes but become less active during winter months. Juveniles, which are the size most eaten by gamefish, are most abundant during summer.

It seems that shrimp are on the diet of just about any gamefish. Juvenile pink and white shrimp (family Penaeidae—common shrimp) are present seasonally in salt marshes. These species use warm-temperate salt marshes as juveniles and migrate to deeper water as adults. Most juvenile common shrimp in salt marshes are from 1 to 4 inches long. The possible colors of juveniles include clear and translucent shades of green, gray, and brown depending in part on the type of bottom where they are living. Juvenile shrimp are most abundant in Gulf salt marshes in autumn and spring and in late summer through autumn in Atlantic marshes. Brown shrimp *(Penaeus aztecus)* is the most common in western Gulf of Mexico salt marshes.

### Mullet

Mullet, described in previous chapters, are also important prey in warm-temperate salt marshes. The most common species are striped mullet *(Mugil cephalus)* and white mullet *(Mugil curema).* Mullet larvae enter salt marshes in winter and grow to large juvenile size by autumn, which is when juveniles are most abundant. Juveniles often undertake migrations out of salt marshes and shallow coastal bays toward warmer areas in autumn, inciting rather dramatic feeding frenzies by gamefish. Mullet leaving Louisiana marshes in September, for example, fall victim to gorging tarpon.

Likewise, the autumn southward migration of tarpon from the southeast Atlantic coast coincides with the evacuation of salt marshes and southward push by white mullet.

## Juvenile Fishes

Juvenile fishes of many species begin arriving in warm-temperate salt marshes in early spring and continue arriving through summer, when they peak in abundance. Common species with spring arrivals include spot, croaker, and pinfish, whereas silver trout arrive in summer. Red drum juveniles arrive in late autumn and early winter. Juveniles that use other shallow coastal habitats will also use salt marshes, particularly if those other habitats are uncommon. Their seasonality is discussed in previous chapters. Many juveniles that survive the summer migrate out of marshes in the autumn, which can induce gamefish to collect along marsh edges and creeks that drain marshes to take advantage of this seasonal bounty.

### Applying What You've Learned

#### Strategies for Murky Water

Once again, because of the often-murky waters of the salt marsh, flies that move water, make noise, or are tied with bright colors or flash can be productive, especially during wet times of year. When fishing marshes, I often use streamers in all white or throw in some chartreuse, yellow, or orange. Flash can certainly help, especially in the most turbid waters, but sometimes it seems that too much flash scares fish away. When I do use extra flash, I always select a color that enhances the local water color. In very murky waters I also use black flies because they present a better silhouette against the backscatter of light that occurs in murky water.

Small poppers can also be productive flies in the salt marsh, especially in the early and late parts of a summer day. I enjoy moving from hole to hole along the edge of a marsh or along a creek bed in the evening, casting a popper a few times into each good-looking spot. The commotion of a fish hitting the fly and the ensuing battle often shuts down the remaining fish in that hole, but the excitement makes it worth it. Plus, there is always another hole a little farther along.

Flies that move water are also good for blind-casting at creek mouths on a falling tide. Casting across the creek and swinging the fly through the current are a good strategy. Be careful not to fish the fly too quickly. In turbid water it may take a bit longer for a fish to find the fly because the fish can't rely so much on site as on its lateral line system.

When a fly (or baitfish) moves through the water, it creates small vibrations that travel through the water in waves—much the same way sound travels through water. At distances of 20 feet or less, the fish's lateral line system picks up the waves as changes in pressure. So, a fly pulsating through murky water is detected by a fish long before the fish can see the fly. As the fish gets closer to the fly, the fish's sight takes over. Slowly fished, bright flies that move water are the top flies for casting to tarpon rolling in marsh creek mouths in summer.

## Applying What You've Learned

### Seasonal Strategies

Because salt marshes occur in warm-temperate climates, they are subject to a wide range of temperatures, which are reflected in obvious seasonal changes. Salt-marsh grasses grow during the warmer months and become dormant or die back in the colder months. The inhabitants of salt marshes undergo similar seasonal changes. Although resident species don't leave the marsh in winter, they decrease their activity or even become dormant in especially cold periods. For example, during cold periods killifish will burrow into sediments and remain there, dormant, until temperatures rise. Likewise, fiddler crabs and mud crabs will wait out cold periods in their shelters and emerge after temperatures rise. Some resident species may occasionally vacate the shallow waters of salt marshes when temperatures drop, waiting out the cold temperatures in deeper, warmer waters. At the other extreme, temperatures can get very warm in shallow waters of a salt marsh in the heat of summer. This condition often results in less activity by residents during the middle part of the day and greater activity at dusk, at dawn, and at night.

During cold months, the dark marsh bottom is warmed by the sun, so temperatures in the shallows can rise quickly during the day, causing a surge in activity. Gamefish, such as red drum and spotted seatrout, will move onto the shallows to take advantage of increased prey activity and to warm up in these shallow, sun-heated waters. Midday through late afternoon is the best time to find gamefish moving into the shallows because a few hours of sun often are needed to warm things up.

Gamefish also take advantage of the warming effect of the sun on the shallows during the dropping tide. After a day of warming in the sun, water falling off a marsh flat with the dropping tide will be warmer than surrounding deep water. Gamefish will wait along current-swept drop-offs or at mouths of creeks to warm up in this water and to feed on prey that is swept off flats.

A somewhat different pattern takes shape during the heat of summer. The summer sun may warm the flats beyond the comfort zone of gamefish and some of their prey. When this happens, gamefish take refuge in cooler waters in deeper holes or along drop-offs. As a rising tide moves the cooler water from deeper areas into the shallows, gamefish often follow the cooler water to feed on the flat. Another strategy employed by gamefish in the heat of summer is to take refuge in cool, deep waters during the day and to invade the shallow marsh flats during cooler temperatures at dawn and dusk. Once again, the coincidence of an incoming tide and dawn or dusk can create a productive time for fly fishing.

In addition to affecting gamefish behavior, seasonal temperature changes often result in peaks and valleys of abundance of gamefish in shallow marshes. For example, red drum abundance and feeding activity in shallow marshes usually peak in autumn because this is the season when many prey are at peak abundance and when adult red drum are collecting in large schools prior to heading to deeper water for spawning season. Spawning makes for hungry fish, so autumn is when you have a good shot at finding large red drum in shallow waters. The best spots to find these prespawn fish are shallows that are close to deep, well-flushed areas that the drum may be using to spawn. Similar seasonal changes in abundance and behavior occur for other gamefishes in warm-temperate salt marshes. For example, tarpon and spotted seatrout are coming off their summer spawning, so they need to fatten up in the autumn in preparation for winter—the trout need the energy to tolerate the cooler temperatures and the tarpon to migrate south into warmer waters.

# 8
# Beaches

In many ways, beaches offer a different experience for anglers than do the habitats discussed so far. In some cases, beaches will simply be avenues by which you reach other habitats, like seagrass or mangroves. Even in these situations, however, beaches can allow a close, land-based approach to actively feeding gamefish. In other cases, beaches will present a great environment for gamefish—a dynamic mosaic of habitats that challenges both angler and gamefish. Fishing along beaches requires an angler's attention to subtle details that can make the difference between success and failure. The gamefish available along beachfronts are mostly the same suspects you've been chasing in more-protected waters of seagrass beds, mangroves, oyster bars, or salt marshes, but a few other species are especially abundant along beaches. In this chapter I will outline the basics of the different types of beaches you'll encounter in each region and hopefully add to your enjoyment of these great fishing locations.

## BEACH BASICS

The dynamic nature of coastal beaches poses different challenges to both gamefish and fly angler. You'll notice that the sediment composition of beaches varies among regions. For example, Atlantic beach sediments change as you move from warm-temperate to subtropical locations. The sands of warm-temperate beaches are composed mostly of fine-grained quartz eroded from continental rocks. Calcium carbonate becomes more common after you reach Florida, where carbonate sands dominate the subtropical beaches of south Florida. Beaches on the barrier islands of southern Florida are dominated by calcareous sands. Much of the sand is from the limestone that makes up the lower Florida peninsula and has been reworked by waves for thousands of years. But you'll also notice the fragmented bits of shells that have been washed shoreward from the abundant bivalves (mostly clams) and gastropods (snails) that live in coastal waters and from coral on southernmost beaches. In the Gulf of Mexico, southern beaches are mostly calcium carbonate, with the influence of Mississippi sediments and sediments from land-based erosion increasing as you move north. In the Caribbean, beaches are mostly calcium carbonate, but you'll find some beaches of land-based sediments as well.

Tidal range (plus slope of the land and wave action) influences the width of beaches. Along the Atlantic coast, much of North Carolina and Florida experience a moderate tidal range and thus have mostly narrow beaches. In contrast, South Carolina and Georgia tend to have wider beaches because of their larger tidal range. In some locations in the Gulf of Mexico, moderate tidal range combines with a shallow sloping coast to create wide beaches—such as the microtidal barrier islands of Texas and the chenier islands of Louisiana.

Sediment size says a lot about a beach's environment: the coarser the sediments, the higher the wave energy. With a bit of investigation you'll soon note differences in sediment types and size not only among beaches but also along a single shoreline. This information provides clues to where you'll find gamefish. Most Atlantic and Gulf coast beaches in our area form the seaward edge of barrier islands that protect estuaries and shorelines from onslaughts of the open ocean, so these beaches are exposed to high wave energy. Because of the ocean's energy, these barrier island systems are very dynamic and are always on the move. The nearly constant bombardment of waves means the sands are constantly in motion, so it is almost impossible for seagrass or other live-bottom habitats to become established. On the Atlantic coast, North Carolina's Outer Banks tend to be the highest-energy beaches, with less-dramatic conditions farther south. Most Gulf of Mexico beaches experience moderate to low surf conditions through most of the year, with largest waves coming from strong cold fronts, hurricanes, and periods of extended onshore winds.

## WAVES

As anyone who has spent time on the beach can tell you, waves crashing onto the beach move sand. The energy from breaking waves and the rush of their wash up the beach displace grains of sand. As the waves' energy dissipates, the sand settles back to the bottom. An individual sand grain is moved only a short distance by any single wave, but the accumulation of many small movements by many grains of sand results in large-scale changes in beach formations and offshore sandbars.

Waves generally approach beaches at an angle, so instead of sand simply being moved up and down the beach with each wave, sand is also transported along the beach. And as the wash from one wave retreats seaward, carrying a load of sand, it is met by another incoming wave. While some of the water will continue its seaward flow along the bottom, some of the wash and the sand it carries will become entrained in the wash from the next incoming wave. And because waves are approaching the beach at an angle, accumulation of water in the wash zone creates a current that moves along the beach. This is called a longshore current.

Every once in a while the volume of water pushed against the shore by so many successive waves becomes large enough that it's able to break through the surf zone and head seaward. This seaward rush of water that interrupts the longshore current is what we call a rip current. You can recognize a rip current by the discoloration of the water because it carries so much sediment or by the change in the appearance of the water's surface due to conflicting currents of the seaward flowing rip and incoming waves. Strong, consistent rip currents cut through longshore bars. Rip currents provide feeding areas for gamefish in much the same way as do current edges around oyster bars. Baitfish and other prey get caught in the rip current and transported offshore, and gamefish wait along edges of the rips to pick off discombobulated prey.

In some cases, conflicting forces of incoming wave energy and seaward flowing rips will cause a sorting of sediments into a pattern of cusps and bowls along the beach. Cusps are small ridges of coarse sediment that rim bowls composed of fine sediment, and these formations often continue into the water. When the cusps and bowls continue into the water, they act like miniature bars and troughs that lie across the longshore current and perpendicular to shore. Baitfish will try to escape the current by collecting on the downcurrent sides of submerged cusps, making for good feeding stops for cruising gamefish.

The movement of sand by waves and longshore current forms longshore bars, which are underwater sand bars oriented parallel to the beach. Sometimes longshore bars become so large they're

*Low tide is a great time to explore beaches to get an idea of the terrain for fishing at high tide. In this location, the high-tide line is revealed by the line of algae washed up onto the beach. Also evident is a small drop-off and then a bar that parallels the shoreline. At low tide the surf is washing against the outer side of the bar, but at high tide the bar will be covered and become a good spot to search for cruising gamefish.*

*The slightly darker swath that is close to and parallels the beach is a trough that can hold gamefish prey and thus attract gamefish. The trough cuts offshore through the longshore bar, as revealed by the open space between the breaking waves. This break in the longshore bar is a good place to find gamefish waiting to ambush prey.*

*The roiled water in the center of the photo marks a small rip current that is transporting water and sediment off the beach. These areas often contain baitfish, which can be disoriented by the rip current.*

exposed at low tide and are then called ridges. Some beaches have only a single longshore bar, whereas others sport a series of parallel bars off their shores. Between the beach and the first bar, and between parallel bars, troughs of deeper water form. To some extent, the deeper water of troughs provides a refuge from turbulence of waves breaking over the bars and thus attracts baitfish and other prey that live along the beach front. More importantly, gamefish travel the edges of troughs looking to pick off baitfish that get caught in turbulence of waves tumbling over the bars.

Longshore bars and troughs often reveal their location to an observant angler. Incoming waves rise up, and even break, as they travel over shallow bars and then subside as they travel over troughs. If there are no waves, look for changes in water color—generally a lighter shade marks bars, and darker water marks troughs—or for breaks in currents marking the edge of a bar.

*Beach profiles*

Those of you experienced with beach fishing already know that wave action can quickly change the shape of beaches. You've probably noticed that beaches change shape most dramatically after storms or during winter. This is because of differences in wave energy. In summer, the dominant wave type is low energy. These low-energy waves deposit sand onto the beach and create a gently sloping shoreline. Check the low-tide lines on these summer beaches for a short but steep drop-off, or lip, at the low-tide mark—anywhere from 6 inches to 2 feet deep. The lip is a good area to spot cruising gamefish in search of a meal on an incoming tide.

The large, high-energy waves associated with winter and with storms cause beach erosion and transport of sand offshore. The result is a steeper beach with waves often crashing right along the shoreline, so, as the calmer seas of summer return, the beaches are slowly built up again. The constantly changing nature of beaches means that some study and frequent exploration are needed for anglers to really know a beach and the best places to find gamefish.

## Applying What You've Learned

### Basic Strategies for Fishing the Surf

The crashing surf and roiled water of beaches can be intimidating to the uninitiated, which leads to confusion in what approach to use when fly fishing these areas. The most common mistake of fly anglers new to fishing beaches is trying to cast as far off the beach as they can. I can't tell you how many times I've watched fly anglers wade out to waist-deep water, fight the waves, and put all their strength into casting as far offshore as possible. This approach makes sense; after all, big fish want to be in deep water, right? Not necessarily. Most of the time this approach is not necessary—by wading off the beach, you may be bypassing most of the fish, which are close to shore. You'd be surprised by the numbers and sizes of gamefish that cruise along the beach in water barely deep enough to keep them wet. Of course, there are times when the fish are feeding off the beach, and casting offshore is necessary, but more often than not you will find good numbers of gamefish within easy casting distance from the beach. Much of this can be sight-fishing. Plus, why throw out your arm trying to cast across the ocean if you don't have to?

My general approach to beach fishing is to walk along the beach edge or perhaps just a step into the water because many fish feed along that little drop-off, or lip, right next to the beach. By staying on the beach I have a good view of fish if the water is clear and can cast to the fish I spot. But even if the water is too murky for me to see fish, chances are they're still in these same areas. For blind-casting, the best strategy is to cast on a line that runs between parallel to the beach and at a 45-degree angle to the shoreline.

There are two schools of thought about what fly line to use for this type of beach fishing. Some anglers prefer an intermediate line to get under the surf. They feel that an intermediate line makes a straight line easier to maintain and gives them a more-direct connection to their fly. Others prefer floating lines and maintain a connection to their fly by mending the line over the surf. If you are sight-fishing, a floating line is definitely best because it allows quick pickups and recasts of the fly. If you are blind-casting, an intermediate line may make life easier by allowing longer drifts in the current. But in the end it's a personal preference, so use whichever works for you. Regardless of the fly line you choose, it is important to keep enough tension on the line to feel a fish take the fly.

If you are using a floating line, you can also detect strikes by keeping an eye on the end of your fly line. Sometimes gamefish will really slam the fly, but often a strike in the surf will be more subtle. And although there are times when a rapidly stripped fly garners the most strikes, unless fish are actively feeding I've found it best to fish the fly slowly. I like to let the fly bounce around in the turbulent water of the surf zone like a disoriented baitfish. Again, the challenge with this strategy is to keep enough tension on the fly line to be sure that you detect the strike while allowing the fly to roll around just inside or just outside the surf zone.

## SHIFTING SANDS

Although many people think the Gulf Stream is the dominant current along the southeastern Atlantic coast, in reality the Gulf Stream is too far offshore to influence the movement of sand along the coastal beaches or to directly influence coastal gamefish in most circumstances. Instead, the northward-flowing Gulf Stream forms the outer boundary to the warm-temperate coastal system. West of the Gulf Stream the off-colored water reflects the influence of coastal rivers and beach sediments, whereas the clear water of the Gulf Stream to the east speaks of tropical influence. Closer to the coast, the dominant coastal current flows from north to south, and this current slowly moves sand southward. The currents of the Gulf of Mexico are a bit more complex, but the general flow is counterclockwise. Why does knowing this matter? The direction of sand transport influences where bars and shoals form, which affects where you will find gamefish.

The dominant longshore current, in concert with the dominant coastal current, transports sand along the coast. I'll use the Atlantic coast as an example of how these currents transport sand along the outer beaches, but the same processes are at work in the Gulf. As this sand moves southward, it builds up against the barrier islands and extends seaward as shoals. These shoals act as reservoirs of sand that maintain a ready supply of new sand for beaches farther south. Because of the wave and current action, longshore bars often radiate southward from these shoals. The longshore bars, which are really trails of southward-moving sand, eventually wrap around the southern tip of the barrier island in the form of a spit. In many cases sand is transported behind the islands, forming a large sand flat on the back side of the inlets.

These backside shoals provide shelter for small baitfish looking to escape gamefish lurking in the deep water of the adjacent inlet. Outgoing tides sweep unwitting baitfish to the waiting mouths of gamefish cruising the edges of these flats, but sometimes gamefish swim forays into tightly packed schools of baitfish in the shallow water. Drifting a streamer the size and color of the bait over the edge can be productive on the dropping tide. During the shallow-water feeding frenzies, just getting a fly into the path of a gamefish is usually enough. An early rising tide is a good time to sight-fish these backside sand flats as gamefish come out of the deeper inlets to feed on the sand flat.

Many shallow, sloping beaches have extensive sand deposits extending seaward that allow an angler to wade a considerable distance off the beach at low tide. The sand flats that remain a constant depth for a considerable distance tend to hold fewer prey and fewer gamefish, however. The best fishing on these flats tends to be along the edges, where you may find gamefish moving along the drop-off hoping to surprise prey, hanging in a current waiting for prey to wash off the flat, or perhaps cruising across the flat on a rising tide.

In contrast, shallows that roll away from shore as bars and troughs hold considerably more gamefish, even if they possess only minor contours. These types of shallows are especially common in the Gulf of Mexico. Although the bars and troughs tend not to be of the magnitude of many of their higher-energy Atlantic coast counterparts, the change in bottom from bar to trough collects and holds baitfish, crabs, and other prey just the same, which attracts gamefish.

If surf is moderate or low, many of these beachside flats are wadeable on either side of the low tide. These areas are most common off sandy points and where normal wave action is moderate to minor. Sight-fishing is a good challenge during calm, clear-water days, whereas casting into troughs can be productive when the water is turbid. Often, baitfish are scattered across these shallows, especially when the water is murky. Under such circumstances you won't find gamefish attacking tightly packed schools of panicking baitfish. Instead, keep an eye open for swirls from gamefish feeding on the scattered schools of loosely packed baitfish or for wakes from gamefish moving over a bar.

Wading and sight-fishing the beachside flats require careful attention to the tides. Because of the larger tides of South Carolina, pay extreme attention to tide tables to avoid becoming stranded by high water between the bar and the beach. Even on Gulf beaches with relatively minor tides, you need to be vigilant about the tides so that you don't get stranded on an outer bar on an incoming tide.

Along subtropical and warm-temperate beaches, Spanish mackerel, ladyfish, red drum, speckled trout, snook, bluefish, and crevalle jacks are typical gamefish roving these shallows from late spring through early autumn. Tarpon can be abundant along beaches in summer but require stealthy techniques to get close enough for a cast. You might even come across a cobia, especially in the spring or autumn, which is also when pompano run along the beaches.

Large spotted seatrout can provide some fantastic action along subtropical and warm-temperate beaches in late summer and autumn. The trout hang out in deeper sections of troughs and dart out to grab small fish that pass along the edge of bars or even right next to shore. Unlike their green- or bronze-back coloration when they are feeding in the grass beds, these trout have a radiant pale silver coloration that allows them to blend in well to the background of light-colored sand.

Some beaches that are consistently exposed to moderate surf have slightly different profiles. Rather than slope evenly from the backshore into the water, these beaches often have a steep, 1- to 2-foot drop-off marking the low-tide line. The shallow sandy bottom then tends to slope gradually deeper away from shore. Although it might seem the least likely of places to find gamefish, this little ledge at the edge of a beach can be a gamefish hot spot.

## Applying What You've Learned

### Summer Beachside Snook

In summer in the subtropics, snook will cruise back and forth along beach edges in search of mojarras, scaled sardines, juvenile permit, small gulf kingfish, mullet, other small fish, mole crabs, and other prey unlucky enough to cross their path. I think the edge gives snook a place to corner the small fish, but the safety of deeper water is easily reachable. Although these snook are available along these beaches throughout summer, the fishing is best around new and full moons.

New and full moons are the best times because snook gather along beaches during summer not only to take advantage of abundant prey fish but also to spawn. In southern Florida, snook spawn in aggregations in or near passes and inlets from late afternoon into evening, with an apparent peak in activity near new and full moons. All that spawning takes a lot of energy, and beachside snook can be especially voracious as they replenish their energy stores.

As you might expect from a species famous for its preference for the shade of mangroves, snook along beaches seem to be most aggressive in the low light of dawn and dusk. I've spent many dawns searching for large snook along south Florida's outer beaches near inlets and passes. In the early dawn, snook give themselves away as they chase baitfish onto the beach or explode through a school of sardines. As the sun lights the water, this becomes a sight-fishing opportunity. Depending on the action, it may be sufficient to stand in a spot with the sun at my back and wait for the snook to cruise by. If the fish are more scattered or not as much on the move, I slowly walk along the beach and cast to fish that I spot cruising the shoreline or hanging in troughs between bars. Regardless of whether I stick to one spot or move along the beach, I'm sighting and casting to snook within a couple of feet of the shoreline.

*Sight-fishing for snook along sandy beaches can be great fun and on calm days is perfect for fishing with a six-weight rod. Identical strategies can be used for striped bass along many northern beaches.*

White deceivers or similar flies of 3 inches or less are the best bets. Make sure you take a handful because the rough mouth and sharp gill plates of snook will cause a number of break-offs in a typical day. Similar-size, all-white Clouser Minnows and white Woolly Buggers are also good imitations of the small, silver-colored fish eaten by snook along these beaches. Though these small flies produce the most action, I always pack a couple of larger flies in my fly box. Large, all-white half-and-halfs, tied on 2/0 hooks, do a decent job of imitating the small gulf kingfish that live along these beaches and are eagerly eaten by larger snook. Regardless of the fly I choose, a slow retrieve is best. Lead a cruising fish by a few feet and twitch the fly to get the fish's attention. A short strip or two may spur a following fish into action. A resting fish will require a cast just beyond the fish and a slow strip of the fly across the fish's field of vision. In either scenario, short casts of 30 to 40 feet are usually sufficient.

## GAMEFISH PREY OF SUBTROPICAL AND WARM-TEMPERATE BEACHES

As I'm sure you've surmised by now, the mostly open sand bottom adjacent to beaches means that potential gamefish prey are always on the move or burrow into the bottom for refuge. Mole crabs and swimming crabs are tops on the list of crustaceans that live along beaches. Silver-hued, mobile fishes are potential prey as well.

### Crustaceans

#### *Crabs*

##### *Mole Crabs*

Mole crabs (family Hippidae), also known as sand crabs, are oval in shape, generally tan, brown and white, or gray (often with a purplish hue) in color, and grow to 1 inch long. These crabs live in the swash zone and use the wash from waves to move up and down the beach. They ride the wash either up or down the beach and then burrow into the sand to feed on detritus among the sand grains. As you might expect, these crabs are most vulnerable to gamefish when they are moving from place to place. The common mole crab *(Emerita talpoida)* occurs throughout the Atlantic coast, the Cuban *(Hippa cubensis)* and Puerto Rican *(Emerita portoricensis)* mole crabs are limited to Florida and the Caribbean, and the purple surf crab *(Albunea gibbesii)* ranges southward from North Carolina. In addition, Webster's mole crab *(Lepidopa websteri)* is found in the surf zone from North Carolina southward. Overall, mole crabs tend to be more abundant along Atlantic than Gulf beaches because these beaches typically have more wave energy. Mole crabs are a favorite prey of pompano, which tend to travel the surf zone in large, loosely arranged schools, and of gulf *(Menticirrhus littoralis)*, southern *(Menticirrhus americanus)*, and northern kingfish *(Menticirrhus saxatilis)*. Pompano are migratory and spend their summers along the North Carolina coast, often remaining in small home ranges during the summer season. In autumn, pompano head south to Florida and return northward in spring, providing great sport to beach-going fly anglers in the process. Subadult and young adult red drum also search out mole crabs along sandy beaches.

Anglers are often surprised when I tell them that snook and striped bass also eat mole crabs along sandy beaches. In fact, during research of snook along sandy beaches of southwest Florida, we found that a large portion of snook we captured had recently eaten mole crabs. In some cases, individual fish had eaten ten or more mole crabs.

#### *Swimming Crabs*

Numerous species of swimming crabs also inhabit coastal beaches. Among the most common along the Atlantic coast, lady crabs *(Ovalipes ocellatus)* are limited to the warm-temperate beaches north of Georgia. Lady crabs are common just outside the surf zone, often lie buried in the sand waiting to ambush passing prey, and feed mostly at night. Their sand-colored carapace is covered with dark, purplish dots, so they are well camouflaged on the open sand bottom. The related speckled crab *(Arenaeus cribrarius)* follows a similar ambush strategy but tends to be more active, is tan to gray with white or yellow spots, and is present along warm-temperate and subtropical beaches. Of course, the ubiquitous blue crab (or other members of the *Callinectes* genus) is also present along low-energy beaches.

### ***Shrimp***

#### *Ghost Shrimp*

In fine-grained sand below the low-tide line on moderate- to low-energy beaches, you may find burrows of ghost shrimp. These shrimp are clear to white in color and can reach 3 inches in length.

## Prey Fishes

As you might expect along sandy shorelines, baitfish and other small fishes dominate gamefish diets. Red drum, spotted seatrout, and other species that munch on crabs and shrimp in other habitats will continue to do so along beaches; they'll be especially tuned in to the movements of these small fishes. Moreover, the larger members of these gamefish species tend to focus more on eating baitfish than on eating crustaceans, so it pays to focus on deceivers, Clousers, and other fish-imitating flies. So, although there are certainly times for crab and shrimp patterns, fish-imitating streamers are the dominant flies in a beach angler's fly box.

Many of the prey fish that occur along beaches are the same as or closely related to species already discussed in previous chapters. And although the particular species of fish eaten by beach-going gamefish will vary by location and time of year, most of these prey fish are similar enough in size and appearance that they can be imitated with the same flies used to imitate baitfish in other habitats. The only difference may be that when living along sandy beaches, many of these prey fish will be pale to match their surroundings and may have little or no coloration, so all-white flies are usually my first choice.

### Herrings (Family Clupeidae)

Scaled sardines may be the most common large herrings (family Clupeidae) along subtropical and warm-temperate beaches from early summer through autumn. Threadfin herring *(Opisthonema oglinum)* are also common warm-weather prey along beaches but tend to stay a bit farther off the beach than the sardines and can be especially abundant in the autumn. Other herrings found along beaches, especially in the autumn, include Spanish sardine *(Sardinella aurita)* and gulf menhaden *(Brevoortia patronus)* in the Gulf of Mexico. Round scad *(Decapterus punctatus)*, members of the jack family, are occasionally found along the beach as well but are usually in deeper water. Present along warm-temperate beaches in late summer and autumn are blueback herring *(Alosa aestivalis)*.

### Mullet

Although both striped and white mullet are found along sandy beaches, the white mullet is the species of legendary autumn runs. Juvenile white mullet flood out of their summer estuarine hideaways in the autumn, heading south. After you've seen and heard the chaos and carnage of large gamefish (tarpon, sharks, cobia, snook, red drum) feeding on schools of panicked mullet right along the beach, the image will be burned into your mind forever.

### *Anchovies and Silversides*

Anchovies and silversides, collectively often referred to as glass minnows, can also be common along low to moderate-energy beaches, especially in the autumn. Common species are dusky anchovy *(Anchoa lyolepis),* bay anchovy *(Anchoa mitchilli),* striped anchovy *(Anchoa hepsetus),* and, north of Florida on the Atlantic coast, Atlantic silverside *(Menidia menidia).* It's an amazing sight to see large tarpon rolling through schools of glass minnows that have been pushed up against the beach. The glass minnows scatter in all directions as tarpon, mouths open, roll through panicked baitfish in what looks like slow motion. Cast to the edges of the schools and the surrounding waters rather than into the school of glass minnows to give your fly a chance at getting noticed amid the commotion.

### *Mojarra*

Numerous species of mojarra, including mottled mojarra *(Eucinostomus lefroyi)* and silver jenny *(Eucinostomus gula),* are common along sandy shorelines in summer. As in earlier discussions of mojarras, species vary among locations but are similar in size and shape.

### *Miscellaneous Fishes*

On more-protected beaches, like those outside St. Andrew Bay, near Panama City beach, you may find small fishes most often associated with estuaries, including gulf killifish *(Fundulus grandis),* longnose killifish *(Fundulus similis),* and spot *(Leiostomus xanthurus).*

Gulf and northern kingfish are common along sandy beaches and serve a double purpose: Larger fish are good gamefish targets with small shrimp patterns; smaller individuals are prey for gamefish.

Finally, as in other habitats, spring and summer bring juvenile fishes to beaches. Pompano, permit, various species of jacks, yellowtail snapper, triggerfish, and filefish are among the species represented by juveniles during the warm months.

### Applying What You've Learned

#### Seasonality and the Autumn Feeding Frenzy

In many beach locations, gamefish can be found throughout the year, but late spring through autumn are the best times of year, with autumn perhaps the best of all, in warm-temperate and subtropical regions. Many of the gamefish found on beaches in these regions, such as Spanish mackerel, tarpon, pompano, bluefish, and jacks, are most abundant during the warmer months.

Other species that are resident throughout the year, such as red drum and spotted seatrout, can be found along beaches throughout the year, but even these species are most common in beach habitats from late spring to autumn. For example, as the water warms in March and April, schools of small red drum cruise the beaches of the Chandeleur Islands, and spotted seatrout show up in number in April. Elsewhere in Louisiana, many of the red drum and spotted seatrout that roamed the backcountry lakes as the water warmed in spring will move to the cooler water along beaches if the shallow backcountry gets too warm in midsummer.

But autumn is the most exciting season along warm-temperate and subtropical beaches. Autumn is when many fish that have been living, feeding, and growing in coastal waters all summer gather in schools to migrate south or offshore to wait out the cold winter months. The migrating schools of prey fish attract large numbers of gamefish, and the feeding can be frenzied. For example, white mullet leave the protected coastal estuaries where they've summered and head southward along beaches. Tales of broken rods and worn-out anglers from the autumn run of mullet along the Atlantic coast beaches are legend and are well-founded. Tarpon, ladyfish, snook, crevalle jacks, mackerel, red drum, shark, barracuda, and other gamefish take part in this free-for-all. In fact, the southward autumn migration of tarpon from the Carolinas coincides perfectly with the white mullet migration.

My friend Bob Miller grew up along Florida's southeast coast, and he has told me some amazing stories of the autumn run. He's encountered schools of mullet so large that they stretched across acres of water along and just off the beach. Amazingly, the gamefish were often so abundant and feeding so aggressively that he often hooked a fish on the first cast. He said he frequently lamented the long fight after he hooked into twenty-pound crevalle jack. During the twenty minutes it took to land that one jack, he was surrounded by boils and wakes of other gamefish that continued feeding along the beach. I know the gamefish are plentiful when he tells me of losing a hooked fish because another gamefish ran through and broke his leader.

Bob also related to me a story of a beachside tarpon-feeding frenzy, but this occurred in the spring. He was fishing along the beach, hoping to find gamefish feeding on the spring run of sardines. About a half-mile down the beach he heard a tremendous roar and could see commotion in the water just off the beach. He ran to the spot and found 6-foot tarpon that had corralled a school of sardines against the beach. He said the tarpon were feeding in a near-continuous explosion, with water and fish flying everywhere. Although his fly rod was not heavy enough to land such large tarpon, he cast into the fray. It took only that single cast for him to hook up. After it was hooked, the tarpon headed offshore. Bob hung on as long as he could before grabbing the reel and breaking the fish off at the leader with only a few feet of backing left on the reel.

*Schools of anchovies (the dark water in the bottom half of the photo) and other baitfish often collect along beaches, especially in the autumn in the warm-temperate and subtropical regions. These large schools of bait always attract gamefish.*

*When baitfish aren't evident, birds will often show you where the baitfish are being preyed upon by gamefish.*

There are plenty of examples of other gamefish marauding along sandy beaches. Throughout their range, red drum move into coastal waters in autumn and feed voraciously as they get ready to spawn and as they are between spawning events, and they will even stick around after spawning until water temperatures drop and baitfish move off. Spotted seatrout also prowl beaches looking to bulk up after exhausting themselves during a summer of spawning. Bluefish and Spanish mackerel feed with reckless abandon on tightly packed schools of baitfish.

The barrier island beaches of Texas yield their best beach fishing of the year each autumn as monster spotted seatrout, red drum, crevalle jack, ladyfish, tarpon, and other gamefish gorge on schools of mullet, glass minnows (anchovies), and herrings attempting to slip through the gauntlet. The first light of dawn can bring the best action of the day, so it pays to be early. If you arrive late and miss it, you'll have all winter to regret it. After the sun is up, you may find that jacks are the most active gamefish during periods of high sun. Tarpon that fed in early morning may return after light starts to drop in late afternoon, so don't tire yourself out too much on the jacks. These are probably tarpon that have spent much of the summer feeding on menhaden in offshore waters and have moved inshore in autumn to feed on schools of dusky and bay anchovies and then schools of finger mullet gathering to head south.

The best strategies for this autumn frenzy? First, be there early. The first light of day tends to provide the best action. Dusk can be almost as good. Second, take binoculars and occasionally search the shoreline for birds, the splashes of feeding fish, or the dark shadows of tightly packed schools of baitfish. Third, look for troughs, exposed sandbars, or dead-end sand embayments that form in the longshore currents because these are great collecting places for baitfish. Gamefish search out these dead-ends, so even if baitfish aren't present when you arrive, you might intercept a gamefish coming in for a look. Fourth, given the choice, incoming tide is best, especially early in the tide. Fifth, pack plenty of extra leader, some wire tippet, and maybe even an extra fly rod because the variety of gamefish that takes part in this autumn frenzy can challenge an angler who is ready for only the basics, and it may be a long walk back to the truck.

## THE TROPICS

Beaches of the Caribbean and tropical Florida differ somewhat from beaches of the Atlantic and Gulf coasts. The processes of waves and currents are similar, but the type of sand (mostly calcareous), the protection afforded by coral reefs, and the fact that currents on Caribbean islands are due almost entirely to wind and waves make Caribbean beaches a little different.

While living in the Caribbean, I did some wade-guiding on weekends. Most of the anglers who hired me were from the northeastern region of the United States, and most of their saltwater-fishing experience had been along ocean beaches from New England to North Carolina. I quickly learned that my first task was to teach these anglers that shoreline fishing on most Caribbean islands is unlike fishing the beaches of their home fishing grounds and that fishing the habitats found along tropical shorelines would require an understanding of these habitats and a different approach than they were used to.

## EXPOSED BEACHES

Beaches in the Caribbean are of two general types—exposed and protected. Exposed beaches are usually on the windward coast and are areas of high wave energy. They are made of coarse sand, coral rubble, shell fragments, rocks, or various combinations of these materials—the stronger the wave activity, the coarser the makeup of the beach. The slope of exposed beaches is often steep, and because so much sand is moved by wave energy and associated currents, the diverse bottom community that is often found in more-protected areas is replaced by a short list of hardier species. In these respects, exposed beaches of the Caribbean resemble beaches along the Atlantic coast where most of my visitors had prior fishing experience.

Because relatively few bottom-dwelling (benthic) species are able to tolerate these high-energy environments, baitfish dominate the list of gamefish prey on exposed beaches. Higher-energy beaches tend not to hold schools of baitfish close to shore, except perhaps during calm periods. Instead, the small fish congregate just outside the surf zone. The numerous species of anchovies and herrings that make up these schools are easily imitated with streamers, which fool the schools of jacks that regularly cruise these shorelines. Tarpon are common visitors to exposed beaches but tend not to hang around for extended periods. Instead, tarpon appear and disappear at irregular intervals, even if baitfish remain, following a pattern I have yet to figure out. In contrast, after they find a spot they like, snook tend to stay put for a while and prefer murky over clear water. Just inside the edge of clear and murky water can be a hot spot for Caribbean beach snook.

Fishing on exposed beaches can be difficult due to high winds and surf, so choose your days according to conditions. Days when winds are calm or blowing offshore and when ocean swells are negligible are when fishing exposed beaches is most enjoyable and safest and when gamefish come closest to the beach. Methods for fishing exposed beaches in the Caribbean are the same as described for Atlantic beaches.

## Applying What You've Learned

### Tarpon Blitz

An experience with beach-blitzing tarpon when I lived in the Virgin Islands provides a taste of what can happen if you find yourself in the right place at the right time along an exposed beach on a Caribbean island.

In June and again in January, baitfish (sprat and fry, local names for types of herring and glass minnows, respectively) can often be found schooled up against exposed beaches around St. Croix. I once used a castnet to catch some of the sprat, which were full of eggs and milt and thus appeared to be schooled together to spawn. Although these fish appear to be spawning, there doesn't seem to be a pattern to where they might be found. The locations of these schools change from season to season and from year to year.

I found that the most-efficient way to search for schools of baitfish under attack is to look for brown pelicans. I usually did this by driving to good vantage points and using binoculars to scan the shoreline—diving pelicans were sure signs of baitfish schooled below. A lone pelican diving in an area usually meant scattered baitfish, as did a few pelicans flying along a shoreline occasionally diving into the water. Neither was reason to grab the gear and start fishing. What I was searching for was a handful or more of pelicans diving repeatedly in the same small area. This invariably meant that a large school of sprat or fry was being corralled by large fish from below and forced close enough to the surface to attract pelicans. Sometimes, the pelicans were so full that they took some time off, but the sight of a half-dozen or more pelicans resting on the water close to shore signaled the presence of baitfish just as sure as if they were diving.

After I was on the scene, I usually watched the diving pelicans for a few minutes to figure out which type of baitfish lay below and thus which fly to tie on. If, after diving into the water, a pelican quickly tipped up its beak and swallowed the baitfish, I knew the fish were large, probably sprat. If, on the other hand, a pelican hung its beak to slowly drain the water from its pouch before tipping and swallowing, I knew the baitfish were small, probably fry. This is because the sprat are large enough that a pelican can open its beak an inch or so to let the water quickly drain, but the fry are so small that the pelican must drain the water from an almost closed beak. This behavior makes for a quick way to figure out the dominant bait.

After a school of baitfish is found, it's a good bet there are large fish along the outer fringes feasting on the trapped baitfish. Barracuda, various jacks, and snappers are the usual predators on these baitfish, but occasionally groups of tarpon will invade the scene. A deceiver (when sprat are the bait of choice) and Clouser Minnow (when fry are on tap) are all that is needed on most occasions.

The beach near our apartment was part of a long, crescent-shaped bay with coral-covered rocky points at each end and sandy shoreline in between. Palm trees and seagrapes fringed the back of the beach but were sparsely located and thus provided little shade. The road to the apartment passed up and over a hill, which provided a view of much of the bay. On my way out in the morning and then again returning home in the evening, I usually slowed my truck to take a peek. One evening in June as I drove over the hill toward home, I saw pelicans diving off one of the points. Not one pelican, or even a few, but a dozen or more. Many were diving into the water just outside the line of small surf that was breaking on shore. Others were sitting in the water, either at rest or just too full to fly. I sped home to grab my gear.

I arrived at the beach at about 6:30 and began the five-minute walk to the point. The pelicans were still working the school of baitfish, flying up and diving back into the water as quickly as they could manage. As I neared the point, I thought that prospects looked good for some fun with a few big barracuda or maybe some hungry jacks.

As I got closer, I could see that the pelicans were making quick work of the fish they caught—quickly tipping their beaks and swallowing the fish before lurching from the water for another pass. Sprat! Just the same, I made a couple of throws with my castnet and netted a few fish to make sure of their size. They were large, up to 6 inches. As I pulled in the net after the second throw, I saw an unmistakable dorsal fin of a twenty-five-pound tarpon as it rolled through the baitfish about 40 feet off the beach. I threw the castnet up onto the beach and grabbed my fly rod.

My first two casts were to the deep water just beyond the line of frothing surf. There were no takers. I put the third cast right where I had seen the fish roll when I was throwing the castnet—in the middle of the wild water, where waves rolling in collided with the outgoing wash of previous waves in a fury of white foam. This is no place for a fly, I thought.

The fly hit the water and bounced in the chaotic waves and froth for a few seconds as I hurriedly stripped slack out of the fly line snaking over the white foam. Then the churning water erupted in an explosion. I didn't see the fish, just the spray of white water erupting from the roiled surface. The line went tight in my hand, and I instinctively set the hook with a strip strike. The hook found its mark, sending the tarpon airborne. It was strange, but because of the "washing machine" effect of water over the reef, the tarpon never really landed in the water but rather half-rode the bubbling foam and half-launched itself again and again. Eventually, its leaps carried it away from shore and into deeper water. After the fish finally was back in the water, I set the hook twice more. With that, the tarpon headed for deeper water at breakneck speed and then jumped three more times, about 80 yards away.

I suddenly realized my situation: I stood waist deep in the surf, with larger waves breaking at chest level 10 feet out before boiling around my midriff and tugging at me from behind as the water rushed back out over the reef. The backing peeled off the eight-weight reel with amazing speed and disappeared into the white foam before coming into view again outside the surf zone. The line sliced through cresting waves before following the fish into open water beyond the reef.

The fish slowed, and I finally turned it about 100 yards out. Slowly, I began to work the fish back in toward shore. Then came the stalemate—I took in some line, the fish took out a little line.

Just as I thought things were going well, the fish burst toward open water again, as if it had just been hooked for the first time. I briefly lost sight of the fish as it passed behind a wave. My fly line disappeared into the wave's face as the wave rolled toward shore. Then for a brief moment, as it passed through the next wave, I could see the fish clearly. It was suspended motionless for a brief moment as the wave rose to full height before folding forward in crashing white foam. Each large scale on the tarpon flashed silver in the dimming light, the fish framed by the abyssal azure glow emanating from the depths.

And then it was gone. The hook had pulled. As I reeled in the fly line and backing I felt the adrenaline shakes that so often come with big fish that are lost.

I reeled in the line to check the fly and leader, but as I got the fly line to the rod tip, I had another strike. This time I never saw the fish—it never jumped, just headed for deep water at breathtaking speed. I never had a chance. I was unable to set the hook with the fish heading away so fast, and I had no chance at turning this fish, which was even stronger than the last. I held onto my rod and just watched. And then, like the first fish, the line slackened, and it was gone. This time, the tippet had parted.

Some light still remained, so I tied on a new tippet and fly and headed back to my spot on the point. Amazingly, the action continued until it was too dark to see. As darkness painted everything in black ink, I felt my way shoreward, gathered my castnet and fly box, and started home. The stiff breeze had dropped with nightfall, but the surf still raced up the beach in fits of hissing foam.

I was sore and tired and had no fish to show for it. But I was happy. I'd been in the middle of a tarpon blitz and had it all to myself. I'd hooked who knows how many fish and felt the raw power of them all. None of them jumped quite like the first one, but I saw the reflection of a silver-hued sunset and heard the rattling gill plates again and again as the fish jumped through the dwindling light.

I returned to this spot each evening after work for the next five days. With each evening the number of pelicans dropped, and the sight of tarpon rolling through the surf was less frequent. But on each occasion I was treated to feeding tarpon—not quite as chaotic as the first evening but still four or five hookups each time. Then one evening there was just one pelican diving, and I saw no tarpon rolling. I caught a couple of barjacks and lost a barracuda, which are usually fun in their own right but not the same after the tarpon blitz. A half-dozen throws of the castnet netted only a handful of sprat. Most of the bait was gone, and the tarpon with them.

## PROTECTED BEACHES

In contrast to exposed beaches, protected beaches in the tropics are sheltered from waves by an offshore barrier reef or wide shallows, tend to be protected from winds, have more-stable bottoms than exposed beaches, and tend to hold more gamefish prey. The stability often allows the establishment and growth of seagrass and scattered mangroves that support diverse communities discussed in previous chapters. Even if seagrass isn't abundant, the stable sandy bottom supports a rich prey community.

Protected beaches often have lush seagrass beds ending right at the shoreline. As you will remember from the chapter on seagrass, seagrass provides fantastic habitat for fish, shrimp, crabs, clams, and many other prey items for gamefish. Healthy seagrass beds that reach the shoreline bring this productive habitat right to the feet of shoreline anglers. Although these aren't the kind of beaches that resorts prefer, these types of shorelines are fantastic for fly fishing and provide excellent habitat for gamefish and the prey they rely on for food.

In areas with shallow, sloping bottoms, you'll often find a thin strip of sand between the beach and the beginning of the grass bed, especially along semiprotected beaches with small but consistent surf. The lower edge of this strip of sand indicates the low-water mark and the area where the small surf stirs the sand. In many cases, minor wave action has carved out a slight depression in this sand strip, and this slightly deeper indentation can hold baitfish, juvenile fish, and crabs.

In general, the very shallow seagrass beds that abut beaches have a less-diverse community of organisms than will deeper grass beds and often fewer resident fish species. Mobile prey such as swimming crabs and small fish may be more important prey items for gamefish along these shallow, grassy shorelines. This is in part because the shallower areas can be harsh environments. For example, the shallows can become very warm and very low in oxygen during calm, summer periods and during extremely low tides can be completely exposed to air. These phenomena create intolerable conditions for many species. Species that are best able to tolerate these conditions or can easily move in and out of these areas as conditions allow are best suited for these habitats. Prey types that are of interest to fly anglers include swimming crabs, hermit crabs, mojarras, and mullet.

Examine the landward portion of the beach for signs of land hermit crabs—parallel walking tracks on either side of a drag mark (from the heavy shell they carry on their back) is evidence of hermit crabs. Other crabs on the beach—land crabs and ghost crabs—leave only the walking tracks. The land-dwelling hermit crabs will sometimes forage along the water and will search the shoreline looking for new shells to move into. They are most active at night but can be found lingering near the water's edge at dawn. A permit or bonefish foraging along a shoreline may fall for a well-placed fly imitating a hermit crab out of its shell. In addition, these same shorelines are home to marine hermit crabs, which may also be on the menu of some of our favorite gamefish.

Barjacks, bonefish, small snappers, and barracuda are the most common gamefish on these shallow shoreline grass flats, but during higher tides (especially at dawn or dusk) larger fish may venture up to the shorelines as well. Large barracuda sometimes lie in wait in depressions in the sand just off the shoreline and will make a meal out of needlefish and half-beaks that cruise along these shallow shorelines. These large barracuda are especially wary, so it's important that you sight and cast to the fish from at least 60 feet away. Usually, you get only a well-placed cast or two before the barracuda realizes something is amiss and moves off.

## Applying What You've Learned

### Strategy for Fishing Protected Beaches

My favorite strategy for these shallow, grass-lined beaches is to walk slowly along the beach, with the sun at my back, looking for bonefish and other gamefish that are cruising along the shoreline searching for food. Sometimes, fish will meander between the strip of sand and the seagrass, and at other times they will remain over one or the other bottom for long distances. Walking along the beach allows me to be higher up off the water, so I can see approaching fish better (and from farther away) than if I was wading. I am also able to backtrack along the beach to get a second shot at a fish that refused or didn't see my initial offering. By stooping to keep a low profile and backtracking along the beach, I once was able to try three different flies on a group of three bonefish before I finally got a take on a large crab pattern.

Protected shorelines provide great opportunities for using lighter-weight fly rods. My favorite rod for fishing protected beaches is a 9-foot six-weight. It is often a long way to any substantial structure, such as reefs or rocks, along these beaches, so even if you connect with a strong fish, it is unlikely to run into structure and break off. And because you will often be casting small, lightly weighted flies, a six-weight rod is perfectly matched to the flies and conditions and makes for an easy day of casting.

## SEMIPROTECTED BEACHES

Whereas some protected beaches are glass calm under most conditions but receive strong surf multiple times a year, others are exposed to waves during periods of high wind or experience a small but consistent surf. These semiprotected beaches tend to support even higher abundances of prey than do fully protected beaches, in part because the occasional wave energy that washes these beaches also mixes the water column and keeps the bottom waters from becoming depleted of oxygen. This maintains a diverse benthic community. So, as long as the wave energy isn't so great that it harms the adjacent bottom habitats, semiprotected beaches can offer the most varied fly-fishing opportunities. This does not imply that low-energy areas are not healthy ecosystems, only that a wider variety of prey species is able to take advantage of semiprotected areas.

The bottom quickly slopes off some semiprotected beaches, either to a deeper grass bed or to open sand bottom. Because sight-fishing is tough in these conditions, and it is doubtful that you will sight and cast to a fish that is feeding on the deep bottom,

*Although typical of photos in tourist brochures, these beaches are great places for fishing.*

flies that mimic moving prey, such as streamer imitations of baitfish or juvenile reef fish, are most appropriate. Species that cruise the deep grass beds along sandy beaches include barjacks, horse-eye jacks, permit, bonefish, barracuda, snappers, and tarpon. Barjacks and horse-eye jacks cruise the shoreline on hit-and-run attacks on baitfish schools or in search of small fish that wander too far from the safety of the seagrass. Small barracuda will lie motionless in the vicinity of small patch reefs or rocks that are inhabited by small fish and take advantage of any fish that lets down its guard. Permit and bonefish cruise the shoreline in search of crabs, shrimp, or clams that lie hidden in the seagrass. Bonefish will also take advantage of a vulnerable fish (whether a baitfish, juvenile reef fish, or a small goby) as prey. In fact, bonefish will feed on rather large baitfish (sardines large enough to be imitated with a size 2/0 deceiver, for example) along these shorelines.

Along semiprotected sandy beaches with small surf and a sandy bottom, gamefish will often forage just below the drop-off at the shoreline. They will also ride the small surf up into the swash zone in search of prey such as small crabs, shrimp, and small fish. Small shrimp or baitfish imitations, like a Gotcha, small Clouser, or Crazy Charlie, are good flies for this type of fishing.

## GAMEFISH PREY OF CARIBBEAN BEACHES

### Mole Crabs

A couple of interesting prey species occur on semiprotected Caribbean beaches with consistent wave action. If wave action is not too rough, gamefish (including palometa, bonefish, permit, and snappers) will cruise along the beach, riding the wash in and out, and readily slurping up mole crabs. Common species of mole crabs in the Caribbean include Cuban mole crab, common mole crab, Puerto Rican mole crab, and the purple surf crab. There are several mole crab fly patterns made of wool, chenille, spun deer hair, or a combination of these materials and weighted to ride on the bottom. Small, heavily weighted, tan Clousers are also productive. It is rare that I use a sinking line when fishing shorelines in the Caribbean, but dredging the bottom with a mole crab pattern on an exposed beach is one of those rare occasions. A sinking line with a short leader will allow you to fish the fly so that it bounces along the bottom, making a good imitation of a mole crab.

## Clams

I hesitated to include this brief section. After all, clams aren't really something that we typically imitate with flies. And how would you fish a clam fly? But then I thought: Why not? There are a lot of creative fly tiers out there who just might give it a shot.

Caribbean coquina clams *(Donax denticulata)* may be the only clam with the potential for imitation with a fly, although I am not aware of any successful attempts to date. Caribbean coquina clams are small (up to 1 inch long), triangular in shape, and vary in color (from white to purple). They actually move from place to place in the intertidal zone of beaches—they emerge from the sand, wash up or down the beach in the surf, and then reburrow in the sand. They are best imitated by a fly that mimics them on the move. At times, bonefish and permit stomachs are full of these clams.

## Baitfish

If you are lucky, you may come upon schools of baitfish moving back and forth along beaches, especially in larger embayments. Often, smaller fish species (like anchovies or dwarf herring) will be closer to shore, and larger species (like herring) will be farther off the beach. However, this pattern may change depending upon how active predators have been. For example, I have seen schools of large sprat packed tightly against the shoreline when tarpon are present. Finding these baitfish schools is not always easy because they blend in very well with their surroundings; they are often well below the surface and somewhat scattered if they are not being actively pursued by predators. Often, these unmolested baitfish schools appear as shadows over the bottom.

If baitfish schools are near the surface and packed tightly, it's a good bet that gamefish are not far away, and it might be only a matter of time before the action begins. Even if no predators are obvious, it's still worth a few casts because predators sometimes stay in the vicinity of baitfish schools even if they are not obviously feeding.

I like to walk large, semiprotected bays looking for signs of baitfish. If I find baitfish, this is where I concentrate my efforts. If there are no obvious signs of baitfish, I stop along the beach at intervals of 30 yards or so and blind-cast for a few minutes, hoping to pick up cruising fish. The most common catch along these shorelines is jacks, although palometa (a member of the jack family and relative of the permit), small barracuda, cero mackerel, and various types of snappers may also grab the fly. Although it is common to find jacks and barracuda eager to take a fly from midmorning to midafternoon, morning and evening are generally best for tarpon.

## TROPICAL BEACHROCK SHORELINES

Many Caribbean shorelines consist of hard limestone pavement, called beachrock, which is the solidified remains of old sand and coral reefs. One type of beachrock shoreline is low lying and may be intermixed with sandy beach. These shorelines are good for bonefish. On the seaward side, beachrock often drops abruptly into the water. These locations often harbor jacks. This drop may be only 1 foot or may be a few feet, and in deeper spots an undercut has usually been eroded by wave action. At first glance, it doesn't look like great fish habitat, but if the drop-off is deep enough, this undercut can provide shelter to numerous juvenile reef fish and gamefish. With careful examination, you may find small fish in the tidepools along beachrock shorelines, which can give you an indication of appropriate sizes and colors of flies.

Undercut beachrock habitat seems to support more small fishes when it's adjacent to seagrass because beachrock provides

*Rocky shorelines tend to harbor a diversity of prey and thus are good places to search for bonefish and permit, especially on rising tides.*

shelter next to a good foraging area. But leaving the shelter of beachrock to forage in adjacent seagrass carries risks for small fish because jacks, palometa, snappers, barracuda, and other predators are always on the prowl along these shorelines. In areas that have deeper drop-offs (a few feet or more) subadult and adult snappers and groupers may set up residence in holes or crevices and will charge from their shelters if prey swims close by. These small snappers and groupers are experts at charging out to grab a fly and getting back into their shelters before an angler can react, resulting in lost flies. Other gamefish will take advantage of invertebrate communities that can be found here. For example, permit and triggerfish can be found feeding on small urchins that seem to inhabit almost every crevice of some beachrock shorelines.

Although beachrock that is bordered by a sand bottom doesn't support nearly as many small fishes, it does provide a source of shelter on an otherwise open bottom, so small fish will use this habitat as shelter as well. Jacks and palometa are among the most common gamefish found here, but you will also find snook, bonefish, and small tarpon. Beachrock that is bordered by rubble is a popular spot for barjacks and blue runners because the rubble also provides habitat for small fishes. You might also find permit rummaging along beachrock edges or in nearby rubble in search of reef crabs, shrimp, and urchins.

## TROPICAL ROCKY SHORELINES

In some locations, you might find that a rocky shoreline drops dramatically into the ocean. Steep shorelines often occur as points at either end of a sandy beach or may extend for a considerable distance along a coast. The deeper drop-offs usually support fringing coral reefs and thus are home to reef fishes of all shapes and sizes and provide shoreline anglers access to larger fish that inhabit deeper water. In fact, these steep-sloped beachrock shorelines may provide shore-bound anglers their best chance of access to large coral reef fishes. Of course, jacks of various sorts (barjacks, blue runners, horse-eye jacks, and crevalle jacks) can be found cruising the edges of these steep drop-offs, and these jacks are often large, as are the barracuda. Snappers and groupers are usually resident on the reefs below these shorelines but are often well hidden within the reef's many crevices. You must coax them out of hiding by fishing your fly dangerously close to the sharp corals. Once hooked, these snappers and groupers will try their best to quickly get back into the safety of their crevices in the reef.

Fishing along steep-sloping beachrock calls for larger flies than you use along shallow beaches and on grass flats. All-white deceivers, white with blue or yellow backs, and chartreuse over white (size 2/0) will do well along these steep, rocky shorelines. Although the deep water may have you thinking of sinking fly lines, I suggest you stick with a floating line. The shoreline and adjacent reef are full of snags that seem to reach out and grab sinking lines, so when fishing these areas from shore, use a floating line. If gamefish are there and are hungry, they'll come up for the fly. Save the sinking line for fishing these locations from a boat. It's a good idea to use a stripping basket when fishing these areas as well.

These rocky coastlines are often in high-energy areas that can be pounded by heavy seas, so fish these areas with caution and only in calm conditions. In addition, the limestone and sedimentary rock that makes up these rocky shores is constantly being eroded, and loose rocks make for difficult footing. Erosion of limestone often creates sharp, craggy edges and crevices, which makes for tough walking and painful scrapes and bruises should you fall, so choose your steps carefully and wear strong-soled shoes. If you fish these locations from a boat, be sure to have only one person fishing while the other stays at the helm. The swells and surf can be tricky along these rocky shorelines, so it's important to be in full control of the boat at all times.

# 9

# Rubble and Sand Flats of the Tropics

I've included this short chapter to give fair coverage to two habitats that don't really fit in elsewhere but that provide great opportunities for sight-fishing in the tropics. Both habitats support sufficient numbers of prey to provide good feeding areas for bonefish, permit, snappers, and a host of other gamefish that ventures into these shallow habitats to feed at high tide. Sand flats have been well covered in numerous books on flats fishing, so I limit most of my discussion to prey of this habitat. I think that rubble flats, however, have been shortchanged, so I delve a bit deeper into details of rubble flats.

## RUBBLE FLATS OF THE BACKREEF

Rubble flats are my favorite shallow-water habitats of Caribbean islands because they are home to permit. Even if you don't find permit, you may find bonefish, jacks, barracuda, triggerfish, snappers, small sharks, and other gamefish on backreef rubble flats. The typical rubble flat lies behind a coral reef, offshore of which is deeper water. The rubble results from coral being broken away from the reef by large waves and deposited behind the reef in pieces. Eventually, seagrass and algae take hold in the backreef and spread into the lagoon, which results in a further slowing of currents and more deposition of debris and sand. In some spots, small colonies of finger coral grow among the seagrass. When everything works out just right, a shallow rubble flat results.

Water depth is the primary factor determining whether you will find gamefish on a rubble flat. The two factors most important in determining water depth on backreef rubble flats are tides and waves.

## TIDES

Tidal range in the Caribbean is generally narrow, the water level changing 1 foot or less through a normal tidal cycle. Even though water depth on rubble flats doesn't seem to change much with tides, gamefish respond to even minor tidal fluctuations just the same. On shallow flats, gamefish may be completely absent during low tide but may venture far onto the flat in search of food at high tide even thought the water depth changed only a few inches. In fact, I have seen this occur many times when I have been unable to detect any change in water depth between tides.

In general, fishing the backreef flats is best from the latter half of the incoming tide through the first hour or so of the outgoing tide. Backreef flats that hold good water throughout the tidal cycle are great places to search for fish at dawn and dusk, regardless of tides. I am not a big fan of early mornings, but when living in the Caribbean I frequently dragged myself out of bed before dawn to walk my favorite backreef flat at first light, especially when the tide was right.

## WAVES

Waves are almost constantly assaulting the outer edge of the reef that protects backreef rubble flats, and the surf pushes water onto the reef. Some of this water is deflected seaward by the coral reef, but some of the water passes over, through, or around the reef and onto the flat. If the reef is relatively deep, or the tide is particularly high, a considerable amount of water can push over the reef and create an appreciable current on the flat. In addition, the remnants of larger waves that crashed onto the reef can maintain some of their form and roll across the flat. Both the wave-induced current and the small waves continuing across the flat can dislodge prey hiding among the rubble, and feeding gamefish are usually quick to chase any dislodged prey.

In contrast, other reefs and flats are shallow, so under normal conditions there is little wave energy that continues over the reef onto the flat. These shallow, more-protected rubble flats tend to have less current and little wave action. Gamefish on these flats tend to be more deliberate in their movements and more wary of things out of the ordinary.

Whether the reef and flat are shallow or not, extended periods with strong surf can increase the water depth more than tides. The constant surf will actually push more water onto the flat than can escape back to sea through cuts and channels in the reef. This results in higher-than-normal water depths for the duration of the strong surf. Gamefish will often take advantage of these high-water periods just as if the high water were due to an extended high tide. The one caveat to this, however, is that the currents can actually become too strong, and gamefish will move off the flats entirely.

A bonus of the near-constant flushing of new water from the incoming waves is that backreef rubble flats rarely get as warm as nearby shallows with less water flow and thus can be good places to fish when other flats are too warm for permit and bonefish.

## STRATEGIES FOR FISHING FOR PERMIT ON RUBBLE FLATS

Permit like to come through the reef to access backreef rubble flats, often riding the energy of the remnant waves through the reef into the shallow water of the backreef. I have seen large fish swimming sideways to get through particularly shallow areas. This is important to know for two reasons. First, you can look for cuts in the reef that provide easier access from the deeper water outside the reef to the backreef and focus your efforts on the portions of the flat fed by these cuts. Second, when hooked, permit will probably hightail it right back through the reef into deeper water, and you should be prepared for this. Both points can influence your fly-fishing strategy.

After they are on the flat, permit will cruise the flat, often with their dorsal fin above the water, occasionally stopping to feed, digging their noses into the bottom and flipping their large forked tail into the air. Prey items for permit in these areas include small clams and snails, sea urchins, crabs, and mantis shrimp. After feeding along a stretch of flat, the fish usually head back through the reef to deeper water. In my experience, for any particular flat, permit will feed in the same general pattern. They will cross the reef in specific areas, travel along the flat in the same direction, and feed more actively on some sections of the flat than others, often at the same time in the tidal cycle. More intriguing, an individual permit's feeding pattern will often persist on the flat for a few days, so as long as you don't spook a fish while trying to catch it, you can return the next day and have a decent shot at finding the fish again under the same conditions.

After you've spotted a permit, the challenge is to present the fly close enough that the fish will see it but not so close that you spook the fish. When a permit is feeding on the bottom, its circle of vision is limited; permit seem to focus on a rather small section of bottom just in front of, or directly below, their swimming path, so getting the fly close is paramount. It's like casting to a teacup moving across the bottom. One option is to cast your fly directly in front of a slowly cruising fish. This approach requires a soft landing of the fly.

A second option is to anticipate the path of a cruising fish and cast the fly along this path, well ahead of the fish. As the fish approaches the fly, give it a small twitch. Although this approach works well over deeper seagrass, it can be tough to impossible on shallow rubble flats. Either the small waves rolling across the flat will move your fly out of the fish's path, or the fly will settle to the bottom and sink into one of the crevices among the rubble and is never seen by the fish. There is nothing quite as maddening as having to wait for a permit to pass by before wading over to unsnag a fly wedged in the rubble. Invariably, the fish moves on before the angler can regroup.

The third—and best—option is to cast directly in front of or to the side of a feeding, tailing fish, making sure the fly lands so that the waves and current carry the fly toward the permit. Let the fly drop to the bottom. If the permit doesn't react, give the fly a slight twitch and again let it rest. Remember that most of the prey you'll be imitating won't move much after they think they've been spotted. Instead, they try to hide in the bottom. Too much movement to a fly will often send a permit in the other direction. The challenge here is to keep the fly from becoming snagged among the rubble. Using lightly weighted or even unweighted flies is recommended.

For each of these options, small waves rolling across the flat or wave-induced currents can make fly presentation very difficult. Of course, there are times when the sea is calm, and the water surface is like a mirror, but the permit are very wary and easily spooked under these conditions. It's a challenging situation under all conditions, which is part of what makes fishing for permit on backreef flats so much fun.

If you are lucky enough to hook a permit, you will be faced with the challenge of keeping your leader in one piece as the fish heads to deeper water—probably directly through the coral reef. Of the numerous permit I've hooked on the fly on backreef flats, I've lost all to leaders that were cut on corals. The closest I came to landing one of these backreef permit was when the tippet parted as the leader came to the rod tip at the end of a twenty-minute battle.

So, you have two options. One strategy, albeit risky, is to clamp down on the drag and hope your line and rod hold as you prevent the fish from running through the reef. A second strategy is to give the fish plenty of line to run through the reef to deeper water and let the fish tire itself out. After the fish has tired, it will come to the surface, and you can work the fish back over the reef onto the flat. This is the stage of the fight where I have lost many fish, due either to bad luck or impatience on my part. So, take your time, even though all of your senses tell you to hurry.

## Applying What You've Learned

### Losing to a Permit

I began working my way across the flat as the light of the dawn sky slowly overtook the glow of the full moon. There was just enough wind to ripple the surface of the small surf rolling gently across the reef and spreading onto the flat. As I stripped out the usual 50 feet of fly line, I saw movement out of the corner of my eye. Glancing to my left, I saw the wake from a permit slowly cruising across the flat. I checked the knot connecting my urchin fly pattern to my tippet and false-cast to get fly line out of the rod tip. The permit tailed 40 feet away.

I made a false cast and then dropped the fly 4 feet in front of the fish. The unweighted fly dropped slowly to the bottom, but the fish moved off to the left without seeing the fly. I made another cast and placed the fly a little closer in front of the slowly moving fish. As the fly dropped, the fish surged quickly forward. I saw the end of the fly line jump and set the hook with a strip strike.

The fish gave a small head shake, then rubbed its nose in the bottom, then bulled 50 feet, rubbed its nose again, and surged another 50 feet. I followed after the fish the best I could, getting closer to the reef and all of its sharp coral with each step. Then suddenly, the fish had enough of the shallow water and bolted through the reef. The rod captured the vibration of the fly line scraping across the coral as it passed through the reef—fraying leader, shredding fly line, and testing the durability of the backing. I lightened the reel's drag and followed the path of the line as quickly as I could, carefully picking my way through the maze of mostly dead coral, freeing the line from the labyrinthine passage of the fish through the reef. All this time the fish was still heading seaward, by now into the deeper water outside the shallow reef. Then suddenly the line was free, the curve in the backing quickly straightened—the fish was still on!

I was able to apply some pressure as the fish slowed and finally stopped taking out line and began swimming back and forth in the deeper water. As the fish began to tire, its dorsal and tail fins broke the surface. I slowly gained the edge in the battle for backing and finally the fly line. I began to walk back to the flat, and the fish followed, tired now and finning at the surface.

As I guided the permit over the reef, the sight of shallow water gave it new energy, and the fish rubbed its nose on every coral head it passed. I worked the fish onto the flat many times, only to have it regain its strength and rush back into the reef.

Suddenly the situation worsened—after bulling its way into the reef once again, the fish refused my pressure pulling it back to the flat and began to swim back and forth in the reef. I followed the best I could, rod held high as I weaved my way through the coral. Then it happened: I lost track of my footing, tripped on a piece of broken coral, and went down: full body, flat on my face; rod, still in hand, fully submerged, an extension of my sprawled right arm. I was completely soaked. I regained my footing and brought the rod back into the upright position. Water gushed off my wide-brimmed hat and flooded from my soaked shirt. I couldn't believe it: The fish was still on! Then I felt a stinging pain in my legs. A quick glance down revealed a little blood, but it didn't look bad. My attention returned to the fish with even greater focus than before.

The fish continued to move back and forth across the reef, but this time I stayed put. I didn't dare try navigating the reef maze again. And I was starting to feel the pain of the coral cuts on my legs. I eventually gained enough line so only 20 feet of fly line and leader was between us. I could see clearly the iridescent glow of the permit's silvery sides and the yellow hue to its belly brightened by the battle. Even from the side I could see that its shoulders were broad. The fish was tired and had conceded, so I began walking the fish back onto the flat. With only another 30 feet to a safe spot to land the fish, the line went slack. The leader had finally failed, not with a snap, but with a muted parting. It took both me and the fish by surprise. I stared at the leader in disbelief; the permit continued to swim in the direction I had been leading it. Then the fish felt its freedom, veered off, and slowly swam slowly over the reef. I was left with the remnants of the frayed leader dangling from the rod tip and spikes of plastic protruding like cactus spines from the fly line wound tightly on the reel.

The pain suddenly reminded me of my fall, and I realized that the water around my legs was discolored. I looked down to see that most of my left leg and my right thigh were solidly brush-burned, scraped, raw, and bruised but not bleeding. The blood was from a cut on my right kneecap in the distinct pattern of brain coral. I checked for urchin spines but fortunately found none. Defeated, I walked back to shore, sat on the beach and rested, and let the gash in my knee dry closed. After a few minutes I made my way back to my truck and home.

## SHORELINE RUBBLE FLATS

Other rubble flats lie close to or along the shoreline. It is common to come across small flats of coral rubble mixed with sand and seagrass as you drive around a Caribbean island. The topography of the land often continues into the water, so pay particular attention to stretches of flat land where the road passes close to the water. The road may provide shoreline access to a wadeable shallow-water rubble flat.

Flats that are adjacent to busy roads or walkways will be most productive at dawn and dusk, when traffic is low. However, fish that are resident in busy areas sometimes adjust to the activity and are not so easily spooked. That doesn't mean these fish will be easy to catch—they might not be easily spooked, but they might still be picky eaters or wary of poorly presented flies because the flats are so accessible that they might be heavily fished.

Other rubble flats are harder to find but can be worth the effort. The small flats off the beaten track will likely have less fishing pressure and thus may hold more fish willing to take a fly. These isolated flats have provided me with great fishing over the years. If you have time before your trip, do your best to find a boater's map, a topographical map, or some good aerial images from a good website. For U.S. waters, the United States Geological Survey is a good place to start, as is the National Oceanographic and Atmospheric Administration (NOAA). The Internet is a valuable resource for both traditional maps and aerial photos that can reveal the locations of likely flats. Most islands have a government fisheries bureau, which is worth a phone call (results are certainly not guaranteed) to ask if it has any local coastal maps. I've found some very good maps in old fishing and sailing books. You don't need a map detailed enough for navigation, just one that shows you general patterns of inshore water depths and locations of reefs and shoals.

Fly-fishing strategies for these flats will vary. On the narrow flats that parallel the shoreline, I prefer to slowly walk the shoreline searching for signs of fish. Walking on the shore provides a higher vantage point so I can see fish at a greater distance. I am also able to quickly move to a location down the shoreline should I see a tailing fish. And walking the shoreline is definitely easier than negotiating the uneven surface of the submerged rubble. Don't be surprised to see fish right up against the shoreline, especially at high tide or at dawn or dusk. If you don't see fish after a pass along the shoreline, you may want to wade the middle of the flat. If this strategy doesn't work, wade to the outer edge of the flat and try casting into deeper water. Such blind-casting might result in a nice jack, snapper, or barracuda and even the occasional small tarpon if the flat is near a creek or lagoon. If you don't see fish on your first visit to a flat, try again at a different time of day or at a different point in the tidal cycle. I know of a few flats where large

*Rubble flats that are best for fishing have a mix of rubble and seagrass. This flat, shown at low tide, has the perfect mix.*

schools of bonefish cruise the rubble zone in the last hour and a half of the incoming tide but are completely absent at other points in the tidal cycle. Still other flats have feeding fish at dawn and dusk, seemingly regardless of the tide.

## GAMEFISH PREY OF RUBBLE FLATS

The mixture of rubble, seagrass, and scattered corals supports a diverse mixture of prey species. Rubble flats with seagrass mixed in will have the same suite of prey discussed in the chapter on seagrass, whereas rubble flats without seagrass will harbor a subset of seagrass prey species. In addition, the many crevices among the rubble are good hiding places for an assortment of other prey species that deserves mention here.

### Reef Crabs and Porcelain Crabs

Chief among these additional prey species are small members of the spider crab family (Majidae). These crabs feed along the bottom and scurry for the underside of shells and rubble when chased. Reef crabs—green reef crab *(Mithrax sculptus)* and tan reef crab *(Mithrax coryphe)*—and to a lesser extent pitho crabs—gray pitho *(Pitho aculeata)* and pitho crab *(Pitho mirabilis)*—top the list and are eaten by bonefish and permit.

The carapaces of reef crabs are triangular with rounded edges, whereas the pitho crabs are teardrop-shaped, with their eyes at the narrow end of the teardrop. All four species listed here grow to 1 inch but are often smaller. The abundance of each species varies among locations, but the green reef crab is usually the most common in shallow rubble flats mixed with seagrass.

When you choose a fly to imitate spider crabs, your choice of color can be simplified to the basics—dark green, brown, or tan depending upon the species. The pitho crabs listed here are tan to gray in color, the green reef crab is dark green, and the tan reef crab is tan.

Porcelain crabs (family Porcellanidae) also inhabit shallow rubble flats. The lined porcelain crab *(Petrolisthes galathinus)* is especially abundant on finger corals growing on rubble/seagrass flats. The lined porcelain crab is small (⅔ inch), medium green, with an oval carapace and oversized, flattened claws.

When fishing flies that imitate these small crabs, the action you give to the fly should be minimal—all species of walking crabs remain close to shelter (whether under a rock, among seagrass blades or algae, or burrowing into the bottom) and don't scurry over long stretches of open bottom when chased. At most you may want to give the fly a couple of twitches to get the attention of the bonefish or permit and then let the fly sit still.

## Mantis Shrimp

Mantis shrimp live in holes among the rubble or shells and are similar in appearance to the praying mantis land insect (thus the name). When living among sparse seagrass with coral rubble or open sand bottom, the golden mantis *(Pseudosquilla ciliata)* is tan in coloration. The rock mantis *(Gonodactylus oerstedii)* is usually dark green or black but also varies to match its habitat and is mostly found among rock and coral crevices. Mantis shrimp usually don't venture far from their burrows and are most active at night, but enough are active during the day that permit eat a lot of them. When they are chased, their defense posture is to turn and face their adversary while retreating backward toward their burrow. Although these species of mantis shrimp can reach 4 inches, usually only the smaller mantis shrimp are eaten by bonefish and permit.

## SAND FLATS

At first glance, sand flats are pretty simple habitats. There's not much structure to shelter prey or to hold gamefish. Yet, sand flats can be great places to fish for bonefish, permit, snapper, and a host of other species. So what's going on? There are numerous species of prey on sand flats, and the open nature of sand flats presents an easy habitat for gamefish to feed. You'll remember from the chapter on seagrass that the more complex the shelter of the habitat, the harder it is for predators to find and catch prey. So, although open sand bottoms don't host as many prey as seagrass, a gamefish's chance of finding and catching prey is much higher.

Spend some time wading sand flats, and you'll soon conclude that not all sand flats are created equal and that there are subtle-yet-important complexities to the bottom that influence the type and amount of prey. The type of open bottom reveals the typical wave and current conditions an area experiences and can give you a good idea of whether it is a good feeding area for bonefish. Sandy bottom with closely set waves or ridges is frequently exposed to waves or current that causes shifting sands. Shifting sands tend to have fewer prey organisms than more-stable sediments. Stable sediments also tend to be softer because of detritus and mud that is mixed (due, in part, to the activities of the resident animals), which makes these bottoms more hospitable to more organisms.

In areas with stable sand bottom, the survival strategies of species that live here provide clues to their presence. Many of the

*Sand flats are the ultimate for sight-fishing for bonefish.*

species that live on sand flats dig burrows and thus show themselves by the presence of a hole that is the entrance to their burrow. These species filter-feed, feed on detritus that is delivered by tides, or emerge from their burrows to feed on the surrounding bottom. Clams bury themselves in the sand but extend tubular siphons to the sand surface in order to filter plankton and other food from the water. Some worm burrows are as big around as a penny. The burrows of mantis shrimp are perfectly round and may be as big around as a quarter. And some species of shrimp and worms discharge large amounts of sand out of their burrows. These clues indicate that you are on a sand flat with a "live bottom" that supports gamefish prey.

Finding a live flat is an essential first step to finding gamefish. Most gamefish try to get away with as little travel as possible in their search for a meal, so after they've found a good place to feed they'll use the area repeatedly. So, after you've found a live flat, you can set about figuring out when and how gamefish take advantage of the food source.

## GAMEFISH PREY ON SAND FLATS

### Polychaetes (Marine Worms)

Polychaetes are segmented worms that come in many body shapes, but for our purposes we will divide the many species into two general categories: tube-dwellers and free-moving. Among the most recognizable tube dwellers are the numerous filter-feeding species with large, bushy crowns that extend from the worm's tube or burrow (Christmas tree worms are typical of this group). The colorful crowns quickly retract into the tube if the worm senses danger. Bonefish will chomp the tops off these worms. Weighted flies with marabou plumes are good imitations of these polychaetes. The second group of polychaetes searches for food along the bottom or filter-feeds and either lives in a tube, burrows into the sediment when seeking shelter, or simply lives on the bottom and is shaped as variations on the earthworm theme. Bonefish are the most notable gamefish that eat polychaetes with regularity.

### Crustaceans

Numerous species of crustaceans that occur in other habitats also live on sand flats. As you might suspect, sand flats that border grass beds or mangroves will receive an overflow of prey from these habitats, whereas sand flats far removed from other habitats will harbor a smaller list of prey species. Golden mantis shrimp dig tunnels in the sand and emerge at night to feed. Mantis shrimp on sand flats are tan to closely match the color of the bottom. Ghost shrimp are responsible for many of the mounds of sand that look like ski moguls. Snapping shrimp also inhabit sand flats. On hard-sand bottoms snapping shrimp will shelter in pieces of shell or rubble, as will reef and pitho crabs. In softer-bottomed sand flats, snapping shrimp will dig burrows. Juvenile common shrimp (up to 3 inches long) also burrow into soft sand, leaving a small hole for water exchange, and emerge at night to feed. Numerous species of swimming crabs also inhabit shallow sand flats and match their surroundings with excellent camouflage coloration.

## Gobies and Wrasses

Numerous species of small fish are specially adapted to the sand flats, including a few species of small gobies that are either clear or blandly colored to match the sand bottom. The goldspot goby *(Gnatholepis thompsoni),* dash goby *(Gobionellus saepepallens),* and orange-spotted goby *(Nes longus),* which makes itself comfortable in the burrows of snapping shrimp, are examples of gobies that live in burrows on sand flats. Pearly razorfish *(Hemipteronotus novacula)* and rosy razorfish *(Hempiteronotus martinicensis)* are members of the wrasse family (Labridae) and live on sand flats 4 feet deep or more. Razorfish hover above the bottom and dive into the sand when threatened. When living over sand, both species are pale in coloration.

Because so many of the prey that live on sand flats either live permanently underground or emerge at night to feed, it makes sense that gamefish that feed on sand flats have a good sense of smell. They use this sense of smell to find prey. For example, filter-feeding prey, like clams and some species of worms, draw water into one opening of their burrow, filter plankton and other food from the water, and expel the water out another burrow opening. I believe that gamefish that feed on these species can detect the outflow. In contrast, small organisms that must search out their food, such as crabs, shrimp, and small fishes, can be seen by gamefish and chased down. Bonefish and permit are especially noted for their ability to both smell and sight their prey.

### Applying What You've Learned

#### Strategies for Sand Flats

Because sand flats don't offer much in the way of shelter, their primary use by gamefish is as a feeding area. Granted, bonefish can get into such shallow water that they can escape sharks, dolphin, large barracuda, and other larger predators, but when they are that shallow they can be targeted by ospreys, so they remain wary. Another characteristic of sand flats is that because they are so shallow they can quickly become very warm in the heat of the summer sun and very cold after the passing of a cold front, in both cases making the flats inhospitable to gamefish. Given the wide-open character of sand flats, gamefish are usually on the move, and the challenge for fly anglers is to interpret the flats to figure out the best places to intercept these traveling gamefish.

The biggest factor influencing the use of sand flats by gamefish is tides. As mentioned in the discussion of rubble flats, it doesn't take much of a tidal change to influence the coming and going of gamefish. The well-known standard behavior for gamefish on sand flats is to follow the rising tide onto a flat and reverse course and leave the flat with the dropping tide. Early in the incoming tide the edges of the flat are the first places to look for fish coming onto the flat. As the tide rises, fish will come over the edge and onto the flat, often using traditional routes to access the shallows. At the very least, this behavior pattern means that even exploring

*Exposed at low tide, the shrimp mounds of this sand flat are very evident. As the tide rises, bonefish will eagerly move onto these types of flats in search of the crabs, shrimp, and small fish that wait out the low tide in the pools of water between the mounds of sand.*

a flat at low tide can bring rewards. If you happen upon fish concentrated along an edge, you're probably close to one of these traditional avenues of access. With a little searching you'll probably find nearby a small channel that, even if very shallow, serves as the first access point to the flat on the rising tide. But before you get too excited, there's a catch—the locations of these avenues may change depending on the magnitude of the tide.

Spring tides occur with every new and full moon and cause higher-than-normal high tides and lower-than-normal low tides. The high spring tides flood more of the sand flats than those at any other time in the tidal cycle, so gamefish tend to venture farther onto the flats in search of prey. And because more water moves onto and off the flats during spring tides, the currents are stronger. The combined higher water and stronger currents can cause a shift toward shallower avenues of access and exit. In contrast, neap tides occur at the first and last quarters of the moon and cause lower-than-normal high tides and higher-than-normal low tides and thus tend to limit gamefish to deeper access areas and smaller portions of the flat.

Each type of tide has its advantages. During spring tides, gamefish know they can access parts of the flat that are normally unreachable and thus are eager to move onto the flat after the tide begins to flood. But because the amount of time between high and low tide stays the same, regardless of tide height, the permit, bonefish, snapper, or crevalle jack must cover a lot of more ground in a limited amount of time. In the worst case, although the shallow sand flat has a lot of live bottom, it is too far from the safety of deep water to attract gamefish in all but the most extreme tides. In the best case, gamefish will flood the flat with the tide and feed aggressively as they move through. And although you might expect bonefish to leave these backwater areas as soon as the tide turns to ebb, you may be surprised by what a little patience on your part reveals. I have many times seen bonefish coming out of backwater areas when the dropping tide was almost too low for them to escape—backs out of the water, almost crawling as they emerge from the mangroves. They seem to know just how long they can wait before heading to deeper water to wait out low tide.

Bonefish and other sand flats gamefish are still keyed to the tides during the neap tides but tend not to venture as far onto the flat nor to feed as aggressively on the rising tide. Although this behavior might seem like a negative, it's not—gamefish are more likely to feed throughout tidal cycle than to focus on the rising and early falling tides, as they often do during spring tides. This is especially true of bonefish and permit.

The one caveat to following the tides in your fishing is the weather. Specifically, atmospheric pressure and wind can affect water level more than the tides in much of the tropics where the normal tidal range is minor. As you'll remember from previous chapters, high pressure and strong offshore winds will cause lower-than-expected high and low tides, whereas low pressure and onshore winds will cause higher water levels than expected for both tides. Given the tuned-in nature of shallow-water gamefish, these weather changes can influence gamefish behavior much the same as spring and neap tides.

Finally, tides and wind move water, which creates currents. Your first thought will probably be that you'll find gamefish on sand flats moving into the current. Much of the time this is true, but take an occasional peek behind you as you wade a sand flat for that occasional fish that rides with the current.

A less-obvious aspect of currents is that they influence water temperature. During warm times of year the water on sand flats can become too warm during the day for many species of gamefish. Rather than abandon the food-rich flats for the season, gamefish use the currents to their advantage.

Tidal currents carry cooler water from adjacent deeper areas onto the flats with the rising tide, and if the incoming tide is strong enough, gamefish will ride the cooler water onto the flat to feed. As the water is warmed by the sun, gamefish may move off the flats early in the dropping tide before the water becomes too warm.

In contrast, during cold seasons, the midday sun will heat the shallow water over the sand flats. As the tide rises and is warmed by the sun and by the sun-baked sand, gamefish will move onto the flat to feed. When sun-warmed water begins to drain the flat on a dropping tide, it's worth searching out channels that drain the flat. Gamefish holding at the ends of these channels get not only the benefit of intercepting prey that is washed off the flat but also the extra warmth of the solar-heated water.

So, in summary, when creating a strategy for fly fishing a sand flat, you need to consider tides, wind, atmospheric pressure, currents, and temperature. Whether you find fish or not, it is worthwhile to make notes of the conditions on the flat and to fish the flat under different conditions. It won't take long for you to figure out the patterns of the fish. If you are traveling to an unknown area for just a couple of days, take the time to figure out the local tides and weather conditions and to make a best guess on where the fishing conditions will be best. By getting enough practice and noting conditions when fishing different areas, you'll develop a knack for picking the right times and places.

# 10
# Stewardship

We long ago passed the point where we could go fishing and return home without further thought and expect the fisheries and habitats to remain healthy. There are increasing stresses on the coastal environment and a lot more people fishing now (and not all of them fishing responsibly). Habitat loss and degradation are the biggest factors threatening our coastal fisheries. As anglers we are the primary users and beneficiaries of these coastal environments, so we must also be their stewards.

## HABITAT CONSERVATION

Any fisher who's spent much time on the water knows that healthy habitats are essential to having quality fisheries. Unfortunately, too few anglers truly understand how habitat loss has damaged the fisheries, and even fewer are doing anything about it. If anglers want to ensure that there are recreational fisheries in the years to come, they need to become involved in protecting the habitats that are the factory producing our coastal fisheries.

Let's look at this as if we were newly hired managers at an assembly-line factory that has been successfully churning out a product. Our job is to make sure the assembly line continues to function efficiently. Wanting to use some factory resources for other ventures, we remove a few stations from the assembly line to put into use elsewhere. For a while, this change is fine—the production process can handle a few kinks in the chain. But eventually our meddling causes wholesale changes in the way the assembly line operates, and factory production becomes inefficient, total output falls, some products cease altogether, and the company stock goes into a tailspin. In a sense, this is what we've done with our coastal fish stocks—the loss and degradation of coastal habitats (the assembly line) have resulted in a drop in the quantity and quality of the product (the fisheries). As both the managers of the factory and the consumers of the product, anglers have the most responsibility and the most to benefit by getting the factory back on track. In a sense, it's like we're the employees who own the company stock, but we're not protecting our investment.

Most species of coastal gamefish have at least one life stage that is especially vulnerable to habitat loss and degradation. Tarpon is a good example. Adults use most coastal and coastal ocean habitats and are able, to some extent, to adapt to changes in coastal habitats. But even these changes can be troublesome—changes in freshwater flow into estuaries, for example, cause changes in baitfish abundance, which in turn affects tarpon migrations and feeding.

But as with many coastal gamefish, juvenile tarpon are most at risk. Juvenile tarpon are dependent upon shallow mangrove and marsh backwaters for the first year or two of their lives. These habitats are already significantly less abundant than they once were, and loss and degradation continue. Without these habitats, few juvenile tarpon survive, and the future fishery suffers.

Mangroves are critically important habitats for many of the gamefish we pursue, but unfortunately mangroves are among the most-threatened coastal habitats in the world. Diverting fresh water from mangrove and marsh areas, filling in mangrove wetlands and salt marshes for development, cutting mangroves for wood products, and polluting are all immediate threats to these habitats and to the communities that depend on them. Without these fragile habitats, many species will not be able to survive, and we will lose a fantastic habitat for fishing. To fragment these important fish habitats into ever-smaller, low-quality parcels is to invite disaster for coastal gamefish and is an outcome we should try our best to prevent.

Indirect effects are tougher to see and generally don't cause concern until long after the damage has been done. Alteration of freshwater flow into estuaries, for example, has been affecting the world's fisheries for many years but only relatively recently has become a major public issue. Alterations of freshwater flows into estuaries change the types of species and the numbers of organisms that are present, and this change has far-reaching impacts. Most species of seagrass, for example, can't tolerate salinities of less than 15 parts per thousand (ppt) for more than a couple of weeks. (Normal ocean salinity is 30–35 ppt; freshwater salinity is 0 ppt.) So, if too much fresh water is released into estuaries for long enough, the seagrasses will die, and the organisms that rely on seagrass habitats will also die or leave the area. This, of course, will result in fewer gamefish because there is less for them to eat and no places to hide if larger predators come into the area.

The same holds true for mangroves and salt-marsh grasses—they can handle total fresh water for a while but will be outcompeted by other plant species if the system changes to fresh water. And even if the plants are able to remain, many of the organisms that provide habitat and food for fish and their prey will die—the oysters that grow on mangrove prop roots or line salt-marsh shorelines will die if exposed to salinities of less than 15 ppt for more than a week or two. When these organisms go, so do the gamefish.

Research in Florida showed that the diet of juvenile snook was half as diverse and that more snook had empty stomachs in creeks with altered freshwater flows than did juvenile snook in creeks with natural flows. This alteration might not only hinder the growth of juvenile snook but also lessen their survival, which can impact the adult population.

Just as in human medicine, proactive care is most effective for fisheries conservation. The top priority should be protecting what habitats are left. Although it's not always feasible, the next-best thing is restoring what has been damaged—emergency medical care—and this is a lot more expensive. There are plenty of opportunities to fix past wrongs, but none of this will happen without anglers at the front.

*Destruction of coastal habitats is probably the biggest threat to our fisheries and is something that anglers must actively oppose. This photo shows the loss of habitat essential to juvenile tarpon.*

Florida, for example, has lost approximately 50 percent of mangroves already due to direct habitat impacts. In a worst case scenario, because we have lost so many mangroves and wetlands, we may have already lost some of our ability to manage these fisheries—if juvenile habitat is a limiting factor in adult abundance, then loss of juvenile habitat may put a cap on the total number of adults even under the best management strategy. Unfortunately, data are not yet sufficient to determine exactly how much habitat loss contributes to how many fewer fish.

What it comes down to is this: Without healthy habitats we can't have healthy fisheries, regardless of fisheries management actions that might be taken. Fish hatcheries may be a useful tool, if used correctly, to get fish populations back on track to recovery. But if the fish don't have healthy habitats in which to live, the stocking won't be effective in the long term. If for nothing other than selfish reasons, anglers should be the most concerned about habitat loss and be the most ardent supporters of habitat protections: Continued loss of habitats will result in continued declines in our fisheries.

## SEAGRASS STEWARDSHIP

Seagrasses are an integral part of the environment that sustains the gamefish that so many of us ardently pursue. It's impossible to overstate how much communities in seagrass beds depend on the food and shelter that only a healthy environment can provide. Unfortunately, seagrass beds are under threat from a number of sources. Sedimentation from coastal development can smother seagrass. Too many nutrients from sewage, fertilizer runoff, and other sources can cause algae blooms that decrease the clarity of the water, causing the seagrass to die due to lack of light. Too many nutrients can cause so many epiphytes to grow on the grass blades that the blades are smothered and die. Water management practices that remove all fresh water from an estuary or release too much fresh water create conditions that are unsuitable for growth of seagrass. These threats to seagrass are associated with various nonfishing human activities, but they affect the seagrass that gamefish depend on and should be of concern to anglers. Concerned anglers should become involved in local conservation efforts to address these problems.

But anglers can directly address one of the increasing threats to seagrass beds—scarring of the grass beds by boat propellers, called prop-scarring. Prop-scarring is caused by running a boat in water that is too shallow, so that the propeller digs a trough through the seagrass. Because the rhizomes (rootlike structures) of seagrasses don't grow down into depressions (they grow only horizontally), a deep propeller scar may remain barren bottom for over a decade. In a worst case scenario, wave action or currents work at the edge of the prop scar and erode the adjacent grass bed, creating a large area of open bottom. Anglers can significantly decrease the amount of prop-scarring by boating responsibly and by educating others who don't seem to know any better.

## MANGROVE STEWARDSHIP

Maintaining healthy mangroves for healthy fisheries starts at home, so anglers need to practice responsible fishing while on the water. First, don't break off your leader and leave it dangling in the mangroves. Far too many birds have become entangled in monofilament left dangling from mangrove branches—I've personally cut far too many bird carcasses from webs of fishing line strung through mangrove branches. Second, because we have already lost so much of the mangrove habitat that gamefish depend upon, as responsible stewards of gamefish habitats we should report destruction of mangroves. Enforcement agencies aren't able to be in all places at all times, so when we are on the water we must report the destruction of gamefish habitats.

As in all of our coastal environments, the connections between healthy habitats are essential to the success of gamefish populations. For example, juvenile tarpon and snook require shallow, protected, low-salinity areas during at least the first year of life but must be able to move to somewhat deeper areas with higher salinity as they grow. Eventually, adults use the various habitats provided by estuaries and the coastal ocean, but even adults have specific habitat requirements. A fish's chances of survival are much greater if it can move from one habitat to another without having to negotiate large, inhospitable areas, such as seawalls where mangrove shoreline used to be. This is especially true for the juvenile and subadult stages of the life cycle that depend on the very mangrove shorelines that are under such extreme threat.

Despite some changes in environmental laws, development continues to eradicate important mangrove habitats. In many areas, only small sections of mangroves remain where once the entire shoreline was a continuous stretch of undisturbed mangrove habitat. In other areas, poor water quality from too much sediment or pollution or from too much or too little fresh water due to channelization has altered the communities associated with mangrove prop roots. In addition, dredging to allow more boat access removes the shallow habitats that are essential to both juvenile and adult gamefish. Often, these destructive forces act in concert, resulting in sparse coastal landscapes.

## OYSTER BAR STEWARDSHIP

Because oyster bars that are made up of live oysters support more prey than oyster bars made up of dead shell, any threats to oyster bars will harm gamefish. Unfortunately, numerous threats to oysters exist. Too much sediment can bury oysters, and many estuaries are inundated with sediment-laden water draining farmland, housing developments, and urban areas. Too many nutrients can cause plankton blooms that create hypoxia (low oxygen) or anoxia (no oxygen) that last for periods long enough to kill oysters. Runoff heavy in nutrients comes from farms and suburban lawns, from urban sewage outfalls, and from livestock. The herbicides and pesticides that often accompany this runoff can also stress oysters. Boat wakes from channels that border oyster bars can prevent juvenile oysters from colonizing reefs, thus dooming a reef to eventual death. Too much physical disturbance from tonging, dredging, and frequent boat groundings can damage or even destroy reefs as well.

Because oysters and their predators and diseases are so affected by salinity, changing the flow of fresh water into estuaries can have dire consequences. If, for example, release of water from dams causes long periods of high freshwater flows, salinities may drop enough to kill oysters in the upper portions of an estuary. If, on the other hand, so much fresh water is diverted from rivers by cities or agriculture, salinities in the estuary may become high enough to allow predators and disease to become established farther into the estuary than they would under natural conditions. In both scenarios (which are already realities in some areas), the health of oysters and oyster bars declines.

Oyster bars influence water current patterns, so changing their location, size, or orientation (by dredging, for example) can have unpredictable impacts on the flow of water and sediments, causing unpredictable problems that affect gamefish and prey. For example, currents may become stronger and carve deep holes in the bottom or wipe out areas of seagrass that had previously been protected by the removed bar. Or currents may be completely blocked, creating a stagnant area behind an altered bar that holds few prey and gamefish.

As we are learning in so many of our estuaries, oysters are an essential component of a healthy coastal ecosystem. They are also important habitats for gamefish and their prey. In some areas, they are *the* most important gamefish habitat. Effective stewardship means making sure these habitats remain viable parts of our coastal ecosystems. And remember that after an oyster bar is gone it's probably gone for good because oyster larvae need the hard substrate provided by previous generations of oysters to survive.

## SALT-MARSH STEWARDSHIP

Salt marshes are excellent protectors of shorelines against erosion and efficient collectors and depositories of sediments that might otherwise smother other habitats or quickly fill in estuaries and other coastal areas. Moreover, marsh plants stabilize the transition between land and sea and by doing so provide valuable habitat to both marine and land animals. In fact, many marine gamefish have come to depend on salt marshes for part or all of their life cycles. In other words, salt marshes are an indispensable habitat in the coastal environment. With all that we know about the importance of salt marshes for sustaining healthy fisheries and healthy coastal ecosystems, you might think that these habitats are well protected. Unfortunately, this couldn't be further from the truth. Salt marshes are under continuing threats from many sources, and threats to salt marshes are threats to gamefish.

Development in and around salt marshes and other wetlands is perhaps the most-obvious effect on the health of these habitats. Development simply wipes out the marsh by converting it to land, resulting in wholesale habitat loss. Development also removes the protection from erosion that a salt marsh naturally provides. Unfortunately, salt marshes are still sometimes used as disposal areas for spoil from channel dredging, which has the same effect on the salt marsh as development—the covering and filling in, and thus destruction, of salt-marsh habitat.

Less obvious, but also damaging, is the digging of drainage ditches and canals to drain the water from the marsh—either for control of mosquitoes or for flood control of neighboring areas. Salt marshes depend on tidal flushing and the mixing of salt water and fresh water, and draining the marsh prevents these. It is doubtful that apparent benefits of drainage ditches outweigh long-term negative effects on the salt-marsh communities and associated gamefish. In fact, drainage ditches may convert low marsh into high marsh, completely removing gamefish habitat.

The diversion of freshwater flows and the sediments they carry also threatens salt marshes. Without fresh water, the high marsh deteriorates. And without the infusion of sediments to maintain the marsh's structural integrity, the marsh begins to erode. The shrinking of salt marshes of the Mississippi delta, for example, has been linked to diversion of freshwater flow resulting from channelizing of the Mississippi River. In the past, the river would deposit most of its sediments in the delta's marshes, but now the channelized flow is so strong that sediments are carried far into the Gulf (which causes additional problems offshore). Without new sediments to replace portions of salt marshes that are eroding, the marshes are shrinking, and so is gamefish habitat.

Finally, pollutants can harm or even kill some of the organisms that live in the salt marsh. For example, chemicals sprayed to kill mosquitoes also kill invertebrates that are food for juvenile gamefish in these marshes. Housing developments adjacent to marshes that use septic systems can introduce far too much nitrogen into the groundwater that flows into adjacent salt marshes. The excess nitrogen creates blooms of algae and phytoplankton, which can cause severe depletions of oxygen when it dies and decays. Lack of oxygen can cause rather severe die-offs of marsh organisms, including juvenile gamefish.

By now it should be obvious that saltwater gamefish in the warm-temperate region have an intricate relationship with salt marshes. It should also be obvious that the degradation of salt-marsh habitats has negative effects not only on the species of gamefish that we pursue with a fly rod but also on the overall health of coastal ecosystems. The decisions we make now about these important coastal habitats will influence many generations of saltwater fly anglers.

## BEACH STEWARDSHIP

Beaches are the launching point from which we begin many of our journeys into the saltwater world. By absorbing the force of the oceans, beaches protect barrier islands and the estuaries that lie behind them and buffer the land from the erosive forces of the sea. A suite of animals has evolved into beach specialists and has come to depend on the ecological integrity of these environments. Alterations that affect beaches also affect these animals.

Beaches also protect marine habitats from land-based human activities. As we breach the protective bulwark between land and sea, we harm both the land habitats and sea habitats that depend on the nature of the beaches. For example, it is a common practice for hotels to import sand to create beaches for tourism. In the tropics, imported sand covers and smothers seagrass and corals, and as the sand erodes it is carried by currents to adjacent areas, where it further damages habitats.

Beach (re)nourishment activities also damage beach-dependent organisms, such as mole crabs. Mole crabs may be absent or in low abundance for years following beach renourishment, which has direct implications for gamefish that prey on mole crabs, including pompano, juvenile permit, and snook. Alterations of the longshore flow of sand can dramatically affect coastal habitats as well. Jetties, for example, interrupt the transport of sand via the longshore current. The beach may build up nicely around a new jetty, but beaches downstream starve for new sand and slowly lose ground. Longshore bars are similarly affected by changes in sand transport. These are just some of the factors we have to consider when we weigh the benefits and disadvantages of alterations of our beaches.

## FINAL THOUGHT

For each piece of habitat lost, the capacity of the fisheries is diminished, as are the opportunities you have to go fishing and the long-term economic value of these fisheries. Habitat protection is an investment in the future of the fisheries, no different than investing in a 401k for retirement. It's time that recreational anglers make major investments in the future of their fisheries.

# REFERENCES AND FURTHER READING


Adams, A. J. *Fly fisherman's guide to saltwater prey*. Mechanicsburg, PA: Stackpole Books. 2008.

Adams, A. J., J. E. Hill, and C. Samoray. Characteristics of spawning ground fidelity by a diadromous fish: A multi-year perspective. *Environmental Biology of Fishes*. 2011.

Adams, A. J. and J. P. Ebersole. Mechanisms affecting recruitment patterns of fish and decapods in tropical marine ecosystems. In I. Nagelkerken (ed.), *Ecological linkages among tropical coastal ecosystems*. New York: Springer. 2009.

Adams, A. J. and J. P. Ebersole. Resistance of coral reef fishes of back-reef and lagoon habitats to a hurricane. *Bulletin of Marine Science* 75(1):101–113. 2004.

Adams, A. J. and J. P. Ebersole. Use of back-reef and lagoon habitats by coral reef fishes. *Marine Ecology Progress Series* 228:213–226. 2002.

Adams, A. J., J. V. Locascio, and B. D. Robbins. Microhabitat use by a post-settlement stage estuarine fish: Evidence from relative abundance and predation among habitats. *Journal of Experimental Marine Biology and Ecology* 299:17–33. 2004.

Adams, A. J. and R. K. Wolfe. Occurrence and persistence of non-native *Cichlasoma urophthalmus* (Family Cichlidae) in estuarine habitats of southwest Florida (USA): Environmental controls and movement patterns. *Marine and Freshwater Research* 58(10):921–930. 2007.

Adams, A. J. and R. K. Wolfe. Cannibalism of juveniles by adult *Centropomus undecimalis*. *Gulf of Mexico Science* 24(1–2):11–13. 2006.

Adams, A. J., R. K. Wolfe, N. Barkowski, and D. Overcash. Fidelity to spawning grounds by a catadromous fish, *Centropomus undecimalis*. *Marine Ecology Progress Series* 389:213–222. 2009.

Adams, A. J., R. K. Wolfe, and C. A. Layman. Preliminary examination of how human-driven freshwater flow alteration affects trophic ecology of juvenile snook (*Centropomus undecimalis*) in estuarine creeks. *Estuaries and Coasts* 32(4):819–828. 2009.

Adams, A. J., R. K. Wolfe, G. T. Kellison, and B. C. Victor. Patterns of juvenile habitat use and seasonality of settlement by permit, *Trachinotus falcatus*. *Environmental Biology of Fishes* 75:209–217. 2006.

Adams, D. H. and D. M. Tremain. Association of large juvenile red drum, *Sciaenops ocellatus*, with an estuarine creek on the Atlantic coast of Florida. *Environmental Biology of Fishes* 58:183–194. 2000.

Anonymous. *Red drum*. North Carolina Division of Marine Fisheries publication.

Anonymous. *Spotted seatrout*. North Carolina Division of Marine Fisheries publication.

Arrivillaga, A. and D. Baltz. Comparison of fishes and macroinvertebrates of seagrass and bare-sand sites on Guatemala's Atlantic coast. *Bulletin of Marine Science* 65(2):301–319. 1999.

Austin, H. M. A survey of the ichthyofauna of the mangroves of western Puerto Rico during December, 1967-August, 1968. *Caribbean Journal of Science* 111(2):27–39. 1971.

Austin, H. M. and S. E. Austin. Juvenile fish in two Puerto Rican mangroves. *Caribbean Journal of Science* 111(2):26–31. 1971.

Austin, H. and S. Austin. The feeding habits of some juvenile marine fishes from the mangroves in western Puerto Rico. *Caribbean Journal of Science* 113(4):171–178. 1971.

Baelde, P. Differences in the structures of fish assemblages in *Thalassia testudinum* beds in Guadeloupe, French West Indies, and their ecological significance. *Marine Biology* 105:163–173. 1990.

Baltz, D. M., J. W. Fleeger, C. F. Rakocinski, and J. N. McCall. Food, density, and microhabitat: Factors affecting growth and recruitment potential of juvenile saltmarsh fishes. *Environmental Biology of Fishes* 53:89–103. 1998.

Bass, R. J. and J. W. J. Avault. Food habits, length-weight relationship, condition factor, and growth of juvenile red drum, *Sciaenops ocellatus*, in Louisiana. *Transactions of the American Fisheries Society* 104(1):35–45. 1975.

Beach, D. *Coastal sprawl: The effects of urban design on aquatic ecosystems in the United States.* Arlington, VA: Pew Oceans Commission. 2002.

Bell, S. S., R. A. Brooks, B. D. Robbins, M. S. Fonseca, and M. O. Hall. Faunal response to fragmentation in seagrass habitats: Implications for seagrass conservation. *Biological Conservation* 100: 115–123. 2001.

Bohlke, J. E. and C. C. G. Chaplin. Family Centropomidae: Snooks or robalos. In *Fishes of the Bahamas and adjacent tropical waters.* Wynnewood, PA, Livingston Publishing: pp. 253–254. 1968.

Bologna, P. A. X. and K. L. Heck Jr. Macrofaunal associations with seagrass epiphytes relative importance of trophic and structural characteristics. *Journal of Experimental Marine Biology and Ecology* 242:21–39. 1999.

Bortone, S. A. (Ed.). *Biology of the Spotted Seatrout.* Boca Raton, FL. CRC Press: pp. 1–3. 2003.

Boulon, R. H. J. Use of mangrove prop root habitats by fish in the northern U.S. Virgin Islands. *Proceedings of the Gulf and Caribbean Fisheries Institute* 41:189–204. 1987.

Brook, I. M. Trophic relationships in a seagrass community *Thalassia testudinum*, in Card Sound, Florida: Fish diets in relation to macrobenthic and cryptic faunal abundance. *Transactions of the American Fisheries Society* 1063:219–229. 1977.

Brown, D. *Fly fishing for bonefish.* New York: Lyons & Burford. 1993.

Brown-Peterson, N. J., M. S. Peterson, D. L. Nieland, M. D. Murphy, R. G. Taylor, and J. R. Warren. Reproductive biology of female spotted seatrout, *Cynoscion nenbulosus*, in the Gulf of Mexico: Differences among estuaries? *Environmental Biology of Fishes* 63:405–415. 2001.

Bruger, G. E. *Age, growth, food habits, and reproduction of bonefish,* Albula vulpes, *in south Florida waters* (Research Publication 3). Florida Department of Natural Resources Marine Research Laboratory. 1974.

Carmona-Suarez, C. A. and J. E. Conde. Local distribution and abundance of swimming crabs *Callinectes* spp. and *Arenaeus cribrarius* on a tropical sand beach. *Fisheries Bulletin* 100:11–25. 2002.

Carr, W. E. S. and C. A. Adams. Food habitat of juvenile marine fishes occupying seagrass beds in the estuarine zone near Crystal River, Florida. *Transactions of the American Fisheries Society* 1023:511–540. 1973.

Catano, S. and J. Garzon-Ferreira. Ecologia trofica del sabalo *Megalops atlanticus* (Pisces: Megalopidae) en el area de Cienega Grande de Santa Marta, Caribe Colombiano. *Revista de Biologia Tropical* 42(3):673–684. 1994.

Cocheret de la Moriniere, E. *Post-settlement life cycle migrations of reef fish in the mangrove-seagrass-coral reef continuum.* Dissertation. University of Nijmegen, the Netherlands. 2002.

Coen, L. D., K. L. Heck Jr., and L. G. Abele. Experiments on competition and predation among shrimps of seagrass meadows. *Ecology* 626:1484–1493. 1981.

Colton, D. E. and W. S. Alevizon. Feeding ecology of bonefish in Bahamian waters. *Transactions of the American Fisheries Society* 12:178–184. 1983.

Connolly, R. M. Differences in composition of small, motile invertebrate assemblages from seagrass and unvegetated habitats in a southern Australian estuary. *Hydrobiologia* 346:137–148. 1997.

Cowper, S. W. The drift algae community of seagrass beds in Redfish Bay, Texas. *Contributions in Marine Science* 21:125–132. 1978.

Crabtree, R. E. Relationship between lunar phase and spawning activity of tarpon, *Megalops atlanticus*, with notes on the distribution of larvae. *Bulletin of Marine Science* 56(3):895–899. 1995.

Crabtree, R. E., E. C. Cyr, R. E. Bishop, L. M. Falkenstein, and J. M. Dean. Age and growth of tarpon, *Megalops atlanticus*, larvae in the eastern Gulf of Mexico, with notes on relative abundance and probable spawning areas. *Environmental Biology of Fishes* 35:361–370. 1992.

Crabtree, R. E., E. C. Cyr, and J. M. Dean. Age and growth of tarpon, *Megalops atlanticus*, from South Florida waters. *Fishery Bulletin* 93:619–628. 1995.

Crabtree, R. E., C. W. Harnden, D. Snodgrass, and C. Stevens. Age, growth, and mortality of bonefish, *Albula vulpes*, from the waters of the Florida Keys. *Fishery Bulletin* 94:442–451. 1996.

Crabtree, R. E., P. B. Hood, and D. Snodgrass. Age, growth, and reproduction of permit *Trachinotus falcatus* in Florida waters. *Fishery Bulletin* 100:26–34. 2002.

Crabtree, R. E., D. Snodgrass, and C. W. Harnden. Maturation and reproductive seasonality in bonefish, *Albula vulpes*, from the waters of the Florida Keys. *Fishery Bulletin* 95:456–465. 1997.

Crabtree, R. E., C. Stevens, D. Snodgrass, and F. J. Stengard. Feeding habitats of bonefish, *Albula vulpes*, from the waters of the Florida Keys. *Fishery Bulletin* 96:754–766. 1998.

Dahlgren, C., G. T. Kellison, A. J. Adams, B. M. Gillanders, M. S. Kendall, C. A. Layman, J. A. Ley, I. Nagelkerken, and J. E. Serafy. Marine nurseries and effective juvenile habitats: Concepts and applications. *Marine Ecology Progress Series* 312:291–295. 2006.

Danylchuk, A. J., A. J. Adams, S. J. Cooke, and C. D. Suski. An evaluation of the injury and short-term survival of bonefish (*Albula* spp) as influenced by a mechanical fish handling device used by recreational anglers. *Fisheries Research* 93(1–2):248–252. 2008.

Dennis, G. D. Island mangrove habitats as spawning and nursery areas for commercially important fishes in the Caribbean. *Proceedings of the Gulf and Caribbean Fisheries Institute* 41:205–225. 1998.

Denson, M. R., W. E. Jenkins, A. J. Woodward, and T. I. J. Smith. Tag-reporting levels for red drum (*Sciaenops ocellatus*) caught by anglers in South Carolina and Georgia estuaries. *Fisheries Bulletin* 100:35–41. 2002.

Doering, P. H. and R. H. Chamberlain. Experimental studies on the salinity tolerance of turtle grass, *Thalassia testudinum*. In M. J. Kennish (Ed.), *Seagrasses: Monitoring, ecology, physiology, and management*. Boca Raton, FL. CRC Press: pp. 81–98. 2000.

Duarte, L. O. and C. B. Garcia. Diet of the mutton snapper *Lutjanus analis* (Cuvier) from the Gulf of Salamanca, Colombia, Caribbean Sea. *Bulletin of Marine Science* 65(2):453–465. 1999.

Durako, M. J., M. O. Hall, F. Sargent, and S. Peck. Propeller scars in seagrass beds: An assessment and experimental study of recolonization in Weedon Island State Preserve, Florida. *Proceedings of the Nineteenth Annual Conference on Wetlands Restoration and Creation*. Hillsborough Community College Institute of Florida Studies: pp. 42–53. 1992.

Durako, M. J., M. D. Murphy, and K. D. Haddad. *Assessment of fisheries habitat: Northeast Florida* 45:51. 1988.

Durako, M. J., R. C. Phillips, and R. R. Lewis III. *Proceedings of the Symposium on Subtropical-Tropical Seagrasses of the Southeastern United States* 42:209. 1987.

Faunce, C. H., J. J. Lorenz, J. A. Ley, and J. E. Serafy. Size structure of gray snapper *Lutjanus griseus* within a mangrove "no-take" sanctuary. *Bulletin of Marine Science* 701:211–216. 2002.

Fay, C. W., R. J. Neves, and G. B. Pardue. Species profiles: Life histories and environmental requirements of coastal fishes and invertebrates (mid-Atlantic)—striped bass. *U.S. Fish and Wildlife Service Biological Report* 82(11.8). U.S. Army Corps of Engineers, TR EL-82-4. 1983.

Fernandez, Chico. *Fly-fishing for bonefish.* Mechanicsburg, PA: Stackpole Books. 2004.

Finucane, J. H. Ecology of the pompano *Trachinotus carolinus* and the permit *T. falcatus* in Florida. *Transactions of the American Fisheries Society* 3:478–486. 1969.

Fonseca, M. S. and S. S. Bell. Influence of physical setting on seagrass landscapes near Beaufort, North Carolina, USA. *Marine Ecology Progress Series* 171:109–121. 1998.

Fonseca, M., P. E. Whitfield, N. M. Kelly, and S. S. Bell. Modeling seagrass landscape pattern and associated ecological attributes. *Ecological Applications* 121:218–237. 2002.

Fourqurean, J. W., A. Willsie, C. D. Rose, and L. M. Rutten. Spatial and temporal pattern in seagrass community composition and productivity in south Florida. *Marine Biology* 138:341–354. 2001.

Franks, J. S., J. R. Warren, and M. V. Buchanan. Age and growth of cobia, *Rachycentron canadum*, from the northeastern Gulf of Mexico. *Fisheries Bulletin* 97:459–471. 1998.

Geary, B. W., J. R. Rooker, and J. W. Webb. Utilization of saltmarsh shorelines by newly settled Sciaenids in a Texas estuary. *Gulf and Caribbean Research* 13:37–49. 2001.

Gilmore, R. G., C. J. Donohoe, and D. W. Cooke. Observations on the distribution and biology of east-central Florida populations of the common snook. *Florida Science* 46(3–4):306–313. 1983.

Gotceitas, V. and Colgan, P. Predator foraging success and habitat complexity: Quantitative test of the threshold hypothesis. *Oecologia* 80:158–166. 1989.

Grabowski, J. H., M. A. Dolan, A. R. Hughes, and D. L. Kimbo. *The biological and economic value of restored intertidal oyster reef habitat to the nursery function of the estuary.* North Carolina Marine Fisheries Commission, Fishery Resource Grant Program, Fishery Grant EP-6. 2001.

Greening, H. S. and R. J. Livingston. Diel variation in the structure of seagrass associated epibenthic macroinvertebrate communities *Marine Ecology Progress Series* 7:147–156. 1982.

Heck, K. L. Jr. Comparative species richness, composition, and abundance of invertebrates in Caribbean seagrass *Thalassia testudinum*. *Marine Biology* 41:335–348. 1977.

Heck, K. L. Jr. and T. A. Thoman. Experiments on predator-prey interactions in vegetated aquatic habitats. *Journal of Experimental Marine Biology and Ecology* 53:125–134. 1981.

Heck, K. L. Jr. and M. P. Weinstein. Feeding habits of juvenile reef fishes associated with Panamanian seagrass meadows. *Bulletin of Marine Science* 453:629–636. 1989.

Heck, K. L. Jr. and G. S. Wetstone. Habitat complexity and invertebrate species richness and abundance in tropical seagrass meadows. *Journal of Biography* 4:135–142. 1977.

Heupel, M. R., C. A. Simpfendorfer, and R. A. Heuter. Estimation of shark home ranges using passive monitoring techniques. *Environmental Biology of Fishes* 135-142. 2004.

Hildebrand, S. F. Family Albulidae. In H. B. Bigelow (Ed.), *Fishes of the western North Atlantic*. New Haven, CT. Memoir Sears Foundation for Marine Research: pp. 111–131. 1963.

Hildebrand, S. F. Family Elopidae. In H. B. Bigelow (Ed.), *Fishes of the western North Atlantic*. New Haven, CT. Memoir Sears Foundation for Marine Research: pp. 132–147. 1963.

Hill, J., J. W. Evans, and M. J. Van Den Avyle. *Species profiles: Life histories and environmental requirements of coastal fishes and invertebrates (south Atlantic) B striped bass.* U.S. Fish and Wildlife Service Biological Report 82(11.118). U.S. Army Corps of Engineers, TR EL-82-4. 1989.

Hindell, J. S., G. P. Jenkins, and M. J. Keough. Variability in abundances of fishes associated with seagrass habitats in relation to diets of predatory fishes. *Marine Biology* 136:725–737. 2000.

Hindell, J. S., G. P. Jenkins, and M. J. Keough. Evaluating the impact of predation by fish on the assemblage structure of fishes associated with seagrass *Heterozostera tasmanica* (Martens ex Ascherson den Hartog), and unvegetated sand habitats. *Journal of Experimental Marine Biology and Ecology* 255:153–174. 2000.

Hixon, M. A. and J. P. Beets. Predation, prey-refuges, and the structure of coral-reef fish assemblages. *Ecological Monographs* 63(1):77–101. 1993.

Hoese, H. D. and R. H. Moore. *Fishes of the Gulf of Mexico: Texas, Louisiana, and adjacent waters* (2nd ed.). College Station: Texas A&M University Press. 1998.

Holt, S. A., C. L. Kitting, and C. R. Arnold. Distribution of young red drums among different seagrass meadows. *Transactions of the American Fisheries Society* 112:267–271. 1983.

Howard, R. K. Diel variation in the abundance of epifauna associated with seagrasses of the Indian River, Florida USA. *Marine Biology* 96:137–142. 1987.

Johannes, R. E. Reproductive strategies of coastal marine fishes in the tropics. *Environmental Biology of Fishes* 31:65–84. 1978.

Jordan, F., M. Bartolini, C. Nelson, P. E. Patterson, and H. L. Soulenet. Risk of predation affects habitat selection by the pinfish *Lagodon rhomboides* Linnaeus. *Journal of Experimental Marine Biology and Ecology* 208:45–56. 1996.

Kalbfleisch, W. B. C. and B. Jones. Sedimentology of shallow, hurricane-affected lagoons: Grand Cayman, British West Indies. *Journal of Coastal Research* 141:140–160. 1998.

Kaplan, E. H. *A field guide to southeastern and Caribbean seashores: Cape Hatteras to the Gulf Coast, Florida, and the Caribbean.* Boston: Houghton-Mifflin. 1988.

Kaplan, E. H. *A field guide to coral reefs: Caribbean and Florida.* Boston: Houghton-Mifflin. 1982.

Kathiresan, K. and B. L. Bingham. Biology of mangroves and mangrove ecosystems. *Advances in Marine Biology* 40:81–251. 2001.

Kilby, J. D. The fishes of two Gulf coastal marsh areas of Florida. *Tulane Studies in Zoology* 2(8):175–247. 1955.

Knowles, L. L. and S. S. Bell. The influence of habitat structure in faunal-habitat associations in a Tampa Bay seagrass system, Florida. *Bulletin of Marine Science* 62(3):781–794. 1998.

Kulczycki, G. R., R. W. Virnstein, and W. G. Nelson. The relationship between fish abundance and algal biomass in a seagrass-drift algae community. *Estuarine and Coastal Shelf Science* 12:341–347. 1981.

Laegdsgaard, P. and C. Johnson. Why do juvenile fish utilise mangrove habitats? *Journal of Experimental Marine Biology and Ecology* 257:229–253. 2001.

Larmouth, D. and R. Fordyce. *Tarpon on Fly*. Portland, OR: Frank Amato Publications. 2002.

Leber, K. M. The influence of predatory decapods, refuge, and microhabitat selection on seagrass communities. *Ecology* 66(6):1951–1964. 1985.

Leber, K. M. and H. S. Greening. Community studies in seagrass meadows: A comparison of two methods for sampling macroinvertebrates and fishes. *Fishery Bulletin* 842:443–450. 1985.

Ley, J., C. L. Montague, and C. C. McIvor. Food habits of mangrove fishes: A comparison along estuarine gradients in northeastern Florida Bay. *Bulletin of Marine Science* 54(30): 881–899. 1994.

Lin, J. and J. L. Beal. Effects of mangrove marsh management on fish and decapod communities. *Bulletin of Marine Science* 571:193–201. 1995.

Linke, T. E., M. E. Platell, and I. C. Potter. Factors influencing the partitioning of food resources among six fish species in a large embayment with juxtaposing bare sand and seagrass habitats. *Journal of Experimental Marine Biology and Ecology* 266:193–217. 2001.

Livingston, R. J. Organization of fish in a coastal seagrass system: The response to stress. *Fish Community Ecology in Estuaries and Coastal Lagoons* 16:367–382. 1985.

Louis, M., C. Bouchon, and Y. Bouchon-Navaro. Spatial and temporal variations of mangrove fish assemblages in Martinique French West Indies. *Hydrobiologia* 295:275–284. 1995.

Luczkovich, J. J., H. J. Daniel III, M. W. Sprague, S. E. Johnson, R. C. Pullinger, T. Jenkins, and M. Hutchinson. Characterization of critical spawning habitats of weakfish, spotted seatrout, and red drum in Pamlico Sound using hydrophone surveys. *Final Report and Annual Performance Report* (Grants F-62-1 and F-62-2). North Carolina Division of Marine Fisheries.

Mackey, G. *Juvenile nursery grounds in the British Virgin Islands, eastern Caribbean: Two sampling strategies reveal complex interactions between mangroves, seagrass beads and backreef habitats of juvenile coral reef fishes.* Master's thesis. University of York, United Kingdom. 1999.

Main, K. L. Predator avoidance in seagrass meadows: Prey behavior, microhabitat selection, and cryptic coloration. *Ecology* 68:170–180. 1986.

Manooch, C. S. III and D. Raver Jr. *Fisherman's guide: Fishes of the southeastern United States.* Raleigh: North Carolina State University Museum of Natural History. 1991.

Marshall, A. R. *A survey of the snook fishery of Florida, with studies of the biology of the principal species,* Centropomus undecimalis *Bloch.* Miami, FL: State Board of Conservation, Marine Laboratory. 1958.

McCoy, E. D., H. R. Mushinsky, D. Johnson, and W. E. Meshaka Jr. Mangrove damage caused by hurricane Andrew on the southwestern coast of Florida. *Bulletin of Marine Science* 59(1):1–8. 1996.

McMichael, R. H. Jr., K. M. Peters, and G. R. Parsons. Early life history of the snook *Centropomus undecimalis,* in Tampa Bay, Florida. *Northeast Gulf Science* 102:113–125. 1989.

Mense, D. J. and E. L. Wenner. Distribution and abundance of early life history stages of the blue crab, *Callinectes sapidus,* in tidal marsh creeks near Charleston, South Carolina. *Estuaries* 12(3):157–168. 1989.

Mercer, L. P. Species profiles: Life histories and environmental requirements of coastal fishes and invertebrates (mid-Atlantic)—weakfish. *U.S. Fish and Wildlife Service Biological Report* 82(11.109):17. 1989.

Mojica, R. Jr., J. M. Shenker, C. W. Harnden, and D. E. Wagner. Recruitment of bonefish, *Albula vulpes*, around Lee Stocking Island, Bahamas. *Fisheries Bulletin* 93:666–674. 1995.

Montague, C. L. and J. A. Ley. A possible effect of salinity fluctuation on abundance of benthic vegetation and associated fauna in northeastern Florida Bay. *Estuaries* 16(4):703–717. 1993.

Moody, K. M. *The role of drift macroalgae as a predation refuge or foraging ground for the seagrass fish,* Gobiosoma robustum. Master's thesis. University of South Florida. 1996.

Mueller, K. W., G. D. Dennis, D. B. Eggleston, and R. I. Wicklund. Size-specific social interactions and foraging styles in a shallow water population of mutton snapper, *Lutjanus analis* (Pisces: Lutjanidae), in the central Bahamas. *Environmental Biology of Fishes* 40:175–188. 1994.

Muller, R. G. *The 2000 stock assessment update of common snook,* Centropomus undecimalis. St. Petersburg: Fish and Wildlife Conservation Commission, Florida Marine Research Institute. 2000.

Mullin, S. J. Estuarine fish populations among red mangrove prop roots of small overwash islands. *Wetlands* 154:324–329. 1995.

Murphey, P. L. and M. S. Fonseca. Role of high and low energy seagrass beds as nursery areas for *Penaeus duorarum* in North Carolina. *Marine Ecology Progress Series* 121:91–98. 1995.

Murphy, M. D. and R. G. Taylor. Reproduction, growth, and mortality of red drum, *Sciaenops ocellatus* in Florida waters. *Fisheries Bulletin* 88:531–542. 1990.

Nagelkerken, I., G. van der Velde, M. W. Gorissen, G. J. Meijer, T. van't Hof, and C. den Hartog. Importance of mangroves, seagrass beds and the shallow coral reef as a nursery for important coral reef fishes, using visual census technique. *Estuarine and Coastal Shelf Science* 51:31–44. 2000.

Nagelkerken, I., M. Dorenbosch, W. C. E. P. Verberk, E. Cocheret de la Moriniere, and G. van der Velde. Day-night shifts of fishes between shallow-water biotopes of a Caribbean bay, with emphasis on the nocturnal feeding of Haemulidae and Lutjanidae. *Marine Ecology Progress Series* 194:55–64. 2000.

Naughton, S. P. and C. H. Saloman. Fishes of the nearshore zone of St. Andrew Bay, Florida, and adjacent coast. *Northeast Gulf Science* 21:43–55. 1978.

Nieland, D. L., R. G. Thomas, and C. A. Wilson. Age, growth, and reproduction of spotted seatrout in Barataria Bay, Louisiana. *Transactions of the American Fisheries Society* 131:245–259. 2002.

Ong, J. E. The ecology of mangrove conservation and management. *Hydrobiologia* 295:343–351. 1995.

Orth, R. J., K. L. Heck Jr., and J. van Montfrans. Faunal communities in seagrass beds: A review of the influence of plant structure and prey characteristics on predator-prey relationships. *Estuaries* 7(4A):339–350. 1984.

Peters, D. J. and W. G. Nelson. The seasonality and spatial patterns of juvenile surf zone fishes of the Florida east coast. *Florida Scientist* 50:85–99. 1987.

Peters, K. M., J. R. E. Matheson, and R. G. Taylor. Reproduction and early life history of common snook, *Centropomus undecimalils* (Bloch), in Florida. *Bulletin of Marine Science* 62(2): 509–529. 1998.

Peters, K. M. and R. H. J. McMichael. Early life history of the red drum *Sciaenops ocellatus* (Pisces: Sciaenidae), in Tampa Bay, Florida. *Estuaries and Coasts* 92–107. 1987.

Peterson, B. J., K. R. Thompson, J. H. Cowan Jr., and K. L. Heck Jr. Comparison of predation pressure in temperate and subtropical seagrass habitats based on chronographic tethering. *Marine Ecology Progress Series* 224:77–85. 2001.

Porch, C. E., C. A. Wilson, and D. L. Nieland. A new growth model for red drum (*Sciaenops ocellatus*) that accommodates seasonal and ontogenic changes in growth rates. *Fisheries Bulletin* 100:149–152. 2002.

Pottern, G. B., M. T. Huish, and J. H. Kerby. Species profiles: Life histories and environmental requirements of coastal fishes and invertebrates (mid-Atlantic) bluefish. *U.S. Fish and Wildlife Service Biological Report* 82(11.94). U.S. Army Corps of Engineers, TR EL-82-4. 1989.

Poulakis, G. R., J. M. Shenker, and D. S. Taylor. Habitat use by fishes after tidal reconnection of an impounded estuarine wetland in the Indian River Lagoon, Florida USA. *Wetland Ecology and Management* 10:51–69. 2002.

Primavera, J. H. Fish predation on mangrove-associated penaeids: The role of structure and substrate. *Journal of Experimental Marine Biology and Ecology* 215:205–216. 1997.

Rakocinski, C. F., S. S. Brown, G. R. Gaston, R. W. Heard, W. W. Walker, and J. K. Summers. Macrobenthic responses to natural and contaminant-related gradients in northern Gulf of Mexico estuaries. *Ecological Applications*. 74:1278–1298. 1997.

Reagan, R. E. Species profiles: Life histories and environmental requirements of coastal fishes and invertebrates (Gulf of Mexico)—red drum. *U.S. Fish and Wildlife Service Biological Report* 82(11.36). U.S. Army Corps of Engineers, TR EL-82-4. 1985.

Robbins, B. D. and S. S. Bell. Dynamics of a subtidal seagrass landscape: Seasonal and annual change in relation to water depth. *Ecology* 81(5):1193–1205. 2000.

Robblee, M. B. *The spatial organization of the nocturnal fish fauna of a tropical seagrass feeding ground*. Dissertation. University of Virginia. 1987.

Robertson, A. I. The structure and organization of an eelgrass fish fauna. *Oecologia* 47:76–82. 1980.

Robertson, A. I. and N. C. Duke. Mangrove fish-communities in tropical Queensland, Australia: Spatial and temporal patterns in densities, biomass and community structure. *Marine Biology* 104:369–379. 1990.

Robins, C. R., G. C Ray, J. Douglas, and R. Freund. *A field guide to Atlantic coast fishes of North America.* Boston: Houghton-Mifflin. 1986.

Rooker, J. R. and G. D. Dennis. Diel, lunar and seasonal changes in a mangrove fish assemblage off southwestern Puerto Rico. *Bulletin of Marine Science* 493:684–698. 1991.

Rooker, J. R., G. J. Holt, and S. A. Holt. Vulnerability of newly settled red drum *Sciaenops ocellatus* to predatory fish: Is early-life survival enhanced by seagrass meadows? *Marine Biology* 131:145–151. 1998.

Rooker, J. R., S. A. Holt, M. A. Soto, and G. J. Holt. Postsettlement patterns of habitat use by Sciaenid fishes in subtropical seagrass meadows. *Estuaries* 212:318–327. 1998.

Ross, D. A. *The fisherman's ocean.* Mechanicsburg, PA: Stackpole Books. 2000.

Ross, J. L. and T. M. Stevens. *Life history and population dynamics of red drum (Sciaenops ocellatus) in North Carolina waters.* Morehead City, NC: Division of Marine Fisheries. 1992.

Ross, J. L., T. M. Stevens, and D. S. Vaughan. Age, growth, mortality, and reproductive biology of red drums in North Carolina waters. *Transactions of the American Fisheries Society* 124:37–54. 1995.

Ross, M. S., P. L. Ruiz, G. J. Telesnicki, and J. F. Meeder. Estimating above-ground biomass and production in mangrove communities of Biscayne National Park, Florida USA. *Wetlands Ecology and Management* 9:27–37. 2001.

Saloman, C. H. and S. P. Naughton. Fishes of the littoral zone, Pinellas County, Florida. *Florida Scientist* 42:85–93. 1979.

Sargent, F. J., T. J. Leary, D. W. Crewz, and C. R. Kruer. Scarring of Florida's seagrasses: Assessment and management options. *Florida Marine Research Institute Technical Report* (TR-1):37. 1995.

Savino, J. F. and R. A. Stein. Behavior of fish predators and their prey: Habitat choice between open water and dense vegetation. *Environmental Biology of Fishes* 24(4):287–293.1989.

Schneider, F. I. and K. H. Mann. Species relationships of invertebrates to vegetation in a seagrass bed. *Journal of Marine Biology and Ecology* 145:101–117. 1991.

Seaman, W. Jr. and M. Collins. Species profiles: Life histories and environmental requirements of coastal fishes and invertebrates (South Florida)—snook. *U.S. Fish and Wildlife Service FWS/OBS-82/11* 16:16. 1983.

Sedberry, G. R. and J. Carter. The fish community of a shallow tropical lagoon in Belize, Central America. *Estuaries* 162:198–215. 1993.

Sexton, W. J. The post-storm Hurricane Hugo recovery of the undeveloped beaches along the South Carolina coast, Capers Islands to the Santee Delta. *Journal of Coastal Research* 114:1020–1025. 1995.

Sheaves, M. J. Patterns of distribution and abundance of fishes in different habitats of a mangrove-lined tropical estuary, as determined by fish trapping. *Australian Journal of Marine and Freshwater Research* 43:1461–1479. 1992.

Shenker, J. M. and J. M. Dean. The utilization of an intertidal salt marsh creek by larval and juvenile fishes: Abundance, diversity, and temporal variation. *Estuaries* 23:154–163. 1979.

Sheridan, P. Comparative habitat utilization by estuarine macrofauna within the mangrove ecosystem of Rookery Bay, Florida. *Bulletin of Marine Science* 501:21–39. 1992.

Sklar, F. H. and J. A. Browder. Coastal environmental impacts brought about by alterations in freshwater flow in the Gulf of Mexico. *Environmental Management* 22(4):547–562. 1998.

Smithsonian Marine Station at Fort Pierce, Florida. Accessed August 25, 2011 at http://www.sms.si.edu/irlspec/index.htm.

Sogard, S. M. Size-selective mortality in the juvenile stage of teleost fishes: A review. *Bulletin of Marine Science* 60(3):1129–1157. 1997.

Sogard, S. M. and K. W. Able. A comparison of eelgrass, sea lettuce macroalgae, and marsh creeks as habitats for epibenthic fishes and decapods. *Estuarine and Coastal Shelf Science* 33:501–519. 1991.

Sogard, S. M. and B. L. Olla. The influence of predator presence on utilization of artificial seagrass habitats by juvenile walleye pollack, *Theragra chalcogramma*. *Environmental Biology of Fishes* 37:57–65. 1993.

Sogard, S. M., G. V. N. Powell, and J. G. Holmquist. Epibenic fish communities on Florida Bay banks: Relations with physical parameters and seagrass cover. *Marine Ecology Progress Series* 40:25–39. 1987.

Stoner, A. W. and I. F. G. Lewis. The influence of quantitative and qualitative aspects of habitat complexity in tropical seagrass meadows. *Journal of Experimental Marine Biology and Ecology*. 94:19–40. 1985.

Taylor, R. G., J. A. Whittington, H. J. Grier, and R. E. Crabtree. Age, growth, maturation, and protandric sex reversal in common snook, *Centropomus undecimalis*, from the east and west coasts of Florida. *Fisheries Bulletin* 98:612–624. 2000.

Taylor, R. G., J. A. Whittington, and D. E. Haymans. Catch-and-release mortality rates of common snook in Florida. *North American Journal of Fisheries Management* 21:70–75. 2001.

Thayer, G. W., D. R. Colby, and W. F. Hettler Jr. Utilization of the red mangrove prop root habitat by fishes in south Florida. *Marine Ecology Progress Series* 35:25–38. 1987.

Tremain, D. M. and D. H. Adams. Seasonal variations in species diversity, abundance, and composition of fish communities in the northern Indian River Lagoon, Florida. *Bulletin of Marine Science* 57(1):171–192. 1995.

Tucker, J. W. J. and S. W. Campbell. Spawning season of common snook along the east central Florida coast. *Biological Sciences* 51(1):1–6. 1988.

Valiela, I. *Marine ecological processes* (2nd ed.). New York. Springer-Verlag. 1995.

Valiela, I., J. L. Bowen, and J. K. York. Mangrove forests: One of the world's most threatened major tropical environments. *Bioscience* 51(10):807–815. 2001.

Virnstein, R. W. and P. A. Carbonara. Seasonal abundance and distribution of drift algae and seagrasses in the mid-Indian River Lagoon, Florida. *Aquatic Botany* 23:67–82. 1985.

Virnstein, R. W., P. S. Mikkelsen, K. D. Carns, and M. A. Capone. Seagrass beds versus sand bottoms: The trophic importance of their associated benthic invertebrates. *Florida Scientist* 46(3–4):363–381. 1983.

Volpe, A. V. *Aspects of the biology of the common snook,* Centropomus undecimalis *(Bloch) of southwest Florida* (Technical Series No. 31). Miami: University of Miami, State of Florida Board of Conservation. 1959.

Walsh, C. J. and B. D. Mitchell. Factors associated with variations in abundance of epifaunal caridean shrimps between and within estuarine seagrass meadows. *Marine and Freshwater Research* 49: 769–777. 1998.

Wenner, C. *Red drum: Natural history and fishing techniques in South Carolina* (Educational Report No. 17). Columbia, SC. South Carolina Department of Natural Resources. 1992.

Wenner, C. and J. Archambault. *Spotted seatrout: Natural history and fishing techniques in South Carolina* (Educational Report No. 18). Columbia, SC. South Carolina Department of Natural Resources. 1995.

# APPENDIX A

Table of the most common coastal gamefish caught by fly anglers, the regions where they typically occur, the habitats they most often use, and the prey groups they eat most.

| Common Name | Scientific Name | Regions | Major Habitats | Major Prey Groups* |
|---|---|---|---|---|
| **Bonefish** | Albula vulpes | T (S) | S, M, O, B, R | crustaceans, fish, echinoderms, polychaetes |
| **Tarpon** | Megalops atlanticus | T, S, W | VO, VC | fish, crustaceans |
| **Permit** | Trachinotus falcatus | T, S | S, M, O, R, B | crustaceans, echinoderms, fish |
| **Pompano** | Trachinotus carolinus | S, W | B, VO | crustaceans |
| **Crevalle Jack** | Caranx hippos | T, S | VO | fish |
| **Blue Runner** | Caranx crysos | T, S | VO | fish |
| **Bar Jack** | Caranx ruber | T | VO | fish |
| **Horse-eye Jack** | Caranx latus | T | VO, C | fish |
| **Snook** | Centropomus undecimalis | T, S | S, M, B, OB | fish, crustaceans |
| **Red Drum** | Sciaenops ocellatus | S, W | S, M, SM, OB, O, B | crustaceans, fish, polychaetes, echinoderms |
| **Ladyfish** | Elops saurus | T, S | VO, VC | fish |
| **Spotted Seatrout** | Cynoscion nebulosus | S, W | S, M, B | crustaceans, fish |
| **Weakfish** | Cynoscion regalis | W, S | SM, S, B | fish, crustaceans |
| **Cobia** | Rachycentron canadum | S, W | VO | fish, squid, crabs |
| **Barracuda** | Sphyraena barracuda | T (S) | VO | fish |
| **Gray Snapper** | Lutjanus griseus | T, S | M, S | crustaceans, fish |
| **Mutton Snapper** | Lutjanus analis | T | S, M, C | crustaceans, fish |

| Common Name | Scientific Name | Regions | Major Habitats | Major Prey Groups* |
|---|---|---|---|---|
| **Yellowtail Snapper** | Ocyurus chrysurus | T | S, C | fish |
| **Bluefish** | Pomatomus saltatrix | W, S | VO | fish |
| **Striped Bass** | Morone saxatilis | W | VO, VC | fish, crustaceans |
| **Spanish Mackerel** | Scomberomorus maculatus | W, S | B | fish |
| **Cero Mackerel** | Scomberomorus cavalla | T | B | fish |
| **Gulf Flounder** | Paralichthys albigutta | S, T | O, S, OB | fish |
| **Southern Flounder** | Paralichthys lethostigma | T | O, S, OB | fish |

**Region:** T = tropics; S = subtropics; W = warm-temperate.
**Habitat:** S = seagrass; M = mangrove; OB = oyster bar; SM = salt marsh; O = open bottom; B = beach; C = coral reef; R = rubble flat; VO = various habitats (mobile species that can be associated with numerous habitats in open areas [e.g., seagrass bed = open area]); VC = various habitats (mobile species associated with habitats in open and enclosed areas [e.g., marsh creeks = enclosed area]).
*Major Prey Groups = most dominant prey in the diet. Only the major prey groups that are amenable to imitation with a fly are listed.

# APPENDIX B

Table of the major groups of prey most eaten by common coastal gamefish by region and by habitat where they occur most often.

| Group | Family | Family Name | Region | Major Habitats | Status |
|---|---|---|---|---|---|
| **Crustaceans** | Mud Crabs | Xanthidae | T, S, W | S, M, OB, SM | R |
| | Swimming Crabs | Portunidae | T, S, W | S, M, SM, B | R/S |
| | Spider Crabs | Majidae | T, S, W | S, OB, R | R |
| | Common Shrimp | Penaeidae | T, S, W | S, M, SM, OB | R/S |
| | Snapping Shrimp | Alpheidae | T, S | S, M, OB, R, C | R |
| | Mantis Shrimp | Squillidae | T | S, R, C | R |
| **Fish** | Killifish | Fundulidae | T, S, W | | R |
| | Mollies | Poecilidae | T, S | | R |
| | Gobies | Gobiidae | T, S, W | S, OB, M, R, C | R |
| | Blennies | Blenniidae | T, S, W | S, OB, M, C | R |
| | Mojarras | Gerreidae | T, S | S, M, OB, O, B | R/S |
| | Herrings | Clupeidae | T, S, W | S, OB, O, B | S |
| | Anchovies | Engraulidae | T, S, W | S, M, SM, O, B | R/S |
| | Silversides | Atherinidae | T, S, W | M, SM, OB, B | R |
| | Mullets | Mugilidae | T, S, W | S, M, O, B | R/S |
| **Worms** | Polychaetes | Various | T, S, W | S, M, R, C, SM | R |
| **Echinoderms** | Brittle Stars | Ophioroididae | | | R |
| | Sea Urchins | Echinoidea | | | R |

**Region:** T = tropics; S = subtropics; W = warm-temperate.
**Habitat:** S = seagrass; M = mangrove; OB = oyster bar; SM = salt marsh; O = open bottom; B = beach; C = coral reef; R = rubble flat; VO = various habitats (mobile species that can be associated with numerous habitats in open areas [e.g., seagrass bed = open area]); VC = various habitats (mobile species associated with habitats in open and enclosed areas [e.g., marsh creeks = enclosed area]).
**Status:** R = resident; S = seasonal.

# INDEX

F



G

# ABOUT THE AUTHOR

For Aaron J. Adams, the line between science and fishing blurred long ago, and Adams uses his fish research to formulate his fishing strategies, and his fishing to help guide some of his research. Adams has a Ph.D. in environmental biology, holds a Coast Guard Captain's license, and has lived, worked, and fished in Maryland, North Carolina, California, Virginia, the U.S. Virgin Islands, Massachusetts, and Florida, and conducted fish research throughout the Caribbean. He is presently a Senior Scientist at Mote Marine Laboratory and Director of Operations for the non-profit Bonefish & Tarpon Trust.